One scandal too many...

the case for comprehensive protection for children in all settings

Report of a Working Group convened by the Gulbenkian Foundation
Published by Calouste Gulbenkian Foundation, London 1993

CW00925810

Contents

Foreword

The passing of the Children Act 1989 has focused attention on the continuing need to protect children. Despite the progressive introduction of statutory safeguards, ill treatment and serious abuse remain prevalent. The NSPCC and the many highly regarded societies and groups listed in this report continue to provide much needed support and protection.

The report is the work of distinguished men and women who are highly experienced in the field of child care. They have achieved a comprehensive result which illustrates the nature and magnitude of the problem and which indicates the need for further safeguards. The Working Group is to be congratulated upon an impressive report which deserves careful study.

Sir Stephen Brown
President of the Family Division of the High Court

The Working Group

The Gulbenkian Foundation convened a working group in July 1991 to produce a report summarising existing safeguards following implementation of the Children Act 1989, and indicating the reforms needed to provide an adequate and consistent framework of protection for all children and young people throughout the UK from injurious and humiliating treatment and punishment. It commissioned Peter Newell to carry out necessary research for the project.

Working Group Members

Christopher Brown has been Director of the National Society for the Prevention of Cruelty to Children since September 1989, following a career in social work and the probation service. Prior to joining the NSPCC he was Chief Probation Officer for Oxfordshire and then for Essex. He served on the Parole Board for England and Wales from 1985 - 1987, and has played a prominent role in social policy issues at a national level.

Paul Curno is Deputy Director of the Calouste Gulbenkian Foundation, UK Branch. He worked as a residential worker in Stamford House Remand Home, West London before qualifying as a Child Care Officer in the mid-1960s. He was Director of the Albany Centre in Deptford, South East London for seven years, before joining the Central Council for Education and Training in Social Work as a Social Work Education Adviser between 1972 and 1978.

Rachel Hodgkin is Principal Policy Officer of the National Children's Bureau. She worked at the Children's Legal Centre from its formation in 1979 until 1992, and has been involved in a range of policy development work including care, education, special education, and health. She was a member of the Health Advisory Service team which reported on services for disturbed adolescents in 1986, and has made successful applications on behalf of children and young people to the European Commission of Human Rights on issues related to penal establishments and secure accommodation.

Dr Zarrina Kurtz is Regional Consultant in Public Health Medicine for South West Thames Regional Health Authority with responsibility for the health of women and children. She is chair of the Management Committee of the Children's Legal Centre, honorary adviser on child health to the National Children's Bureau and immediate past President of the Open Section of the Royal Society of Medicine. She is also a member of the Secretary of State for Health's Youth Treatment Service Group. She was previously Medical Adviser to the Inner London Education Authority, and Senior Lecturer in Epidemiology at the Institute of Child Health, London.

Allan Levy QC is a barrister specialising in child law and medical law who has appeared in many leading cases in these fields. He is a Recorder, and the author of four books on child law and numerous articles. He chaired the recent Pindown Inquiry in Staffordshire, is honorary legal adviser to the National Children's Bureau, chairman of the Intercountry Adoption Lawyers' Association, a member of the Councils of Justice and the Medico-Legal Society and a Fellow of the International Academy of Matrimonial Lawyers.

Lady Lovell-Davis was a member of the Court Committee on Child Health Services, set up by the Department of Health and Social Security (1973 - 76), and of the Children's Committee, appointed by the Secretary of State for Social Services (1978 - 81). She was Director of the National Association for the Welfare of Children in Hospital from 1980 - 88. Since 1985 she has chaired "Caring for Children in the Health Services" a committee of representatives of the major health organisations, which has produced four major reports. She also chaired the Joint British Advisory Committee on Children's Nursing from 1985 - 89. She is an Honorary Member of the British Paediatric Association, and Honorary Secretary of the Royal Society of Medicine.

Kathleen Marshall has been Director of the Scottish Child Law Centre since 1989, and had previously worked as a solicitor in local government. She is also Visiting Professor to the School of Social Work at Glasgow Caledonian University. Her involvement in policy development for children and young people in Scotland has included major submissions to the Child Care Law Review, the Scottish Law Commission and the recent Inquiry into the Removal of Children from Orkney.

Peter Newell has been Co-ordinator of "EPOCH - End Physical Punishment of Children" since 1989. He chairs the Council of the Children's Rights Development Unit, and is a member of the Council for Disabled Children. He previously worked at the Children's Legal Centre, and the Advisory Centre for Education. He is the author of *The UN Convention and Children's Rights in the UK*, 1991; and co-author of *Taking Children Seriously: a proposal for a Children's Rights Commissioner*, 1991.

John Rea Price, OBE, has been Director of the National Children's Bureau since 1991. He was formerly Director of Social Services in Islington from 1972 - 1990, and is a past President of the Association of Directors of Social Services.

Philippa Russell, OBE, is Director of the Council for Disabled Children (formerly the Voluntary Council for Handicapped Children), a member of the National Development Team on mental handicap and has contributed to numerous books and journals on children and disability.

John Tomlinson, CBE, has been Director of the Institute of Education at the University of Warwick since 1985, and was Director of Education for Cheshire from 1972 - 84. He was founder-chairman of the Further Education Unit, 1976 - 78, chairman of the Schools Council 1978 - 82, President of the Society of Education Officers, 1982 - 83, and chairman of the Council of the Royal Society of Arts 1989 - 91. He is chairman of the newly-formed General Teaching Council for England and Wales.

Tom White, CBE, is Principal and Chief Executive of NCH (National Children's Home), former Director of Social Services for Coventry for 15 years, and a past President of the Association of Directors of Social Services and the Association of Child Care Officers. He is currently President of the European Forum on Child Welfare and Deputy President of the International Forum on Child Welfare.

Acknowledgements

The Working Group gratefully acknowledges the information, comments and help it has received from many quarters: in particular from officials in Government departments including the Department of Health, Scottish Office, Welsh Office, and Northern Ireland Office; from all the organisations listed on page xiii; from many other organisations and individuals working in the children's field; and from librarians - in particular at the National Society for the Prevention of Cruelty to Children and the National Children's Bureau.

The Working Group is also very grateful to the Gulbenkian Foundation, without whose support and encouragement this report would never have appeared.

Support for report and recommendations

A draft of the report and recommendations was circulated to organisations working in the children's field. Many made helpful and detailed comments which have contributed to the final draft.

The organisations listed below endorsed the following statement:

"We support the case made in One scandal too many *for comprehensive reform to provide adequate protection for children and young people against ill-treatment and abuse, and arbitrary restriction of liberty, in all settings. We share the Working Group's concern at current inconsistencies and gaps in protection, and above all at the way in which the law and social attitudes continue to condone deliberately hurting children as a form of punishment or treatment.*

"While not necessarily endorsing every detailed recommendation in the report, we do endorse its approach, based on principles in the UN Convention which the Government is committed to implementing, and we hope that appropriate inter-departmental action will follow its publication".

Action for Sick Children
Advice, Advocacy and Representation Service for Children (ASC)
Association of Children's Rights Officers
Association of Metropolitan Authorities
Barnardos
British Association for Community Child Health
ChildCare Northern Ireland
ChildLine
Children in Wales
Children's Legal Centre
Children's Rights Development Unit
Children's Society
Community Development Foundation
Family Rights Group
Grandparents' Federation
Health Visitors' Association
Independent Representation for Children in Need - IRCHIN
Kid's Clubs Network
National Children's Home

National Children's Bureau
National Council for Voluntary Organisations
National Council of Voluntary Child Care Organisations
National Foster Care Association
National Society for the Prevention of Cruelty to Children
Play Matters - National Association of Toy and Leisure Libraries
RADAR
Royal College of Nursing
Royal National Institute for the Blind
Save the Children Fund
Scottish Child and Family Alliance
Scottish Child Law Centre
A Voice for the Child in Care
Voluntary Council for Under Fives
Who Cares Trust

Summary

Background

An apparently unending series of scandals involving serious abuse of children and young people has hit the headlines in the last few years. Despite major reforms in children's law, and a succession of judicial and other inquiry reports, it is clear that children are not adequately protected in our society. The cases have involved abuse, often long-term, of children living at home and in many different institutions, state-run, voluntary and private, in the child care, health, education and penal systems.

The Gulbenkian Foundation commissioned a Working Group of inter-disciplinary experts (see page vii) to consider reforms needed to provide an effective framework for protection of children and young people wherever they spend significant periods of their lives.

The report includes a detailed commentary on existing protection (covering the whole of the UK), which reveals inexcusable inconsistencies and gaps. It reviews and quotes from many of the reports of inquiries and committees. Most were set up in the wake of a particular scandal, and none has attempted to look at protection of children in all settings. The report identifies this as a major impediment to effective reform: that reports have been reactive and tended to focus narrowly on remedying or preventing a particular abuse in a particular setting. Another impediment is the continuing lack of co-ordination of control of children's services and child protection across and within different government departments. But the report identifies as the most pervasive influence inhibiting reform

"the cultural conditioning which affects all of us - legislators, administrators, professionals, parents and children too. We have all been conditioned by a culture in which deliberately hurting children is still accepted both socially and legally, in which concepts of adult 'ownership' of children, who should be 'seen and not heard' persist. The major purpose of this report is to challenge the cultural conditioning which we - and more particularly our children - still suffer from, and to promote instead acceptance of children's right to protection from all forms of physical or mental violence".

The report makes recommendations to improve protection for children in all settings and to change attitudes, to ensure that it is no longer legally or socially acceptable to deliberately hurt children as a form of punishment or treatment. There is an emphasis on legal reform, because the Working Group believes that reforms in policy and practice and changes in attitudes to children will stem from clear principles in the law. But it also underlines the need for positive advice for parents and all other carers.

The case made in the report for comprehensive reform is supported by a wide range of professional and child welfare organisations, to which it was circulated in draft prior to publication (see page xiii). The report seeks to create a consensus in favour of comprehensive and rapid reform of law, policy, practice and above all social attitudes to children.

UN Convention

The Government ratified the UN Convention on the Rights of the Child in December 1991. This commits it to full implementation of the principles and standards in the Convention which are used as a basis for recommendations and promoted as a framework for policy development (see page 7). In particular the Convention insists that:

all rights in it must be secured for all children without discrimination on any ground;

the best interests of the child must be a primary consideration in all matters;

children's right to express their views freely and have them taken seriously must be respected;

the state must protect the child from all forms of physical or mental violence.

Structure of report

The report is divided into two major parts:

The first covers protection of children's physical and personal integrity and liberty. Children are the only people in the UK whose right to physical integrity - to protection from all forms of physical and mental violence - is not yet supported by the law and social attitudes. Concern over child abuse has escalated, but the definition of child abuse in the law and in child protection policy and practice condones quite a high level of violence to children. A separate section covers bullying - a newly recognised issue which affects children not only in schools but in all institutions. The Pindown affair and various inquiries have highlighted concerns at arbitrary and unlawful restriction of children's liberty, and a third section looks at this issue in detail.

The second part highlights certain key strategies for positive and preventive protection of children and young people:

access to advice and counselling, to advocacy and to effective complaints procedures;

access to independent people;

arrangements for police checks and other ways of preventing people who may threaten children's welfare gaining inappropriate access to them;

arrangements for monitoring and reviewing placement and treatment of children;

arrangements for inspection.

The report and its recommendations do not of course pretend to cover all issues relevant to child protection. In particular it does not attempt to cover quality of life issues - children's and families' standards of living, standards of health, education and other services. Nor does it cover all the civil liberties issues reflected in the UN Convention and vital to children's development wherever they are living. Recommendations do not extend to training, management, pay or status of those who work with children (the subject of other major recent inquiries and reports). And while it emphasises identification of ill-treatment and abuse, the report does not review current procedures for responding to child abuse, although it does call for a full review. The recommendations for legislation to prevent children being deliberately harmed, and to give them access to independent advice, advocacy and complaints procedures provide an essential basis for positive caring:

"Our recommendations propose the development and dissemination of positive advice for all carers. But that process is undermined unless and until the bottom line of respecting children's right to personal integrity is accepted".

Major recommendations

Detailed recommendations follow each section, and a summary of all recommendations starts on page 193. The following are some of the major recommendations made in the report:

Part One

Protecting children's physical integrity
The law concerning child upbringing should be prefaced by a statement of positive principles of care, reflecting rights in the UN Convention and including the right not to be subjected to corporal punishment or any other

humiliating treatment or punishment. The concept of "reasonable chastisement" should be removed and replaced by parental duties to guide and safeguard their children according to their evolving capacity.

Definitions of physical and sexual child abuse should be based clearly on the child's right to physical and personal integrity and should not condone any level of physical or mental violence to children.

The purpose of legal reforms to protect the child's physical integrity are educational, not to increase prosecution or intervention in family life, which are unlikely to benefit children. The Government should provide and/or support information campaigns aimed at encouraging positive non-violent child-rearing. Codes of practice on positive methods of encouraging good behaviour should be issued to all those working with children in institutional settings.

Legislation applying to all institutional and quasi-institutional placements for children should include further controls on sanctions, including temporary or permanent exclusion.

The Department of Health, and appropriate departments in Scotland, Wales and Northern Ireland, should be designated the lead government department with overall responsibility for all aspects of child protection, charged with co-ordinating policy and action across government.

Bullying
All institutional placements for children should be required to have a policy on protecting children and young people from bullying and preventing bullying. Children themselves should be actively consulted and involved.

Restriction of liberty
Restriction of a child's liberty by a parent or other informal carer should only be lawful in so far as it is necessary for the safety and welfare of the child, and in line with the child's evolving capacities. Positive advice should be made available to limit unnecessary and unlawful restriction of liberty.

The prohibition on restriction of liberty in certain institutions (under the Children Act) should be extended to apply to all private and voluntary institutions, and to all schools. Detailed and consistent safeguards (including approval by the Secretary of State) should apply to all lawful restriction of liberty in the child care and health sectors.

The placing of children in solitary confinement in all open institutions should be explicitly forbidden. In any secure institutions in which it is permitted, its use must be limited by strict criteria and detailed safeguards.

Part Two

Children and young people in all settings should have ready and well-publicised access to:

confidential advice and counselling;

help from an independent advocate or representative;

complaints procedures with an independent element;

ultimate access when necessary to the courts.

In all cases special provision should be made for disabled children and young people, and to enable representations to be made on behalf of very young children.

When local resolution of children's complaints fails, there should be a further avenue of complaint, either to a new UK-wide children's ombudsperson service, or by widening the powers of the existing Commissioners for Local Administration (local government ombudspeople).

There should be an obligation to appoint an independent visitor for children in various institutional placements, and in particular for those children and young people judged unable to use the complaints procedures available to them.

All employers of workers/volunteers who have substantial access to children should be required to follow codes of practice on recruitment, induction and supervision. The codes would include arrangements for police checks.

All such employers should be required to report any conduct which suggests that a person may not be suitable for work involving substantial access to children (with appropriate safeguards for individuals).

Health legislation should ensure that there is an obligation to make available specified appropriate developmental checks for all children.

Arrangements for formal review of placement and treatment, involving the children themselves, should extend to all children being accommodated in institutions and quasi-institutional settings throughout the UK.

In addition, in the case of all placements away from home for a significant period there should be an "exit-review" or "leaving interview" at which the child would be invited to comment on the placement, its successes and any problems etc.

An inter-departmental inquiry should consider establishing at central government level an appropriately trained inspectorate, including lay members, for all residential services for children.

(See full summary of recommendations on page 193)

Introduction

It is just over a hundred years since the first law protecting children in the UK from cruelty was enacted. The Prevention of Cruelty to and Protection of Children Act 1889 passed through Parliament 66 years after the first statute protecting animals.

One hundred years on, the Children Act 1989 received Royal Assent, heralded as the "most important piece of legislation affecting children this century". It is in many ways a great Act. But in the months leading up to and following its implementation in October 1991, there was unprecedented publicity for a series of scandals involving ill-treatment and abuse of children: children at home, children in care in children's homes, children in independent and special schools, children in a government-administered youth treatment centre, and children in both a private health institution and a National Health Service unit.

The exercise which has led to this report should have been commissioned by government some years ago, with an adequate research budget, detailed legal advice and a remit extending across the responsibilities of all relevant government departments. If it had been, and its conclusions acted on, it is more than likely that some major scandals would have been averted, and the lives of many children and young people substantially improved. Now that the Government has indicated its commitment to consistent development of children's rights, through its ratification of the UN Convention on the Rights of the Child, there is all the more reason to seek comprehensive, rather than piecemeal, reform and to anticipate, rather than react to, further scandals.

It is clear that, whatever the intention, the protection afforded to children by the law and current policies and practice in all settings is far from adequate. One of the main recommendations of the 1991 report by Sir William Utting, the then Chief Inspector of the Social Services Inspectorate, following the Pindown affair, was that the Department of Health should

"review, with other interested groups, the legislation safeguarding the welfare of children across the full range of residential settings".

This recommendation took account of the progress made in the Children Act - progress which still leaves inconsistencies and gaps in protection. If one looks - as this report does - beyond England and Wales to the whole of the

UK, and beyond residential care to all the places where children spend significant periods of their lives, the inconsistencies become greater and the gaps wider. The law in Scotland and Northern Ireland is under review, providing an immediate opportunity to build on the Children Act reforms and seek to make protection comprehensive.

Calls for comprehensive reform are not new. Back in 1981 for example the government-appointed Children's Committee, in one of its last reports, recommended a progressive programme, governed by a specific timescale, to eliminate the use of corporal punishment on all children and young people. In 1983 the Children's Legal Centre proposed, in response to a Department of Health consultation, that children in all settings should be safeguarded by detailed regulations listing unacceptable sanctions and treatment as well as positive requirements. In 1986 after wide consultation the NHS Health Advisory Service recommended in *Bridges Over Troubled Waters*, a report on services for disturbed adolescents, that in all institutional settings for children and young people there should be a general prohibition on inhuman and degrading treatment, as well as specific prohibitions on physical punishment and other inappropriate sanctions. There should also be "well-publicised complaints procedures" and young people should be given a handbook setting out their rights, any rules of the institution, and how they should set about making a complaint.

Looking at the history of attempts to legislate to protect children it is clear that it has taken the exposure of extreme abuse to provoke many of the reforms. And then the reforms have tended to be limited to remedying, or attempting to remedy the particular abuse in the particular setting.

One serious impediment to action has been the continuing lack of co-ordination of control of children's services. The Home Office, the Department of Health and the Department for Education all have responsibilities for the welfare and protection of children: there has been little sign until very recently of consistent co-operation between departments to promote welfare and enhance protection. Even within departments, it appears that different divisions can defend conflicting policies (eg between health and child care, maintained and independent education etc). It is our view that one Department should be charged with responsibility for co-ordinating policy and action for all aspects of child protection: in England and Wales the obvious department is the Department of Health. It is already acknowledged to take lead responsibility for children, and significantly has been given the task of over-seeing implementation of the UN Convention on the Rights of the Child.

There can be little doubt, however, that the most pervasive influence inhibiting reform has been the cultural conditioning which affects all of us - legislators, administrators, professionals, parents and children too. We have all been conditioned by a culture in which deliberately hurting children is still accepted both socially and legally, in which concepts of adult "ownership" of children who should be "seen and not heard" persist. The major purpose of this report is to challenge the cultural conditioning which we - and more particularly our children - still suffer from, and to promote instead acceptance of children's right to protection from all forms of physical or mental violence.

Concern over physical and sexual child abuse in the home and in institutions has escalated rapidly in the last few years. But the concept of child abuse, as commonly defined in law, policy and practice, still condones a level of physical and mental violence to children. In the parallel issue of protection of women from male violence, there is no question of condoning any level of violence. Children as people have the same right to personal integrity, to protection from all forms of physical or mental violence, as the rest of us take for granted. The task of child protection, and the definition of child abuse should flow from this fundamental human right.

Legal reform to protect children and young people from ill-treatment and abuse has so far been hesitant and inconsistent, when viewed across the UK and across the boundaries of the responsibilities of different government departments. But nevertheless there are many encouraging signs of positive changes in attitudes to children and their rights:

For example:

● a political consensus that law reform is needed, which has already produced the Children Act and led to current reviews in Scotland and Northern Ireland.

● development of the concept of parental responsibility, and landmark legal decisions like *Gillick*, upholding children's rights to growing self-determination, and confirming that parents' rights are subservient to the welfare of the child;

● key reports such as that of the judicial inquiry into the Cleveland affair, which prefaced its recommendations with the phrase: "The child is a person, not an object of concern";

● the growth and influence of organisations specifically committed to the development of children's legal rights, like the Children's Legal Centre and the Scottish Child Law Centre, A Voice for the Child in Care, and most recently the Children's Rights Development Unit, and the Northern Ireland Alliance for Children's Rights;

● the emergence of self-advocacy groups of young people, including the National Association of Young People in Care, Black and in Care, and Who Cares? Scotland;

- the development of policy departments within the major child welfare and child protection organisations, collaborating in lobbying for more coherent policies for children, and supporting, for example, the proposal for a statutory Children's Rights Commissioner;

- the appointment of children's rights officers in some local authorities and the formation of the Association of Children's Rights Officers, to advocate for children's views and interests in services, and the development of local "charters" of children's rights.

The movement to respect the rights of children worldwide has also gained an unstoppable momentum. In 1989, adoption by the UN General Assembly of the Convention on the Rights of the Child provided the world's governments for the first time with a detailed set of internationally-validated principles against which to test their treatment and protection of children.

On 16 December 1991, the UK Government became the 117th country to ratify the Convention. By ratifying, it signified its intention to comply with the provisions of the Convention, to make them widely known to both adults and children, and to report regularly to a UN Committee on the Rights of the Child on progress towards implementation. The Convention in over 40 articles covers every aspect of children's lives; it thus provides a comprehensive framework within which to examine the impact of all legislation, policy and practice on children and their rights.

Principles in the Convention, and in particular the principle that children must be protected from "all forms of physical or mental violence" (Article 19) have provided the starting point for preparing this report. They are outlined below (page 7). Significantly, the first recommendation of the 1992 report of the *Inquiry into the Removal of Children from Orkney* was:

"Reform in the field of child law and in particular in matters of child protection should proceed under reference to the European Convention on Human Rights and the UN Convention on the Rights of the Child".

If the principles in the Convention, reflected in this report, are taken seriously and built on, they should help the UK to move quickly towards completing the job that was started a century ago, giving all our children in all settings the protection to which they have a right from all forms of inhuman and humiliating treatment and punishment.

Aims and scope of the report

The aim of *One scandal too many* is to examine the reforms needed to provide an effective framework for the protection of children and young people, wherever they may spend significant periods of their lives, from injurious or humiliating treatment and punishment, including arbitrary and unlawful restriction of liberty.

By basing the case for reform on the principles in the UN Convention, we hope that this report and its recommendations will command wide support, both from the Government which is committed to implementation of the Convention, from local government and from the wide range of non-governmental interests working in the children's field in the UK. On page xiii we list the many organisations which have already indicated their general support for our recommendations, circulated to them in draft a few months ago, and which share our concern at the way in which the law and social attitudes continue to condone deliberately hurting children as a form of punishment or treatment.

Part One of the report considers the framework for protecting children's physical and personal integrity, and their liberty - protection from arbitrary or unlawful restriction of liberty. It provides a summary of current law and guidance, and recommendations designed to make protection consistent in line with principles in the UN Convention.

Part Two highlights certain key issues for protection: access to advice and counselling, advocacy and effective complaints procedures; access to adults independent of the setting in which children are living; arrangements to prevent people who may threaten children's welfare gaining inappropriate access to them (recruitment procedures, criminal record checks etc); arrangements for monitoring and reviewing placement and treatment of children; arrangements for inspection.

The detailed summary in each section of the varying provisions and guidance applying to children in different settings illustrates the extraordinary lack of consistency of current safeguards for children. This reflects the lack of any attempt at comprehensive reform built on a framework of clear principles.

There is an emphasis in the report on legal reform, because we believe that reforms in policy and practice, and changes in attitudes to children will stem from clear principles in law.

Our recommendations are not of course exhaustive, and there are many issues not covered at all in this report which are relevant to child protection. In particular we have not attempted to cover quality of life issues - children's and families' standard of living, standards of health, education and other services. Nor does the report cover all the civil rights issues reflected in the UN Convention and vital to children's development wherever they are living - issues of participation, freedom of expression, thought, conscience and religion, freedom of association, privacy and so on.

Our recommendations do not extend to the training, management, pay and status of those who work with or for children. Recent reports, including in particular the Howe Report, *The Quality of Care*, and the Warner Report, *Choosing with Care*, provide valuable and detailed discussion of these issues. And while we emphasise the importance of ensuring identification of all ill-treatment and abuse, we have not reviewed current administrative procedures for responding to child abuse. We concur with the National Society for the Prevention of Cruelty to Children and others who believe that a full review is needed urgently. While we advocate increased rights of access to courts for children, we have not considered how courts should treat children, whether they are parties or witnesses.

Finally, while the report says a great deal about how children and young people must not be treated, it does not provide positive advice except by implication on how they should be treated, in easy or difficult circumstances. Our recommendations for legislation to protect children from being deliberately harmed, and to give them access to independent advice, advocacy and complaints procedures provide an essential basis for positive caring. It has become very apparent to us that there is an urgent need for more advice and sharing of good practice, in particular on positive and acceptable ways of controlling violent and disruptive behaviour. The Department of Health recently (April 1993) circulated *Guidance on Permissible Forms of Control in Children's Residential Care*. Our recommendations propose the development and dissemination of positive advice for all carers. But that process is undermined unless and until the bottom line of respecting children's right to personal integrity is accepted.

The UN Convention on the Rights of the Child - setting an agenda for policy development

The UN Convention on the Rights of the Child is the first detailed international treaty to provide comprehensive minimum standards for treatment of the world's children. By April 1993, 134 countries had ratified the Convention. The UK did so in December 1991, thus committing itself to making the rights in the Convention a reality for the UK's 13.2 million children and young people under the age of 18.

In this report, we are concerned with the rights of children in all settings to adequate protection from all forms of ill-treatment and abuse, and from arbitrary and unlawful restriction of liberty. The Convention provides a valuable framework for policy development and one which the Government is now committed to implementing.

Of course, there are some ways in which UK law and practice already exceeds the demands of the Convention, which was drafted for worldwide application and therefore provides no more than minimum standards. As Article 41 emphasises, the Convention does not affect any other provisions, in domestic law or other international law, which are "more conducive to the realization of the rights of the child".

The Convention does uphold clearly children's rights to physical integrity, to protection from "all forms of physical or mental violence", and to protection from arbitrary or unlawful restriction of liberty. The following summary of these and other relevant provisions in the Convention is intended to set out the framework of principles on which our recommendations are built.

Relevant provisions in the Convention

The Convention defines "child" as every person under the age of 18.

Basic principles

Equal rights, special care

The preamble to the Convention emphasises the "equal and inalienable rights of all members of the human family", and also children's rights to "special care and assistance".

No discrimination

Article 2 insists that all the rights in the Convention must be available

"without discrimination of any kind, irrespective of the child's or his or her parent's or legal guardian's race, colour, sex, language, religion, political or other opinion, national, ethnic or social origin, property, disability, birth or other status".

In reviewing the implications of other Articles, this principle must be included throughout.

Best interests

Article 3 insists that

"In all actions concerning children, whether undertaken by public or private social welfare institutions, courts of law, administrative authorities or legislative bodies, the best interests of the child must be a primary consideration".

Children's views

Article 12 insists on enabling the child to be an active participant:

"1 States Parties shall assure to the child who is capable of forming his or her own views the right to express those views freely in all actions affecting the child, the views of the child being given due weight in accordance with the age and maturity of the child.

"2 For this purpose, the child shall in particular be provided the opportunity to be heard in any judicial and administrative proceedings affecting the child, either directly, or through a representative or an appropriate body, in a manner consistent with the procedural rules of national law".

Physical and personal integrity

Article 19 goes beyond children's rights to protection from abuse, to assert their right to personal integrity - to protection against "all forms of physical or mental violence":

"1 States Parties shall take all appropriate legislative, administrative, social and educational measures to protect the child from all forms of physical or mental violence, injury or abuse, neglect or negligent treatment, maltreatment or exploitation including sexual abuse, while in the care of parent(s), legal guardian(s) or any other person who has the care of the child.

"2 Such protective measures should, as appropriate, include effective procedures for the establishment of social programmes to provide necessary support for the child and for those who have the care of the child, as well as for other forms of prevention and for identification, reporting, referral, investigation, treatment and follow-up of instances of child maltreatment described heretofore, and, as appropriate, for judicial involvement".

In addition, Article 37 (a) insists that states parties ensure that

"No child shall be subjected to torture or other cruel, inhuman or degrading treatment or punishment..."

And Article 28(2) emphasises that

"States Parties shall take all appropriate steps to ensure that school discipline is administered in a manner consistent with the child's human dignity and in conformity with the present Convention".

Also relevant to the right to physical integrity, Article 24(3) obliges states

"to take all effective and appropriate measures with a view to abolishing traditional practices prejudicial to the health of children".

This was drafted with particular reference to the practice of female circumcision, genital mutilation of girls and young women, and other practices which may be based on cultural or religious tradition, but which threaten the physical integrity and/or health of the child.

Restriction of liberty

Article 37:

"...(b) No child shall be deprived of his or her liberty unlawfully or arbitrarily. The arrest, detention or imprisonment of a child shall be in conformity with the law and shall be used only as a measure of last resort and for the shortest appropriate period of time;

"(c) Every child deprived of liberty shall be treated with humanity and respect for the inherent dignity of the human person, and in a manner which takes into account the needs of persons of his or her age. In particular every child deprived of liberty shall be separated from adults unless it is considered in the child's best interest not to do so and shall have the right to

maintain contact with his or her family through correspondence and visits, save in exceptional circumstances";*

(* When it ratified the Convention, the Government made a reservation indicating only qualified acceptance of this Article, stating:

"Where at any time there is a lack of suitable accommodation or adequate facilities for a particular individual in any institution in which young offenders are detained, or where the mixing of adults and children is deemed to be mutually beneficial, the United Kingdom reserves the right not to apply Article 37(c) in so far as those provisions require children who are detained to be accommodated separately from adults".)

"(d) Every child deprived of his or her liberty shall have the right to prompt access to legal and other appropriate assistance, as well as the right to challenge the legality of the deprivation of his or her liberty before a court or other competent, independent and impartial authority, and to a prompt decision on any such action".

In relation to the last paragraph, it is important to note that the safeguards provided by the European Convention on Human Rights, Article 5, are clearly "more conducive to the realization of the rights of the child":

"...(4): Everyone who is deprived of his liberty by arrest or detention shall be entitled to take proceedings by which the lawfulness of his detention shall be decided speedily by a court and his release ordered if the detention is not lawful".

Article 40:

"1 States Parties recognise the right of every child alleged as, accused of, or recognised as having infringed the penal law to be treated in a manner consistent with the protection of the child's sense of dignity and worth, which reinforces the child's respect for the human rights and fundamental freedoms of others and which takes into account the child's age and the desirability of promoting the child's reintegration and the child's assuming a constructive role in society".

Parental care

Article 5 respects the

"responsibilities, rights and duties of parents or, where applicable, the members of the extended family or community as provided for by local custom, legal guardians or other persons legally responsible for the child, to provide, in a manner consistent with the evolving capacities of the child, appropriate direction and guidance in the exercise by the child of the rights recognised in the present Convention".

Article 18 also emphasises parental

"responsibilities for the upbringing and development of the child. Parents, or as the case may be, legal guardians, have the primary responsibility for the upbringing and development of the child. The best interests of the child will be their basic concern..."

It goes on to insist on States Parties providing appropriate assistance to parents and guardians.

Separation from parents

Separation of children from their parents, for protection from abuse or other reasons, is subject to the principles in Article 9:

"1 States Parties shall ensure that a child shall not be separated from his or her parents against their will, except when competent authorities subject to judicial review determine, in accordance with applicable law and procedures, that such separation is necessary for the best interests of the child. Such determination may be necessary in a particular case such as one involving abuse or neglect of the child by the parents, or one where the parents are living separately and a decision must be made as to the child's place of residence.

"2 In any proceedings pursuant to paragraph 1 of the present Article, all interested parties shall be given an opportunity to participate in the proceedings and make their views known.

"3 States Parties shall respect the right of the child who is separated from one or both parents to maintain personal relations and direct contact with both parents on a regular basis, except if it is contrary to the child's best interests..."

And under Article 20:

"1 A child temporarily or permanently deprived of his or her family environment, or in whose own best interests cannot be allowed to remain in that environment, shall be entitled to special protection and assistance provided by the State.

"2 States Parties shall in accordance with their national laws ensure alternative care for such a child.

"3 Such care could include, inter alia, foster placement, Kafala of Islamic law, adoption, or if necessary placement in suitable institutions for the care of children. When considering solutions, due regard shall be paid to the desirability of continuity in a child's upbringing and to the child's ethnic, religious, cultural and linguistic background".

Standards for institutions, services and facilities

Article 3(3):

"States Parties shall ensure that the institutions, services and facilities responsible for the care or protection of children shall conform with the standards established by competent authorities, particularly in the areas of safety, health, in the number and suitability of their staff, as well as competent supervision".

Read together with Articles 2(1) and 3(1), this emphasises the need for consistent and non-discriminatory standards for institutions, services and facilities, in which the best interests of all affected children are a primary consideration.

Other articles and issues:

Right to periodic review

Article 25:

"States Parties recognise the right of a child who has been placed by the competent authorities for the purposes of care, protection or treatment of his or her physical or mental health, to a periodic review of the treatment provided to the child and all other circumstances relevant to his or her placement".

Rehabilitation

Under Article 39, States Parties must promote the

"physical and psychological recovery and social reintegration of a child victim of any form of neglect, exploitation, or abuse; torture or any other form of cruel, inhuman or degrading treatment or punishment, or armed conflicts. Such recovery and reintegration shall take place in an environment which fosters the health, self-respect and dignity of the child".

Part One

Three suspended 1,000 school
over sedation of boarders tell
girls in care home of bullying
HEAD LOCKS UP and abuse
HAIRCUT BOY HUNDREDS ABUSED IN CARE

Spot checks to fight children's home abuse

Children Disturbed child
at special centre to close
school after drug ban
'forced to
eat vomit' *Children force-fed*

Child care in *and beaten in home*
Britain 'an illusion' Children's
Up to 2000 children locked up
Troubled home for homewas
children to close 'repressive'
'SCHOOL OF CRUELTY' CONDEMNED
The care Child-care staff 'must be
nightmare vetted for crime record

Protecting children's physical and personal integrity and liberty

Children are the only people in the UK whose right to physical integrity - to protection from all forms of inter-personal violence - is not yet supported by the law and social attitudes. While concern over child abuse has escalated in recent years, the definition of child abuse in the law and in child protection policy and practice commonly condones quite a high level of violence to children.

Similarly, there has been growing concern over the restriction of children's liberty in residential institutions. But legal reforms and safeguards are not yet consistent.

This part of the report covers the legal framework for protection of children's physical and personal integrity (including in section 1.2 protection from bullying by other children and young people), and protection from arbitrary or unlawful restriction of liberty.

1.1 Protecting children's physical and personal integrity

Positive principles for caring for children

Children's law throughout the UK still lacks clear and positive principles of care for parents and all others caring for children, and in particular does not reflect the right of children, wherever they are, to respect for their physical and personal integrity - to protection from all forms of physical or mental violence.

Starting on page 29, we summarise relevant law and guidance which covers children in their homes and in the huge variety of institutional and other placements available in the UK. This demonstrates the illogical inconsistencies and gaps in protection which have come from piecemeal but escalating reform.

The law has moved, rapidly but still hesitantly, away from out-dated concepts of absolute parental rights and "ownership" of children. The Children Act, for England and Wales, introduced the concept of "parental responsibility", following landmark judgments like *Gillick* which had made it clear that parental rights are only granted to safeguard and promote the welfare of the child.[1] But the Act does no more than define parental responsibility in circular fashion as

"all the rights, duties, powers, responsibilities and authority which by law a parent of a child has in relation to the child and his property" (section 3).

The Scottish Law Commission's current proposals for reform of Scottish family law build on this, defining in some detail responsibilities and corresponding rights, and insisting that the child be consulted about major decisions (see page 32).[2]

The preamble to the UN Convention on the Rights of the Child emphasises that children should grow up in a family environment "in an atmosphere of happiness, love and understanding", and that the child

"should be fully prepared to live an individual life in society, and brought up ...in particular in the spirit of peace, dignity, tolerance, freedom, equality and solidarity".

Article 5 emphasises the need to respect the responsibilities, rights and duties of parents to provide *"in a manner consistent with the evolving capacities of the child appropriate direction and guidance in the exercise by the child of the rights recognised in the...Convention".*

And Article 18 states that

"Parents, or as the case may be legal guardians have the primary responsibility for the upbringing and development of the child. The best interests of the child will be their basic concern".

The right of all children to physical and personal integrity is upheld in Article 19, which insists that states must take

"all appropriate legislative, administrative, social and educational measures to protect the child from all forms of physical or mental violence, injury or abuse, neglect or negligent treatment, maltreatment or exploitation, including sexual abuse, while in the care of parent(s), legal guardian(s) or any other person who has the care of the child".

Sexual exploitation of children is also underlined in another Article (Article 34) of the Convention. Legislation in the UK on sexual offences covers sexual abuse of children, and prevailing social attitudes certainly do not condone it. But there is still a major problem of denial of its prevalence, both in families and in institutions, underlined in recent reports including those of the Cleveland and Orkney inquiries.[3]

The UN Convention raises another issue relevant to physical integrity of children: it insists that "effective and appropriate measures" must be taken

"with a view to abolishing traditional practices prejudicial to the health of children" (Article 24(3)).

This provision was inserted in the Convention because of particular concern over the practice of female circumcision, genital mutilation of girls and young women in certain communities. Genital mutilation is specifically prohibited under the Prohibition of Female Circumcision Act 1985, but there are concerns about the effectiveness of enforcement, and guidance was issued under the Children Act for England and Wales in 1991 to alert social workers and others to the issue.[4] This provision in the Convention applies to any traditional practice which may be prejudicial to the child's health, and its implications should be considered seriously in all communities. The anti-discrimination principle in Article 2 of the Convention, that all rights must be available to all children without discrimination on any ground, emphasises that the child's right to physical integrity cannot be undermined by culture, religion or tradition.

To accord children the status they deserve as people, and to implement fully the UN Convention which the Government ratified in December 1991, the law must include a clear statutory basis for children's rights, including their right to physical and personal integrity which is the focus of this report.

We recommend that laws concerning the upbringing of children in England and Wales, Northern Ireland and Scotland should be prefaced by a statement of positive principles of caring, as well as a clear prohibition of all physical punishment and humiliating treatment of children, addressed to parents, others with parental responsibility and all those having care and control of children.

Law in some Scandinavian countries already provides useful examples of positive principles of care for children: in Finland, the Child Custody and Right of Access Act 1983 begins:

"The objects of custody are to ensure the well-being and the well-balanced development of a child according to his individual needs and wishes, and to ensure for a child close and affectionate human relationships in particular between a child and his parents.

"A child shall be ensured good care and upbringing as well as the supervision and protection appropriate to his age and stage of development. A child should be brought up in a secure and stimulating environment and should receive an education that corresponds to his wishes, inclinations and talents.

"A child shall be brought up in the spirit of understanding, security and love. He shall not be subdued, corporally punished or otherwise humiliated. His growth towards independence, responsibility and adulthood shall be encouraged, supported and assisted" (section 1).

Similarly in Sweden, the section on custody and access in the Code relating to Parents, Guardians and Children begins:

"Children are entitled to care, security and a good upbringing. Children are to be treated with respect for their person and individuality and may not be subjected to corporal punishment or any other humiliating treatment".

"Reasonable chastisement"

With the developing concept of parental responsibility and positive principles of care must come a change in attitudes to ensure that it is no longer acceptable to deliberately hurt or humiliate children. The legal concept of "reasonable chastisement" is no longer an appropriate standard for treatment of children. It carries with it overtones of ownership, and a lack of respect. To achieve the necessary change in attitudes, we recommend it should now be abandoned, and replaced with parental duties to "guide" and "safeguard" their children, in line with their evolving capacity. Such a change would signal a new status for children, and provide a logical basis for much-needed education and information programmes to encourage positive discipline, and for child protection.

The right of parents and other carers to use "reasonable chastisement" is rooted in legal cases going back centuries. "Chastisement" does not only cover striking children and other physical punishments, but any other punishment or treatment judged "reasonable" by the courts. In the leading case Chief Justice Cockburn stated in 1860:

"By the law of England, a parent...may for the purpose of correcting what is evil in the child, inflict moderate and reasonable corporal punishment, always, however, with this condition, that it is moderate and reasonable".[5]

When the first legislation against child cruelty was passing through Parliament, the Bill which became the Prevention of Cruelty to and Protection of Children Act 1889, a provision was included confirming parents', teachers' and other carers' right to use "moderate and reasonable" punishment. It is clear from the reports of debates on the Bill that the major pre-occupation of MPs and peers was to ensure that in legislating against cruelty they did not interfere with punishment rights. An amendment was moved and accepted to delete the words "reasonable and moderate" qualifying punishment. And as the Bill passed through the House of Lords, Lord Herschell reassured peers:

"Your Lordships will see that the Bill carefully reserves intact the power which rests in a parent or guardian to administer punishment to a child. In that respect the law is not interfered with by this Bill".[6]

This acceptance of "reasonable chastisement" has been re-enacted without debate in succeeding Acts. Currently in England and Wales it is the Children and Young Persons Act 1933, together with the law on assault, which provide protection for children and young people from cruelty. Section 1 of the 1933 Act makes it an offence for anyone aged 16 or over who has the custody, charge or care of any child or young person under 16,

"to wilfully assault, ill-treat, neglect, abandon or expose the child in a manner likely to cause unnecessary suffering or injury to health".

It is curious and probably significant that legislators found it appropriate to include the word "unnecessary", apparently implying that cruelty to children involving "necessary" suffering or injury is acceptable.

Subsection 1(7) of the Act contains the statutory confirmation of parents' and other carers' common law freedom to use "reasonable and moderate" chastisement:

"Nothing in this section shall be construed as affecting the right of any parent, teacher or other person having the lawful control or charge of a child or young person to administer punishment to him".

(Similar legislation applies in Scotland and Northern Ireland - see page 29).

During passage of the Children Bill (now the Children Act 1989) through Parliament, attempts were made to remove this statutory confirmation of punishment rights, but the Government argued that children were adequately protected under existing legislation.[7]

As within the law on cruelty, the common law defence of "reasonable chastisement" is also available in the law on assault, although there is no statutory confirmation of it. The criminal law covering offences against the person was reviewed in 1980 by the Criminal Law Revision Committee but it made no recommendations for change or limitation of the common law defence of "reasonable chastisement".[8] Currently (February 1993) the Law Commission is considering further reform related to offences against the person, as part of a major project to codify the criminal law, but as yet has not made any suggestions for reviewing or reforming this defence.[9]

Thus while specific laws to protect children from cruelty by parents and other carers have existed for more than a century, the built-in concept of "reasonable chastisement" has continued to permit a high level of violence and humiliation to children, in their homes and in institutions (see page 30 for examples of recent court interpretations of "reasonable"). The concept of child abuse, instead of being based as it should be on the right of the child to physical and personal integrity, to protection from all forms of physical or mental violence, tolerates an arbitrary level of violence.

Institutional abuse

A report on institutional abuse of children published in 1992 by the NSPCC concluded:

"As crisis has followed crisis in public care, and reports have continued to publish recommendations that remain unheard, finally it seems that some of the fundamental problems in residential care are being recognised. The size of the task facing those who must remedy the situation remains enormous, with a genuine shift in public attitudes required..."[10]

The flood of reports acknowledging serious abuse of children in every kind of institutional placement continues in 1993. As the NSPCC report stated:

"...the testimonies of victims show that institutional abuse of children and young people is a significant problem representing a serious violation of human rights".

It reported that the scale of the problem was unknown, but that some professionals had suggested that up to three-quarters of children in residential care suffered some sexual abuse. It quotes a survey by the National Association of Young People in Care (NAYPIC) of a self-referred group of 50 young people in care which found 65 per cent alleging sexual abuse, 75 per cent alleging physical assault and 80 per cent complaining of over-use or wrongful use of restraint.[11]

In institutions, hitting children with implements including canes, leather tawses and slippers, as well as smacking or slapping them with the hand and shaking them, were widespread and legal methods of punishment in the UK until recently. It is only in the last six years that there has been any legislation to prohibit corporal punishment of children (outside the penal system: it ended in prisons and borstals in 1967). In 1987 abolition took effect in all state-supported education in the UK (as indicated on page 51 this reform does not yet - February 1993 - cover all pupils in private schools).

Since then, building on this reform, the Children Act 1989 has effectively ended physical punishment in England and Wales in local authority and private foster care (see page 34), and in all group daycare settings including childminding in England, Wales and Scotland (see page 47). And as another step towards adequate protection of children, regulations which apply to residential children's homes in England and Wales, both local authority, voluntary and private, not only prohibit physical punishment but also for the first time list other unacceptable sanctions (see page 38).

We recommend that this reform should be appropriately and consistently applied to all institutional and quasi-institutional settings for children, throughout the UK, together with a general prohibition of any form of humiliation (the 1992 review of residential child care in Scotland proposes this - see page 44).

In relation to institutions, it is also important to emphasise very clearly, as we do in our recommendations, that unacceptable sanctions do not become any more acceptable or legal when they are described as "treatment" or advocated as part of a "behaviour modification programme". In the case of Pindown in Staffordshire children's homes, the "treatment methods" of Frank Beck in Leicestershire children's homes, and in other child care, education and health institutions, interpretations of behavioural psychology have been used to justify regimes or practices which abuse and humiliate children, restrict their liberty and deny them basic rights.

In addition to making the legislation protecting children in institutions consistent, it is essential to ensure that all carers as well as children are aware of the legislation. In relation to those employed to care for children, there must also be mechanisms to ensure respect for the legislation, for investigation of all breaches, and to ensure that serious breaches can constitute grounds for preventing the perpetrator gaining further employment with children. Our recommendations address these issues, as do others in Part Two of the report.

Reform in the home

Most recently, moving reform into the family home, the Scottish Law Commission proposed in its report presented to Parliament in May 1992 that there should be strict limits on parents' and other carers' punishment rights, and that it should become a criminal offence to strike a child with an implement, or in a way which causes or could cause injury, or pain or discomfort lasting more than a very short time (see page 31).[12] While there is now wide support among non-governmental organisations in the children's field for prohibition of all physical punishment, this is the first detailed proposal from a governmental body in the UK, and deserves careful consideration.

If implemented, the Commission's proposal would undoubtedly provide clarification and limitation of the right to use "reasonable chastisement". But while the Commission emphasises that it does not see itself as supporting smacking as a child-rearing technique, it refers in its report to "safe disciplinary smacks", "ordinary safe smacks", "a safe parental smack on the bottom" and "careful smacks".[13] Yet the Commission

"accepts and regards as important, the arguments to the effect that physical punishments tend to escalate in severity, that parents using physical force may inadvertently cause damage, and that much abuse starts as ordinary punishment".[14]

Talk of "safe" or "ordinary" smacking is disrespectful to children: if we accord children less protection than the rest of us enjoy from all forms of inter-personal violence, we accord them a lower status as people. Nowadays our society would not for a moment countenance making distinctions in the law between hitting a wife or partner with an implement, and giving her "a little slap" or a "safe smack". Violence against women persists, but the principle of equal status and equal protection in the eyes of the law is established.

When considering Article 19 of the UN Convention on the Rights of the Child, which insists that states should protect children from "all forms of physical or mental violence", the Commission argues

"it is by no means clear that an ordinary smack, which causes no injury, would come within the category of violence, abuse or maltreatment...The

question of when physical contact, even physical contact intended to cause temporary pain, becomes physical violence is, in our view, a question of degree".[15]

But this view, which makes a special case for mild inter-personal violence when directed at children reflects rather than challenges current social attitudes and is certainly not based on principle.

There has been no proposal to include in the law on criminal assault a definition of the seriousness of assault that would constitute a prosecutable offence. Yet it is clear that in relation to minor assaults of adults by adults, the law does not intervene, although a technical offence may have been committed. The same would of course be true if "little smacks" directed at children were to be classified technically as criminal assaults.

The Commission, seeking to justify a different level of protection for children, quotes parents' rights to confine their child in a playpen

"in circumstances in which one private citizen could not lawfully confine another adult in a wooden cage".[16]

But the analogy is flawed: there is nothing protective involved in hitting a child, whatever the motive. Carers often justify physical punishment on grounds of safety, but raising a hand to hit a child who is crawling towards a fire or running into a road both dangerously delays the necessary protective physical intervention, and confuses rather than clarifies the message the child gets about the danger.

The Commission itself recognises

"the force of the argument that, as a matter of policy, a child's interest in not being hit by others should be taken fully into account and given the fullest respect".[17]

Implementation of the Commission's proposals would certainly mark a substantial step forward in child protection, and the Commission is to be warmly congratulated for tackling what it knew would be a controversial and emotive issue.

To provide children, as people, with the same protection as adults from all forms of inter-personal violence, the common law defence of "reasonable chastisement" needs to be removed in statute from both civil and criminal law, in so far as it justifies physical punishment or other punishments involving humiliating treatment of children.

Equity for children demands that the law makes no distinction between assaults where the perpetrator is an adult and the victim a child, and assaults where both perpetrator and victim are adults.

If providing children with equal protection from all physical punishment in both criminal and civil law as we recommend proves unacceptable in the current social and political climate, then we propose that a reform similar to that proposed by the Scottish Law Commission should be applied to criminal law throughout the UK and the civil law should be used to emphasise that physical punishment and other humiliating treatment of children is not acceptable. This was the method adopted (in the Education (No 2) Act 1986 and the Education (Corporal Punishment) (Northern Ireland) Order 1987) to end corporal punishment in state-supported education; the legislation does not make "reasonable" physical punishment by teachers a criminal offence, but removes their defence of "reasonable chastisement" in any civil proceedings brought against them.

One advantage of reform in civil law is the pragmatic one that it avoids the emotive concept of "criminalising little smacks". But this concept is a red herring, promoted to obscure the argument of principle. Nobody is suggesting creating a new criminal offence of smacking - just that the law on assault should be applied to children without the limits uniquely imposed by concepts of "reasonable" corporal punishment. The disadvantage of following the civil law route is the principled one that it falls short of giving children the same legal protection of their physical integrity as the rest of us.

But perhaps more important, given that the primary purpose of these reforms is educational - to change attitudes and practice - using civil law would ensure that children themselves retain the maximum control over any legal action for minor assaults, which is more than likely to affect them adversely. It is obviously extremely difficult for a child to pursue a civil action against his or her parents, and most unlikely that any would. But that is not the point of the provision, which is simply to make clear that physical punishment of children is unlawful. We note that in relation to the prohibition of physical punishment in children's homes, regulations simply state, without elaboration, definition or means of enforcement, that "any form of corporal punishment...shall not be used".[18]

The Scottish Law Commission rejected use of the civil law. During its consultation it received a number of proposals that all corporal punishment of children by parents should be made unlawful for civil law purposes but not for criminal law purposes. The Commission argued first that if these proposals were followed:

"Even conduct at the extreme end of what is permitted by the present law, involving perhaps the use of belts, sticks or other implements, would not be made a criminal offence".

The Commission suggested that to place the reform in civil law only would convey a confusing message to parents, *"who would be told, in effect, that the lawfulness of smacking, belting or caning their children depended on what court they came before...This solution would give the quite false impression that the state is not greatly interested in the matter and that it is simply a private matter between parent and child. The whole reason for setting a legal limit is that the state is interested in protecting children. If the state is sufficiently interested to intervene and set a limit, it should not, in our view, simply leave it to beaten children to enforce the limit by taking civil proceedings against their parents. It would not be acceptable to say that moderate corporal punishment of a wife by her husband was a civil wrong but not a criminal offence".[19]*

Pursuing such arguments logically from a children's perspective surely lends support to giving them the same protection that adults have under criminal and civil law from all inter-personal violence. But the Commission, while arguing correctly that the seriousness of some physical punishment involving use of implements, risk of injury etc merits criminal prosecution, goes on by implication to defend a degree of violence towards children as different from any other form of inter-personal violence, and meriting neither criminal prosecution, nor civil action, nor even necessarily discouragement.

The Commission's dismissal of the use of civil law to determine parental rights to punish seems harsh and out of line with their other proposals for reform. Civil law clearly does reflect "the state's interest" in that it is drafted and implemented by the state. The Commission does not propose that its provisions defining parents' rights and responsibilities, and its radical proposal that parents and others should be obliged to consult children and take their views seriously, should be sited in the criminal law.

Thus it accepts the point of using family law to change behaviour and attitudes. The purpose of such law is not enforcement through the courts, but increased respect for children as people, and improved family relations. This, precisely, is the purpose of a clear ban on all physical punishment and humiliation of children. In addition it will provide an unambiguous basis for child protection work and for information campaigns on positive ways of child-rearing.

Reform in other European countries

Whether the civil law or criminal law, or both as we favour, should be used is largely an academic matter: the major purpose of legal reform in this area is to achieve a rapid change in attitudes and practice, and there is evidence from other countries to suggest that this could be achieved by reform of either civil or criminal law. The five European countries which have completely prohibited all physical punishment of children have generally used their civil law to do so. In some cases, as in Sweden, this has led to the criminal law on assault being applied to any physical punishment of children without distinction. The researched effect of these reforms has been to change attitudes and practice, without increasing prosecution of parents or intervention in family life.[20]

An official of the Swedish Ministry of Justice, explaining the motivation for their legal reform which was implemented in 1979, said:

"By the prohibition of physical punishment, the legislator wanted to show that a child is an independent individual who can command full respect for his or her person, and who should thus have the same protection against physical punishment or violence as we adults see as being totally natural for ourselves".[21]

As the law came into effect in Sweden in 1979, a group of parents made an application to the European Commission of Human Rights, alleging that the legislation breached rights guaranteed to them by the European Human Rights Convention, including the right to respect for family life. The Commission rejected the application in a decision released in May 1982. It concluded that

"the actual effects of the law are to encourage a positive review of the punishment of children by their parents, to discourage abuse and prevent excesses which could properly be described as violence against children".

The official summary of the decision stated:

"The existence of legislation prohibiting all corporal punishment of children, but which does not provide for any sanction in this respect, cannot be considered as an interference in the exercise of the parents' right to respect for family life. Neither does the fact that corporal punishment of a child by his parents may expose the latter to criminal prosecution for assault, by the same standards as assault of a person outside the family, constitute an interference with the exercise of this right".[22]

In Sweden, in the 13 years since the law came into effect in 1979, there has been just one prosecution of a parent for "ordinary" physical punishment (a father was fined the equivalent of £10 for spanking his 11 year-old son, who felt sufficiently aggrieved to report him). A pamphlet circulated by the Swedish Ministry of Justice to all families with children explained the effect of the new law:

"Should physical chastisement meted out to a child cause bodily injury or pain which is more than of very temporary duration it is classified as assault and is an offence punishable under the Criminal Code. In theory at least, this was also true before the new Bill came into force, although it was not generally known. However, the advent of the new law has now swept all doubt aside, although as before trivial offences will remain unpunished,

either because they cannot be classified as assault or because an action is not brought".[23]

In the other countries which have so far prohibited all physical punishment (Finland, Denmark, Norway and Austria) it appears there have been no prosecutions for "ordinary" physical punishment.[24]

In a 1985 recommendation, the Committee of Ministers of the Council of Europe proposed that member states, including the UK,

"should review their legislation on the power to punish children in order to limit or indeed prohibit corporal punishment, even if violation of such a prohibition does not necessarily entail a criminal penalty".

The explanatory memorandum to the recommendation stated:

"...It is the very assumption that corporal punishment of children is legitimate that opens the way to all kinds of excesses and makes the traces and symptoms of such punishment acceptable to third parties".[25]

This was echoed in a further recommendation of the Committee of Ministers in 1990:

"The importance should be emphasised of the general condemnation of corporal punishment and other forms of degrading treatment as a means of education, and of the need for violence-free education".[26]

Recently in several countries, governmental commissions have been appointed to investigate the causes of high levels of violence in society, and to propose ways of preventing or reducing them. After sifting the considerable evidence, they have recommended in every case that physical punishment of children must end. This was the first recommendation of the West German Government's Commission on "Prevention and Control of Violence" in 1990:

"The parental right to chastise, which makes violence a legitimate means of child-rearing, implies the risk of abuse. The borderline between permitted correction and forbidden abuse is neither fixed nor defined clearly".[27]

In August 1992, the German Minister of Justice committed her country to introduce legislation to prohibit all physical punishment within two years.[28]

In Australia, the National Committee on Violence stated in a 1989 report:

"The greatest chance we have to prevent violence in society is to raise children who reject violence as a method of problem-solving, who believe in the right of the individual to grow in a safe environment".

The Committee

"strongly condemns the use of physical violence in disciplining children. The long-term aim should be to abolish such practices. In the interim, this objective is best achieved by education..."[29]

Education not prosecution

The purpose, as we have stressed, of the reforms we recommend is educational. And to be effective, there must be an immediate commitment, alongside legal reform, to positive programmes to support parents and other carers with advice and information on discipline which does not involve violence or humiliation. Guidance issued under the Children Act breaks new ground in providing some positive advice for those working in institutions, and for foster carers and daycare workers. Sir William Utting in his report *Children in the Public Care*, emphasised the importance of training in conflict avoidance and the management of aggression for residential staff:

"even more important is training in approaches which reduce the incidence of violent behaviour".

Sir William reflected that

*"there is an understandable feeling (**among residential workers**) that, while antiquated and inappropriate methods of physical control have quite properly been forbidden, staff have had very little help, advice or training in better methods to replace them.*[30]

More recently, the Warner Report, *Choosing with Care*, recommended that the Government

"should issue full guidance for staff on the issues of control, restraint and physical contact with children in residential care; keep this up-to-date; and reinforce it by ensuring the provision of authoritative training material that allows staff to apply the guidance in real situations".[31]

In April 1993 the Department of Health circulated guidance on permissible forms of control for dealing with extreme situations in residential care. And late in the same year the Scottish Social Work Services Inspectorate also published draft guidance for consultation.[32] Early in 1993 the National Association of Head Teachers produced a memorandum on *Care and Control of Pupils/Students*. This strongly recommends that every school and college should have its own "behaviour management policy", and includes a detailed section on coping with challenging behaviour. The references in the memorandum indicate that a number of individual local authorities have produced detailed guides on these issues already.[33]

So far the Government has not lent its weight to campaigns to discourage physical punishment and humiliation of children in all settings, and to encourage positive discipline. We recommend that it should, both for parents and all other carers. The evidence from other countries suggests that doing so could quickly achieve a change in attitudes and practice of huge benefit not only to children, but to our society as a whole.

Summary of current protection of children's physical and personal integrity

Children at home

Children in the UK living at home have no legal protection against "reasonable and moderate" physical punishment, nor against any other punishment or treatment unless it amounts in the eyes of a court to an offence of cruelty within the terms of section 1 of the Children and Young Persons Act 1933, or the similar provisions applying in Scotland and Northern Ireland: the Children and Young Persons (Scotland) Act 1937 (section 12) and the Children and Young Persons (Northern Ireland) Act 1968 (section 20).

Punishment rights appear to extend to parents, including step-parents, other relatives, and babysitters and nannies caring for the child on behalf of the parent.

Child psychologists John and Elizabeth Newson, who have been studying all aspects of child-rearing, including discipline, for 40 years, have found high rates of commitment to physical punishment:

"The majority of British parents we have interviewed seem to believe that physical punishment is an inevitable and probably necessary aspect of ordinary child upbringing".

As recently as 1985, they interviewed a sample of over 300 mothers with one year-old children: 63 per cent of them said they already smacked their babies. Earlier research by the Newsons found that 22 per cent of seven year-olds had been hit with an implement by their mother; in social classes 1 and 2 (professional and managerial) the proportion of boys already hit with an implement rose to 29 per cent. A further 53 per cent of seven year-olds had been threatened with an implement (implements used or threatened in order of preference were strap or belt, cane or stick, slipper, miscellaneous object).[34]

A Gallup Poll commissioned by the organisation "EPOCH - End Physical Punishment of Children" in 1989 found that 75 per cent of the representative sample polled "believed in" physical punishment. This proportion reduced to 59 per cent of respondents aged 16 - 24, and to 42 per cent of those who reported they had not been physically punished as children. Over 90 per cent of respondents believed that children should never be hit with implements, and that babies under one year old should never be smacked.[35] Surveys conducted by parents' or women's magazines have found similar or large majorities committed to smacking. A survey of *Woman's Own* readers in 1990 found that a quarter of the "thousands" who admitted smacking their children said they had lost control at least once while disciplining. (The magazine also reported that "more than half of mums who smack have regretted doing so".)[36]

In 1990 the Department of Health commissioned a large-scale

"normative study of the nature, extent and background factors of physical violence to children in the home".

The first results should be available late in 1993.

Judges have continued in general to look leniently on parents and other carers who hit children, even with implements. In October 1991 for example, a mother who admitted beating her 11 year-old daughter with a garden cane and an electrical flex was acquitted of assault and cruelty at Brighton Crown Court; in March 1993, North Avon magistrates acquitted a father who admitted using a leather belt on his sons aged five and eight, causing severe bruising.[37] But in contrast, in February 1990 Sir Stephen Brown, President of the High Court Family Division, upheld a local authority decision to place two children on their child protection register after their mother had smacked one of them three times with a wooden spoon. The judge emphasised that the injuries were not very serious:

"But what they did suggest was that there was a basis of concern as to the treatment this boy might receive, even though he well merited some form of reprimand".[38]

And a father who pleaded guilty to two charges of assault after beating his nine and 12 year-old sons with a belt was sentenced to 140 hours of community service in December 1992 in Lincoln.[39]

Scotland

In 1989, Lord Emslie, then Scotland's most senior judge, defended a mother's use of a belt on her 10 year-old daughter, commenting:

"It is evident that the girl richly deserved punishment and the mother's intention was to inflict on her the punishment she deserved".[40]

This case can be contrasted with two other recent Scottish judicial decisions: one in which slapping a two year-old child in the face, knocking him over, was held to be as remote from reasonable chastisement as could possibly be imagined;[41] and a case reported in 1991 in which a father who had whipped and caned his son and two daughters from the age of seven onwards was jailed for four years by Lord Morton of Shuna at the High Court in Dunfermline. Lord Morton told the accused that his violence to the children "went far beyond anything that could have been described as reasonable".[42]

In May 1992, the Scottish Law Commission published and presented to Parliament its proposals for reform of family law which contained a draft Bill.[43] A Discussion Paper circulated by the Commission in October 1990 had asked whether parents' rights to administer "reasonable" corporal punishment should be retained or abolished.[44]

In its 1992 report, the Commission published findings of an opinion poll carried out in September 1991, which reflected the results of EPOCH's poll referred to above, and showed overwhelming support for making any punishment with a belt, stick or other object illegal (94 per cent thought it should be illegal to hit a three year-old with an implement; 91 per cent to hit a nine year-old with an implement, and 85 per cent to hit a 15 year-old with an implement). On the other hand 83 per cent felt that it should be lawful to smack a three year-old with an open hand in a way not likely to cause lasting injury (87 per cent approved smacking a nine year-old, and 68 per cent a 15 year-old).[45]

The Commission's report, which is currently (February 1993) under consideration by Ministers in the Scottish Office, advocates limits but not complete abolition of the right to use physical punishment: it proposes that the defence of "reasonable chastisement" should be removed for the purposes of both the criminal and civil law,

"if the conduct complained of involved striking a child:

(a) with a stick, belt or other object; or

(b) in such a way as to cause, or risk causing, injury; or

(c) in such a way as to cause, or to risk causing pain or discomfort lasting more than a very short time".[46]

The report emphasises the wide public support for banning the use of implements in disciplining children, but states:

"outright abolition of all corporal punishment, for both civil and criminal law purposes, would not be in accord with the overall results of our consultation..."[47]

The Commission proposes, in addition to limiting the defence of "reasonable chastisement", that section 12(7) of the Children and Young Persons (Scotland) Act 1937 which provides statutory confirmation of the defence, should be repealed, together with the references to "assault" in section 12. Section 12 begins:

"If any person who has attained the age of 16 years and has the custody, charge or care of any child or young person under that age, wilfully assaults, ill-treats, neglects, abandons, or exposes him, or causes or procures him to be assaulted, ill-treated, neglected, abandoned, or exposed, in a manner

likely to cause him unnecessary suffering or injury to health...that person shall be guilty of an offence..."

The Commission explains:

"We are in favour of repealing section 12(7). At best it is unnecessary. At worst it conveys the message that cruelty to children is acceptable if done in the name of punishment. If the repeal was accompanied by the other changes we are recommending there would be no risk of confusion so far as those exercising parental responsibilities or rights are concerned".

The Commission also proposes that those who have care or control of a child but do not have parents' responsibilities or rights in relation to the child

"should have no greater right than a parent to administer corporal punishment to the child".[48]

Elsewhere in the report, following principles in the UN Convention on the Rights of the Child, the Commission proposes developments in the concept of parental responsibility, and respect for the views of the child, emphasising that parental rights arise from responsibility: it proposes that a parent should have defined responsibilities towards his or her child:

"so far as is practicable and in the interests of the child:

(a) to safeguard and promote the child's health, development and welfare;

(b) to provide, in a manner appropriate to the stage of development of the child, direction and guidance to the child;

(c) if the child is not living with the parent, to maintain personal relations and direct contact with the child on a regular basis;

(d) to act as the child's legal representative".

Responsibilities defined in (a) and (b) would apply up to 18; those in (c) and (d) up to 16.

In order to fulfil these responsibilities, the Commission proposes that parents should have defined rights over children up to the age of 16:

"(a) to have the child living with him or her or otherwise to regulate the child's residence;

(b) to control, direct or guide, in a manner appropriate to the stage of development of the child, the child's upbringing;

(c) if the child is not living with the parent, to maintain personal relations and direct contact with the child on a regular basis;

(d) to act as the child's legal representative".

The Commission also proposes that

"before a person reaches a major decision which involves fulfilling a

parental responsibility or exercising a parental right, the person shall, so far as practicable, ascertain the views of the child concerned regarding the decision, and shall give due consideration to those views, taking account of the child's age and maturity".

The report states:

"There are great attractions in such an approach. It emphasises that the child is a person in his or her own right and that his or her views are entitled to respect and consideration".

It quotes the obligation in Article 12(1) of the UN Convention on the Rights of the Child to ensure that children have a right to express their views freely in all matters affecting them,

"the views of the child being given due weight in accordance with the age and maturity of the child".[49]

Guidance

There is as yet no official guidance discouraging the use of physical punishment and other undesirable sanctions by parents, although the Children Act bars physical punishment by foster carers (see below) and childminders (see page 47). The campaign "EPOCH - End Physical Punishment of Children" has circulated over 700,000 leaflets to individual parents and carers discouraging physical punishment and offering advice on positive ways of encouraging good behaviour since it was launched as a national campaign in 1989.[50] Some other organisations - notably the National Society for the Prevention of Cruelty to Children, the Health Visitors' Association and the National Foster Care Association - have also published and distributed positive advice.

While the Scottish Law Commission report does not specifically advocate an education campaign against physical punishment, it does state that its proposals

"would not be inconsistent with education campaigns aimed at discouraging corporal punishment generally and emphasising the benefits of alternative child-rearing practices".[51]

Children in care but living at home

Children who are in care but placed with their parents or other relatives have no additional protection, except that their care authority is placed under a welfare duty towards them and is obliged to consult them about decisions affecting them. For England and Wales, the Placement of Children with Parents etc Regulations 1991, issued under the Children Act, list in schedules 1 and 2 *"particulars to be taken into account in considering suitability of persons and households"* and *"particulars on which there should be agreement with the person with whom a child is to be placed"*,

but neither makes any mention of unacceptable sanctions.[52]

Foster care - local authority and voluntary organisation

England and Wales

Law

The Foster Placement (Children) Regulations 1991 oblige local authorities/voluntary organisations in England and Wales to get written agreement from prospective foster carers that they will not use corporal punishment on any child placed with them (regulation 3 and schedule 2).[53] The Children Act allows both local authorities and voluntary organisations to place children with foster carers - under sections 23 and 59 of the Act. In the latter case placements must be monitored by the local authority (section 62). Until recently only a small number of major voluntary organisations (Barnardos, Children's Society etc) were involved in making arrangements for fostering on behalf of local authorities. But over the last few years there has been a growth, at least in some areas of England, of smaller independent agencies recruiting, assessing and reviewing fostering arrangements for local authorities. If an agency operates on a "not for profit" basis, it is classified under the Children Act as a voluntary organisation. The National Foster Care Association is concerned that arrangements for local authority monitoring of placements made by such agencies may not be sufficient to safeguard the welfare of the children involved.[54]

Guidance

Guidance issued under the Children Act goes into more detail about acceptable discipline:

"The applicant's views on discipline should be explored including a readiness to accept that corporal punishment is inappropriate for children in foster placements and to undertake not to use such a form of punishment. The term 'corporal punishment' should be taken to cover any intentional application of force as punishment including slapping, pinching, squeezing, shaking, throwing missiles or rough handling. It would also include punching or pushing in the heat of the moment in response to violence from young people. It does not prevent a person taking necessary physical action, where

any other course of action would be likely to fail to avert an immediate danger of personal injury to the child or another person, or to avoid immediate danger to property. It is well established that the enjoyment of eating and drinking is fundamental to a child's healthy physical and emotional development. Meal times are an important social occasion in the life of a child and it would be quite inappropriate for a child to be refused meals. Deprivation of food and drink should be taken to include the denial of access to the amounts and range of foods and drinks normally available to children in the home but would not include instances where specific food or drinks have to be withheld from a child on medical advice. Similarly, restriction of contact ie visits to and from family and friends should not be used as a punishment".[55]

Scotland

The Boarding Out and Fostering of Children (Scotland) Regulations 1985 make no reference to punishment or treatment of foster children.[56] (The law in Scotland is under review - February 1993.)

Northern Ireland

There are no statutory controls on punishment by foster-parents. Current policy, according to the Northern Ireland Department of Health and Social Services, forbids corporal punishment in foster homes. (The law in Northern Ireland is under review - February 1993.)

Private fostering

England and Wales

Law

The Children (Private Arrangements for Fostering) Regulations 1991 provides (regulation 2) a list of matters on which the local authority must satisfy itself. These include

*"the standard of care which the child is being given...the suitability of the foster parent to look after the child and the suitability of the foster parent's household...(**and**) the ascertainable wishes and feelings of the child regarding the fostering arrangements"*.[57]

But the list does not cover unacceptable sanctions.

The legislation only covers children privately fostered for periods of 28 days or more. There are concerns about children (some from abroad) placed with individuals or families for shorter periods with no safeguards applying.

Guidance

Guidance issued under the Children Act repeats almost word for word the advice on discipline in the guidance on local authority foster care (see above):

"The social worker should explore the foster parent's views on discipline, including a preparedness to accept that corporal punishment is inappropriate for children who are privately fostered..."[58]

The National Foster Care Association has expressed concern that the involvement of local authorities in the regulation of private foster carers is in practice so limited that it is likely that the private foster carer's views on corporal punishment will not be explored, nor will they be provided with the training and support necessary to encourage them to use alternative and acceptable forms of discipline.[59]

The guidance includes an additional sentence:

"Verbal abuse, derogatory remarks and pointed jokes can cause psychological harm to the child".

This appears to be the only official guidance issued to those caring for children which specifically discourages verbal abuse.

Scotland

The Foster Children (Scotland) Act 1984 and the Foster Children (Private Fostering) (Scotland) Regulations 1985 make no reference to punishment or treatment of private foster children.[60]

Northern Ireland

There are no statutory provisions or safeguards covering private foster care arrangements (apart from an obligation to give notice of such arrangements to the relevant authority under section 1 of the Children and Young Persons Act (Northern Ireland) 1968). With "certain exceptions" fostering arrangements are made by the Health and Social Services Boards or by voluntary organisations (with the approval of the Health and Social Services Boards).[61]

Children's homes

England and Wales

Law

The Children's Homes Regulations 1991 cover maintained, controlled and assisted community homes, voluntary children's homes and registered (private) homes.[62] Until implementation of the Children Act in October 1991, private children's homes were entirely unregulated. The Children Act places a duty to safeguard and promote the welfare of children on local authorities providing homes, on voluntary organisations and on proprietors of private homes.

Section 53 of the Children Act sets out local authorities' duty to ensure that

"homes (community homes) are available:

(a) for the care and accommodation of children looked after by them; and

(b) for purposes connected with the welfare of children (whether or not looked after by them)..."

It is not clear whether all accommodation provided by local authorities for children is therefore covered by the Children's Homes Regulations (eg hostels). The regulations define "children's home" as a registered children's home, a community home or a voluntary home. The only stated exclusion (under regulation 3(s)) is that:

"These regulations shall not apply to premises used only to accommodate children for the purpose of a holiday for periods of less than 28 days at a time in the case of any one child".

There are concerns that this leaves private and voluntary schemes providing residential holidays entirely unregulated, if children are accommodated for less than 28 days. They also fall outside the definition of private fostering.

The Act currently requires independent boarding schools with less than 51 boarders to register as children's homes, and thus come within the scope of the regulations, unless they are approved under the Education Act 1981 to take children with statements of special educational needs (but see page 57).

The Children's Homes Regulations are the first legislation to prohibit a range of specified unacceptable sanctions, in addition to physical punishment: regulation 8 covers "Control and Discipline". It states that only such disciplinary measures as

"are for the time being approved by the responsible authority shall be used in a children's home".

"Responsible authority" means: local authority for maintained community homes; board of managers for controlled and assisted community homes; voluntary organisation for voluntary homes; and the "person carrying on" a registered home.

The only exceptions are that the Secretary of State can issue directions in relation to children detained under section 53 of the Children and Young Persons Act 1933 and accommodated in a children's home (no such directions had been issued by February 1993); the Secretary of State also has exceptional powers under section 22(7) of the Children Act

"...for the purpose of protecting members of the public from serious injury, to give directions to a local authority with respect to the exercise of their powers with respect to a child they are looking after..."

Regulation 8 goes on to list in paragraph (2) measures which

"shall not be used in a children's home -

(a) any form of corporal punishment;

(b) any deprivation of food or drink;

(c) any restriction on visits to or by any child or any restriction on or delay in communication by telephone or post with -

> *(i)   his parent,*
>
> *(ii)   any person who is not a parent of his but who has parental responsibility for him,*
>
> *(iii)   his relatives or friends,*
>
> *(iv)   any visitor appointed for the child in accordance with paragraph 17 of Schedule 2 to the Act, (**independent visitor**),*
>
> *(v)   any social worker for the time being assigned to the child by the local authority who are looking after him or voluntary organisation who are caring for him,*
>
> *(vi)   any guardian ad litem of the child,*
>
> *(vii)   any solicitor for the time being acting for the child or whom the child wishes to instruct;*

(d) any requirement that a child wear distinctive or inappropriate clothes;

(e) the use or withholding of medication or medical or dental treatment;

(f) the intentional deprivation of sleep;

(g) the imposition of fines (except by way of reparation);

(h) any intimate physical examination of the child" .

Paragraph (3) provides some exceptions:

"Nothing in this regulation shall prohibit -

(a) the taking of any action by, or in accordance with the instructions of, a registered medical or dental practitioner which is necessary to protect the health of a child;

(b) the taking of any action immediately necessary to prevent injury to any person or serious damage to property;

(c) the imposition of a requirement that a child wear distinctive clothing, for purposes connected with his education or with any organisation whose members customarily wear uniform in connection with its activities;

(d) the imposition by the responsible authority or the person in charge of the home having obtained a court order where necessary of any prohibition, restriction or condition upon contact between the child and any person if they or the person in charge of the home are satisfied that the prohibition, restriction or condition is necessary in order to protect or promote the welfare of the child".

And paragraph (4) sets out recording obligations:

"Full particulars of the use made of any disciplinary measures including -

(a) the date on which they were used;

(b) the reason why they were used; and

(c) the person by whom they were used;

shall be recorded by a duly authorised person on behalf of the responsible authority in permanent form in the home within 24 hours of their use and shall be signed by him".

Guidance

Guidance issued under the Act includes a lengthy and detailed section on "good order and discipline", including commentary on permitted and prohibited disciplinary measures. This is the most detailed official guidance so far issued on positive discipline, and is therefore quoted in full:

"Good order and discipline
"Different homes will have different philosophies of care. It is vital that staff have a sound understanding of the principles and procedures employed in the home for the care and discipline of the children and the treatment methods used so that they can respond to a child with confidence. Difficulties in control will arise where the objectives of the home are not well defined and consequently not well understood by staff or where the children do not understand the reason for their placement. Systems of control and discipline cannot be divorced from systems of management and systems of care practice and planning within the home. It is important that staff should set standards by their behaviour.

"Physical restraint should be used rarely and only to prevent a child harming himself or others or from damaging property. Force should not be used for any other purpose, nor simply to secure compliance with staff instructions. Homes should have a particularly clear policy on how and when restraint may be used. Training should be provided and managers should regularly and formally monitor staff awareness of the rules governing this aspect of their duties. Where children in homes have suffered particularly damaging experiences and have difficulty developing the self-control or good personal relationships which diminish the need for physical

restraint it is important that sufficient, able staff are employed to ensure that the children are dealt with sensitively and with dignity.

"The successful conduct of any home is dependent on a combination of sound management, high standards of professional practice and care planning and upon caring relationships. It is for the responsible body, having regard to the role and purpose of each home and to the nature and characteristics of the children accommodated therein, to develop written policies for each home and for the officer in charge of the home to implement these in the day to day management of the home.

"A major determinant of good behaviour and positive ethos of the home is the quality of the relationships between the staff and the children. Relationships between the staff and the children need to be based on honesty, mutual respect and recognised good professional practice. Many children in homes need to experience care which compensates for the loss of the attention and security they would otherwise receive through the direct care of their parents.

"Good order is unlikely to be achieved unless there is an established framework of general routines and individual boundaries of behaviour are well defined. Children need to be aware of what is expected of them and how the arrangements for their care actually work. There must be proper provision for the social, physical, emotional and intellectual needs of the children. It is important there should be a structure to the child's day and that the correct balance should be achieved between free and controlled time. There should be ample opportunity for children to participate in a range of appropriate leisure time activities. This will aid the maintenance of control.

"Problems will occur when expectations of behaviour are unrealistic or inconsistent or insensitive methods of control are used. Good professional practice would recognise that often misbehaviour by young people stems from a failure by adults to be sufficiently receptive to the needs and problems of the young people rather than from a wilful defiance of authority. The need to avoid labelling children as disruptive or seeking to resolve misbehaviour by moves to new placements without the original behaviour being properly addressed must be recognised. One of the principle purposes of control and discipline is to enable individual children to develop inner controls so that in time they learn self-control, establish feelings of worth and self-respect and are motivated towards improved behaviour and enabled to live in harmony within a group. They should be encouraged to develop a proper awareness of their rights and responsibilities and those of others.

"It is essential that children should be consulted and their wishes and feelings ascertained in matters concerning them. Good order is much more *likely to be achieved in homes where children are routinely involved in decision-making about their care. They should be encouraged to accept responsibility for their own care, appropriate to their age and understanding...*

"Permitted disciplinary measures

"It is recognised that some form of sanction will be necessary where there are instances of behaviour which would in any family or group environment reasonably be regarded as unacceptable. Often such unacceptable behaviour can be prevented by the use of mild or more severe verbal reprimand. The imposition of formal disciplinary measures should be used sparingly and in most cases only after repeated use of informal measures has proved ineffective. For example there is no intention to reduce the authority of staff in applying reasonable mealtime discipline or in the discretionary use of special treats. There should be a system of rewards (commendations, extension of privileges etc) as well as sanctions. In normal circumstances children should be encouraged to behave well by the frequent expression of approval by staff and by the generous use of rewards rather than by the extensive imposition of disciplinary measures. Where sanctions are felt to be necessary, good professional practice indicates that these should be contemporaneous, relevant, and above all just. Children in homes are likely, because of the system, to be confronted as to the consequences of their actions by numerous adults; this often serves merely to compound misbehaviour and undermine the child's self-esteem. Staff should appreciate when a misdemeanour is finished and the subject should be dropped. The responsible body should detail in writing the disciplinary measures which it approves for use in the home; other measures may not be used. The measures approved for use in the home should be appropriate to the age and circumstances of the individual children accommodated. Appropriate measures could be reparation, restitution, curtailment of leisure extras, additional house chores, and use of increased supervision. The responsible body must ensure that staff are aware of the measures which are acceptable, the extent of their discretion in administering them and the requirement to record their use on each occasion. The record of sanctions administered should be kept in a log book (but separately from the home's daily log) and should include in each entry the name of the child, details of the inappropriate behaviour, names of the staff present, and date and nature of the sanction. Each entry should be signed by a person authorised to sign on behalf of the responsible authority. All entries should be written in appropriate language, and all names, including that of the signatory, should be clearly identified. The responsible authority should keep under annual review the appropriateness of the disciplinary measures approved.

Responsible authorities should regularly monitor the use of sanctions and other measures of control in their homes, which should also be scrutinised by the inspecting body. Authorities should seek legal advice about the measures to be approved and their use and should ensure that staff responsible for monitoring, managing or inspecting homes also have access to legal advice".[63]

In August 1992, the Department of Health issued further draft guidance on permissible forms of control which attempts to distinguish between different forms of intervention involving physical control or the restriction of liberty.[64] It also sets out principles to determine the circumstances in which any intervention should be carried out. The Department hopes to issue the guidance in 1993.

Refuges

In England and Wales, the Children Act allows the Secretary of State to issue a certificate defining a voluntary children's home or registered (private) home, or a designated foster parent, as a "refuge" to be used for children who appear to be at risk of harm, generally children who are missing from home or care. The certificate exempts those involved from being prosecuted for harbouring absconding children etc.[65] Such refuges are covered by the appropriate children's homes or foster placement regulations (see above).

These refuges, which are not yet available under Scottish or Northern Ireland legislation (we recommend that they should be), provide a temporary safe haven for children whose living situation has become untenable, for example because of domestic violence and abuse. Negotiations about the child's future can take place from the refuge without necessarily revealing the child's whereabouts.

(Children may also be living with their mothers in "refuges" from domestic violence provided by voluntary agencies like Woman's Aid; such arrangements are not covered by children's legislation, unless the children are under a court order.)

Scotland

Law

The Social Work (Residential Establishments - Child Care) (Scotland) Regulations 1987 apply to any residential establishment providing residential accommodation for children which is controlled or managed by a local authority, which is required to register under section 61 of the Social Work (Scotland) Act 1968 (homes providing "personal care"), or is an independent or grant-aided school which has registered voluntarily under section 61(A) of the Act.[66]

These regulations state:

"(1) Arrangements for discipline, relevant to the care and control of children resident in a residential establishment, shall be determined by the managers in accordance with the statement of functions and objectives formulated under regulation 5(1).

(2) The arrangements shall not authorise the giving of corporal punishment and corporal punishment shall for this purpose have the same meaning as in section 48(A) of the Education (Scotland) Act 1980" (regulation 10).

There are no other controls on discipline in these homes.

The law is currently under review in Scotland.

Guidance

A circular issued in 1988 by the Scottish Social Work Services Group provides two paragraphs of advice on "discipline and other control arrangements": in general

"Staff should view intervention not as punishment or sanctions but as measures to assist the child's personal development, since controlled behaviour is necessary to successful functioning in society and to forming relationships with other children and adults".

The circular emphasises that physical restraint should be carried out in a non-aggressive way and should be authorised by the senior member of staff present. Its use should be recorded. Restriction or curtailment of correspondence or visitors should not normally be applied as a control measure.[67]

Late in 1992 the Social Work Services Inspectorate for Scotland published a review of residential care which included draft guidance on "care sanctions and constraints". It proposes to establish a working group to review the draft guidance in the light of responses, and recommends that once the guidance is issued, local authority inspection units

"should review at least annually the adherence by each home to the guidance and should involve young people and children in this review. They should also review staff training undertaken in respect of implementing the guidance".[68]

The review reports a survey of "measures used to control children and young people" in residential children's homes in Scotland. It found the most used measures were: restricted leisure activities (82 per cent of responding homes); early to bed (74 per cent); physical restraint (67 per cent); control of pocket money (62 per cent); extra tasks (46 per cent); isolation (20 per cent - in some cases with staff presence); withholding of normal clothing (11 per cent).

The review comments:

"Some establishments, especially small children's homes, use no sanctions except staff disapproval. Effective controls depend upon the effectiveness of disapproval, not on physical restraint. For disapproval to be effective approval must in the first place be important. Young people and children must know they are cared for if they are to care about themselves and their behaviour. They can only learn respect for others, through respect for themselves. They must also learn the boundaries of acceptable behaviour. The key skill so often is to be able to show disapproval of the behaviour without disapproval of the person".[69]

The draft guidance suggests that

"Sanctions are found in every group, including families. Within residential care establishments sanctions should be measured and appropriate. They should not be used as a matter of routine, should be used sparingly, and their usage should be monitored and reviewed".

It lists permitted sanctions and controls, and also controls which are not permitted, including: any kind of physical punishment; deprivation of meals; deprivation of contact with professionals or parents and other adults with whom children have a significant relationship; withdrawal of communication; being sent to bed early -

"This can be a more frightening and lonely experience than may be evident from the young person's behaviour. It is effectively unsupervised exclusion from the group and therefore carries potential dangers. Young people may be disallowed from staying up late to watch TV etc";

withholding or use of medication; any form of humiliation. The guidance also covers when and how to use physical restraint, and the need for overall consistency and training.[70]

Northern Ireland

Law

In Northern Ireland the relevant regulations do not prohibit corporal punishment or other undesirable sanctions. In practice however it has been forbidden in all statutory homes for a number of years, and strongly discouraged in voluntary homes.[71]

The four training schools (which include children convicted of criminal offences) are governed by the Children and Young Persons Act (NI) 1968, as amended, and by rules made in 1952.[72] These include powers to use corporal punishment, but it has not been used, according to the Northern Ireland Office, since 1981.

The law is currently under review in Northern Ireland.

Secure accommodation

England and Wales

Accommodation provided for the purpose of restricting the liberty of children in community homes must be approved by the Secretary of State: the Children (Secure Accommodation) Regulations 1991 apply in addition to the Children's Homes Regulations but do not include any additional provisions on control or punishment of children.[73]

Scotland

Similarly, the residential care regulations described above (page 42) apply to all establishments providing secure accommodation. There are no additional provisions on control or discipline applying specifically to secure accommodation.

Northern Ireland

Of the four Training Schools in Northern Ireland, one (Lisnevin), operates within a secure campus. Two others (Rathgael Centre and St Patrick's) have limited secure facilities. As indicated above the Training School Rules currently in force provide a power to use corporal punishment, but it is not in fact used.

(For detailed discussion of secure accommodation and legal safeguards against arbitrary/unlawful restriction of liberty see section 1.3.)

Youth treatment centres

Law

There are currently two youth treatment centres in England, administered by the Department of Health. The Secretary of State has the power (under section 82 of the Children Act) to arrange for the "provision, equipment and maintenance" of homes

"for the accommodation of children who are in need of particular facilities and services which...in the opinion of the Secretary of State are unlikely to be readily available in community homes".

No regulations control the care of children in the youth treatment centres, or define unacceptable sanctions. In March 1992 the Department of Health issued a "Policy and Management Specification" for the Youth Treatment Service.[74] This indicated that in relation to the rights of young people placed in the Service, the Secretary of State would be advised by a non-departmental group of lay-people (termed the "Secretary of State's YTS Group"). A Chief Executive has been appointed, responsible to the Secretary of State for management of the Service.

Residential care homes

Law

These homes, mostly for elderly residents but also including disabled children, are required to register under the Registered Homes Act 1984 and are covered by the Residential Care Homes Regulations 1984.[75] These regulations state that

"every home shall be maintained on the basis of good personal and professional relationships between the person registered and persons employed at the home and the residents" (regulation 9(3)).

The regulations oblige homes to keep

"a statement of the sanctions used in the home to control bad behaviour and a book in which shall be entered a record of any sanction administered to a child and the name of that child" (schedule 2, para 3).

The Residential Care Homes (Amendment) Regulations 1988 state that homes must

"ensure that corporal punishment is not used as a sanction in relation to any child in the home".[76]

Guidance

Detailed guidance on treatment of residents in these homes is given in a Code of Practice published in 1984.[77] In a foreword by the then Secretary of State, authorities were asked to regard the Code as having the same status as a Department of Health circular. A section on controls and sanctions (para 4.5.4) states that they should not be applied in such a manner as to undermine the self-respect of children or to lessen their sense of responsibility. The guidance was written before the regulations were amended to prohibit corporal punishment, and is silent on the issue. It emphasises that

"where possible, intervention should be based on reward rather than punishment, with the emphasis placed on good relationships and honesty,

*trust and respect. However, where sanctions have to be introduced, these
should have as their objective the growth of self-discipline otherwise they
become merely repetitive. Early bedtime, the setting of additional tasks, the
restriction of entertainments and the temporary withholding of pocket money
are preferable to other measures which might humiliate the child in the eyes
of himself and his peers. Restricting a child's contact with his parents or
depriving him of food should not be used as forms of correction, nor should
restriction of liberty be used..."*

The guidance adds that behaviour modification should only be undertaken on
the instruction of a medical practitioner or psychologist and under strict
supervision:

*"It should not be practised loosely by untrained workers as a means of
discipline"*.

A clear and written policy on sanctions is required.

Medication must never be administered for purposes of social control or
punishment (see also section 1.3.)

Scotland and Northern Ireland

In Scotland and Northern Ireland it appears there are no residential care
homes including both children and elderly patients.

Daycare

England and Wales

Law

The Children Act provides a new legislative framework for registration and
review of group daycare in England and Wales (and Scotland, see below).
The Act allows the Secretary of State to make regulations setting out
requirements which must be imposed by local authorities when considering
the registration of childminders and group daycare providers (sections
72(3)(a) and 73(4)(a)). But no regulations have as yet been issued (February
1993).

The requirement to register covers childminders looking after one or more
children aged under eight for reward on domestic premises, and anyone
providing daycare or supervised activities for one or more children under
eight on non-domestic premises (whether for reward or not). This covers, for
example, day nurseries, playgroups, permanent creches in shopping centres,
leisure centres, further and higher education establishments, temporary
creches set up for special events such as conferences, out of school clubs,

holiday playschemes, and adventure playgrounds. Those providing daycare but not required to register include parents or close relatives, foster parents in relation to foster children, and people (nannies etc) employed by a parent (or by two sets of parents) to look after a child mainly in the child's home.

Guidance

Guidance issued under the Act for England and Wales states:

"People responsible for running a daycare facility need to have an agreed policy on its day to day operation and to develop procedures for modifying unacceptable behaviour in the children which will include appropriate sanctions. It will encourage development of a sense of right and wrong behaviour if children are encouraged to co-operate in the social organisation of the facility. The sanctions applied in the case of unacceptable behaviour must take account of the age and stage of development of the child, be given at the time, be relevant to the action or actions and be fair. The child should always be told why his behaviour is not acceptable and the reasons for applying a particular sanction. Providers and childminders should ensure that parents are fully informed about and support the policy on modifying unacceptable behaviour and the range of sanctions.

"Corporal punishment (smacking, slapping or shaking) is illegal in maintained schools and should not be used by any other parties within the scope of this guidance. It is permissible to take necessary physical action in an emergency to prevent personal injury either to the child, other children or an adult or serious damage to property".[78]

The guidance appears to cover local authority day nurseries, playgroups, private nurseries, childminders, out of school clubs and holiday schemes, parent-toddler groups, toy libraries, drop-in centres and playbuses. The Department of Health issued a circular in 1993 "clarifying" the purpose of the guidance on daycare, with an emphasis on expanding daycare facilities "of an acceptable standard". It provides some additional guidance, none of it directly relevant to the above.[79]

Scotland

Guidance

In Scotland, similar guidance for implementation of the daycare provisions of the Act has been issued by the Scottish Office. In a section on "behaviour" of children, it states:

"...There are no circumstances in which sanctions such as smacking, slapping or shaking can be justified. Under section 12 of the Children and Young Persons (Scotland) Act 1937 a person aged over 16 who is looking

after a child and who ill-treats him or causes him to be ill-treated is guilty of an offence. It may however be necessary to take preventive physical action to avoid the risk of injury to the child or to some other child or a carer".[80]

Northern Ireland

Guidance on daycare issued under the Children and Young Persons (Northern Ireland) Act 1968 does not cover sanctions, but the Northern Ireland DHSS reports that Health and Social Services Boards in practice operate a "no smacking" policy. The law in Northern Ireland is under review (February 1993).

Residential nurseries

There are a small number of institutions offering residential accommodation for babies and very young children (sometimes in association with daycare). Some have advertised themselves as "hotels" for babies. Under the Children Act for England and Wales the definition of (private) children's home in section 63 suggests that they are required to register as children's homes, and are thus subject to various regulations (see above page 37).

Health service

National Health Service (NHS) institutions

Law

There is no legislation specifically covering treatment or punishment of children and young people in NHS institutions, which include hospitals, adolescent units, and some locked provision, apart from a general ban on ill-treatment of patients with mental disorders in NHS and private health institutions (Mental Health Act 1983, section 127).

Guidance

Recently the Department of Health issued guidance which states:

"The physical punishment of children in maintained schools, including hospital schools, is now illegal. As in all other areas of a hospital, children should never be punished by smacking, slapping or shaking".[81]

The NHS Management Executive drew the attention of co-ordinators, purchasers and providers of health services to the guidance in a circular.[82]

Private health institutions

Law

There are private nursing homes and hospitals for those suffering from sickness, injury or infirmity, and also maternity homes. There are also private mental nursing homes for those with "mental disorders" as defined in the Mental Health Act 1983. A number of mental nursing homes contain only disabled children and young people, some placed by local authorities, some by parents, and some detained under the Mental Health Act. Concerns about treatment of children and young people in some private health institutions, including in particular use of sedation and restriction of liberty, have been raised over the last few years (see page 87). These institutions are required to register under the Registered Homes Act 1984. Regulations applying are the Nursing Homes and Mental Nursing Homes Regulations 1984.[83] These do not cover unacceptable sanctions. It appears that some nursing homes are also registered as residential care homes (see page 46).

Similar legislation on private health institutions in Scotland and Northern Ireland does not cover unacceptable sanctions.

Education

Maintained schools

Law
Throughout UK

In August 1987 legislation came into effect which protects pupils in state-supported education from corporal punishment. The legislation is contained in the Education (No 2) Act 1986 (section 47 for England and Wales, and section 48 for Scotland: later amended by the Self-Governing Schools etc (Scotland) Act 1989 schedule 10 para 8(18)), and in the Education (Corporal Punishment) (Northern Ireland) Order 1987 for Northern Ireland.

The legislation defines corporal punishment as

"doing anything for the purpose of punishing the pupil concerned (whether or not there are other reasons for doing it) which, apart from any justification, would constitute battery".

A subsection makes clear that

"a person will not be taken as giving corporal punishment by virtue of anything done for reasons that include averting an immediate danger of personal injury to, or an immediate danger to the property of, any person (including the pupil concerned)".

(The effect of this subsection in education legislation is reflected in the regulation prohibiting corporal punishment in children's homes, and in the guidance on unacceptable sanctions in other settings.)

The legislation did not take the simple course of defining any corporal punishment as assault, by removing the traditional defence of "reasonable chastisement" from teachers and others working in schools. Its effect is only to remove this defence in any civil action taken against a teacher for giving corporal punishment. A subsection protects teachers from criminal liability:

"A person does not commit an offence by reason of any conduct relating to a pupil which would, apart from this section, be justified on the ground that it is done in pursuance of a right exercisable by a member of the staff by virtue of his position as such" (section 47(4)).

Nor does the legislation protect all school pupils. It covers all maintained schools, including grant-maintained schools (and self-governing schools in Scotland) and also non-maintained special schools (see page 53). In the private sector, only those pupils whose fees are paid in whole or in part by the state, or who attend private schools supported by the state (eg certain music schools and city technology colleges), come within its scope. Parents can still pay to have their children beaten in independent schools, and a number of schools still advertise their use of corporal punishment (see page 54).

England and Wales

Apart from legislation on exclusion from school (see below), there are no other specific limits on sanctions to be used in maintained schools. The Education (No 2) Act 1986 states that articles of government for all county, voluntary and maintained special schools must give the head teacher the duty of determining measures,

"which may include the making of rules and provisions for enforcing them to be taken with a view to -

(i) promoting, among pupils, self-discipline and proper regard for authority;

(ii) encouraging good behaviour on the part of the pupils;

(iii) securing that the standard of behaviour of the pupils is acceptable; and

(iv) otherwise regulating the conduct of pupils..."

The head teacher must act in accordance with any written statement of general principles from the governing body, and have regard to any guidance offered on particular matters. The head teacher must also make disciplinary measures "generally known within the school". The "standard of behaviour which is to be regarded as acceptable" at the school is to be determined by the head teacher, "so far as it is not determined by the governing body". The head and governing body must consult the local education authority about any disciplinary measures which may lead to increased expenditure, or which may affect the responsibilities of the authority as an employer (Education (No 2) Act 1986 section 22).

The same Act gives LEAs "reserve powers" to

"take such steps as they consider are required to prevent the breakdown, or continuing breakdown, of discipline"

in any school maintained by them, where the education of pupils may be "severely prejudiced" (section 28).

There is no other legislation limiting disciplinary measures in maintained schools, including maintained boarding schools. Maintained special schools (and non-maintained special schools - see page 53) are required to keep a punishment book in which must be recorded "disciplinary measures" taken against pupils, by the Education (Approval of Special Schools) Regulations 1983, as amended by the Education (Approval of Special Schools) (Amendment) Regulations 1991.[84] A circular states:

"The punishment book is intended to record disciplinary measures taken by a member of staff against a pupil in the enforcement of school discipline. The use of corporal punishment as a disciplinary measure is no longer valid. Section 47 of the Education (No 2) Act 1986 prohibits the use of corporal punishment in maintained and non-maintained special schools. While major measures, such as fixed term, indefinite or permanent exclusions, should be recorded, it is not intended that this book should include minor measures employed in day-to-day classroom management. The punishment book should not deal with sanctions or privileges withheld as part of any general social procedures developed within the school community nor part of any individual behavioural or treatment programme (which might nevertheless be recorded in pupils' treatment or other records)".

Our recommendations emphasise the importance of not treating sanctions differently because they form part of a "treatment" programme.

Incident books should also record "serious or recurrent disciplinary problems involving pupils or staff".[85]

Exclusion from school

The Act also introduced for the first time detailed provisions on suspension and exclusion from school. Only head teachers can exclude pupils. There are no appeals against temporary or indefinite suspensions, but parents (and pupils from the age of 18) have a right to appeal against permanent exclusion (expulsion) to a tribunal set up by the local education authority, or in the case of voluntary schools, by the governing body; (grant-maintained schools' governing bodies must also make arrangements for appeal).

In November 1992 the Department for Education issued a discussion paper on school exclusions, seeking views on possible changes in legislation, and on the need for further guidance on discipline and exclusions.[86] Certain changes may be included in the Education Bill currently (February 1993) before Parliament.

There does not appear to be any legislative framework to allow children or their parents to challenge exclusion/expulsion from any other category of institution, except that proprietors of independent schools approved to take children with statements of special educational needs are required to consider representations from parents and local authorities before deciding to exclude a child.

Scotland

Aside from the legislation on corporal punishment already described (page 50), matters of discipline are left to schools and education authorities. Scottish schools have a positive statutory duty to take reasonable care for the safety of pupils when under their charge (Schools (Safety and Supervision of Pupils) (Scotland) Regulations 1990.[87] A local authority may only exclude a pupil from school if satisfied that the parent of the pupil refuses or fails to comply, or to allow the pupil to comply, with the rules, regulations or disciplinary requirements of the school, or if they consider that allowing the pupil to remain at the school would be likely to be seriously detrimental to order and discipline in the school or the educational well-being of other pupils: Schools General (Scotland) Regulations 1975.[88]

Non-maintained special schools

This anomalous group of schools - neither maintained nor independent - are generally boarding schools run by voluntary organisations not for profit for children with special educational needs, and must be approved by the Secretary of State for Education and Science. The legislation against corporal punishment in the Education (No 2) Act 1986 applies to pupils at these schools.

The Education (Approval of Special Schools) Regulations 1983 as amended by the Education (Approval of Special Schools) (Amendment) Regulations 1991 place a duty on the governing bodies of these schools to

"make such arrangements for safeguarding and promoting the welfare of the pupils at the school as shall have been approved by the Secretary of State".

The regulations also oblige schools to keep a punishment book; information to be published by the governing body must include details of *"general arrangements as to school discipline and the arrangements for bringing school rules to the attention of pupils and parents"* (schedule 3).[89]

Because voluntary organisations are "accommodating" pupils at these schools, certain provisions in the Children Act (sections 61 and 62) also apply to them. The voluntary organisation is placed under a general duty to safeguard and promote the children's welfare, and also to give due consideration to the ascertainable wishes and feelings of children regarding decisions made about them. Certain regulations issued under the Children Act also apply to these schools - the Arrangement for Placement of Children (General) Regulations 1991; the Review of Children's Cases Regulations 1991, and the Representations Procedure (Children) Regulations 1991.[90] But none of these relates to treatment of children in the school, and the Children's Homes Regulations do not apply to these schools, although they do apply to some small independent boarding schools (see page 57).

Independent schools

As noted above, the legislation against school corporal punishment does not protect pupils in the private sector whose fees are paid by their parents. Regulations issued under the Education (No 2) Act 1986 detail the pupils protected.[91]

Current Government policy, expressed in a letter from the Department for Education, is that abolition of corporal punishment for all pupils in independent schools would be inappropriate

"on the grounds that parents of such pupils are better placed than those in the maintained sector to act on their philosophical convictions about corporal punishment by sending their children to schools with corresponding discipline policies".[92]

The European Commission of Human Rights has declared admissible two applications from independent school pupils and their parents alleging that the use of corporal punishment in their schools breached the European Human Rights Convention. The cases were referred by the Commission to the European Court of Human Rights. In its judgment in the case of Costello-Roberts v UK, announced in March 1993, the Court found by five votes to four

"that the particular corporal punishment inflicted on the applicant had not given rise to a violation of Article 3 of the European Convention of Human Rights".

Jeremy Costello-Roberts had been slippered three times on his buttocks at a boarding school when he was seven. The four dissenting judges stated that

"...in the present case, the ritualised character of the corporal punishment is striking. After a three-day gap, the headmaster of the school 'whacked' a lonely and insecure seven year-old boy...In our view the official and formalised nature of the punishment, meted out without adequate consent of the mother, was degrading to the applicant and violated Article 3".

The decision does not in any sense support retention of corporal punishment in schools: all nine judges emphasised that

"the Court did not wish to be taken as approving in any way corporal punishment as part of the disciplinary regime of a school".[93]

The European Court decided not to hear the other case, Y v UK, after the applicant and the Government agreed a financial settlement involving a payment of £8,000 plus legal costs amounting to over £12,000,

"on condition that the case is withdrawn from the Court and no further cases are instituted against the Government in respect of this matter in any national or international court".[94]

In this case, the European Commission found the caning which the boy "Y" received at an independent day school amounted to inhuman and degrading treatment in breach of Article 3 of the European Convention on Human Rights. It reported:

"The applicant was hit with such force with the cane that four wheals appeared on his buttocks, with swelling and bruising, causing considerable pain for some time after the act itself. The Commission considers that such injury to a teenage boy is unacceptable whoever were to inflict the punishment, be it parent or teacher. The Commission sees no justification for treating the applicant in this way. In particular it can find no pedagogical reason for dealing with the applicant's bullying behaviour with a punishment on the same bullying level, ie the use of superior strength to hurt and degrade another".

It is clear, given the very narrow decision in the Costello-Roberts case, that if this case had gone to the Court, the caning would have been found to be in breach of the European Convention.[95]

Attempts are being made during the passage of the Education Bill, currently (February 1993) before Parliament to extend legislation against corporal punishment to cover all pupils in independent schools.

There is no legislation limiting disciplinary measures in independent day schools, nor in all independent boarding schools. The Children Act places new welfare duties on the proprietors of independent schools in England and Wales which "provide accommodation for any child" (ie boarding schools), to "safeguard and promote the child's welfare" (section 87), and the local authority for the area has a corresponding duty to take steps to ensure that this obligation is fulfilled. These duties do not apply to independent schools obliged to register as children's homes, or under the Residential Homes Act 1984 as residential care homes providing personal care for children who are disabled or mentally disordered (see below).

Guidance issued under the Act on the interpretation of the general duties in section 87 is addressed to proprietors and to local authority social services departments (SSDs). The section on discipline goes into some detail, eg:

"Schools should have a clear policy on what standards of behaviour are expected of pupils, how these standards are to be maintained and how unacceptable behaviour is to be tackled. Schools should ensure that parents are aware of their policy on behaviour and discipline and should aim to secure parents' support in putting it into practice..."

SSDs are advised to have regard to the principles and practice regarding control and discipline in the Children's Homes Regulations (see page 37). The guidance suggests there should be a system of rewards as well as sanctions:

"In normal circumstances children should be encouraged to behave well by the frequent expression of approval by staff and by the generous use of rewards rather than by the extensive imposition of sanctions. The latter might reasonably include: temporary removal of privileges, mild or moderate verbal reprimand, additional household chores and restriction of leisure activities. Sanctions which are unproductive, eg writing out of lines, or which involve the use of educational activities, such as essay-writing, should be avoided as a means of punishment. If in exceptional circumstances it is decided to use corporal punishment, it should not be unreasonable (for trivial offences or applied indiscriminately to whole classes) or excessive. In all circumstances punishments and sanctions need to be applied fairly and consistently, making the distinction between minor and serious offences clear, yet at the same time allowing a degree of flexibility for individual circumstances.

*"In deciding how these criteria are to be applied some allowance needs to be made for the cultural ethos and declared policy of the school. Corporal punishment is widely regarded as particularly inappropriate for children with sensory, physical and intellectual impairment and those with emotional and behavioural difficulties. Details of corporal punishment - date, nature of offence, nature of punishment - should be recorded in the punishment book and the record witnessed by another adult. In normal circumstances corporal punishment should only be administered by the head teacher. The imposition of sanctions (but **not** corporal punishment) by prefects or teachers is permissible providing that these punishments are reasonable. Sanctions administered or imposed should be recorded stating clearly the nature of the transgression and the nature of the sanction, and be subject to monitoring by*

a senior member of staff who is concerned with care of children within the school. The record should be available to parents".[96]

Regulations on the inspection of independent schools by SSDs (the Inspection of Premises, Children and Records (Independent Schools) Regulations 1991) state that those carrying out inspections may inspect records which contain, amongst other things, "details of punishments administered to any child in the school".[97] But there is no regulation requiring all independent schools to keep punishment books: this is a requirement for special schools including non-maintained special schools, for independent schools approved to take children with statements of special educational needs, and for those independent schools required to register as children's homes (see below).

Independent schools required to register as children's homes

The Children Act obliges independent schools in England and Wales which have less than 51 boarders to register as children's homes (section 63), unless they are approved by the Secretary of State for Education and Science under section 11(3)(a) of the Education Act 1981 to take children with statements of special educational needs. Also exempt are those independent schools which are registered under Part I of the Registered Homes Act 1984 as residential care homes providing personal care for children who are disabled or mentally disordered (see below).

In January 1993, the Department of Health indicated that the Education Bill currently (February 1993) before Parliament was to be used to amend the requirement to register, so that independent schools with boarders would only have to register as children's homes if four or more pupils normally remain for more than 295 days during the year, irrespective of the number of boarders accommodated for shorter periods (ie during term-time only).[98]

Those independent schools currently obliged to register as children's homes (the Department of Education and Science estimates that there are approximately 250 of them, representing about 10 per cent of all day and boarding independent schools, and approximately a quarter of all independent schools with boarding accommodation) come within the scope of the Children's Homes Regulations 1991, and guidance issued under the Children Act (see page 37). Thus the use of corporal punishment and other specified sanctions is prohibited, a punishment book must be kept etc.

Independent schools required to register as residential care homes

Independent schools with 50 or fewer pupils, not approved to take children with statements of special educational needs under the 1981 Act (see below) are required to register as residential care homes under the Registered

Homes Act 1984 if they are providing both board and "personal care" for four or more persons

"in need of personal care by reason of...disablement...or past or present mental disorder".

These schools come within the scope of the Residential Care Homes Regulations (see page 46). Thus corporal punishment is prohibited and there is a requirement to keep a statement of sanctions and a record of their use. The Code of Practice *Home Life* applies (see page 46). (Schools which are registered as Residential Care Homes cannot be registered as children's homes - Children Act section 63(5)(c).)

Independent schools approved to take children with statements of special educational needs

Under the Education Act 1981, the Secretary of State for Education has power to approve independent schools to take children with statements of special educational needs (and under the Act local authorities may only place children with statements in independent schools which are approved, unless the Secretary of State has approved the particular placement - section 11(3)).

Regulations set out the grounds for approval (Education (Special Educational Needs) (Approval of Independent Schools) Regulations 1991). The proprietor must arrange

"in the case of a school which is also a boarding school, for such steps as may be necessary to be taken to safeguard and promote the welfare of the boarders at all times".[99]

The schools are required to keep

"a punishment book in which there shall be recorded disciplinary measures taken against children in the school" (schedule 1, para 10(2)).

The school must publish a prospectus; amongst the information it must contain are

"particulars of the general arrangements as to school discipline including, especially, the practice of the school as respects corporal punishment where permitted by law and the arrangements for bringing to the attention of children and parents school rules made in respect of such punishment" (schedule 2, para 12(2)(g)).

The proprietor must also ensure that children are not excluded from the school "otherwise than on reasonable grounds". Before any decision to exclude a child is taken, the proprietor must "unless it would not be appropriate to do so in any case", give written notice to parents, local education authority or placing authority, and the local authority in which the school is situated, giving the grounds for the proposed exclusion. The proprietor must take into account any representations made by any of these parties (schedule 1, para 5).

(The major Education Bill presented to Parliament in November 1992 reenacts most of the 1981 Act, including requirements for the approval of independent schools to take children with statements, but the legislation may be amended during the Bill's passage through Parliament.)

Guidance

Guidance on the interpretation of the regulations is given in a DES Circular.[100] The guidance on sanctions including corporal punishment (where legal) is similar to that issued under the Children Act (see page 55).

Scotland and Northern Ireland

There is as yet (February 1993) no legislation similar to that in the Children Act applying to independent schools in Scotland or Northern Ireland.

Penal institutions

Young offender institutions

Law

The Young Offender Institution Rules 1988 (for England and Wales) include detailed provisions on discipline and control, systems of privileges, personal letters and visits etc.[101] The section on "order and discipline" states:

"Order and discipline shall be maintained but with no more restriction than is required in the interests of security and well-ordered community life. In the control of inmates, officers shall seek to influence through their own example and leadership, and to enlist their willing co-operation".

Force must not be used "unnecessarily", and

"when the application of force to an inmate is necessary, no more than is necessary shall be used".

In addition,

"no officer shall act deliberately in a manner calculated to provoke an inmate" (rule 47).

Temporary confinement to a special approved cell or room is permitted in certain circumstances (see section 1.3, page 95).

No inmate aged under 17 may be put under restraint. Removal from association with other inmates is also controlled under rule 46.

The rules list offences against discipline, including the general one of in any way offending against good order or discipline. They also list the "awards" which the governor can make for an offence against discipline, including caution, forfeiture of privileges, extra work, confinement to a cell or room for not more than three days etc. Charges against discipline must be inquired into, first by the governor, and the inmate must be given

"a full opportunity to hear what is alleged against him and of presenting his own case" (rule 52).

Graver charges must be referred to the Board of Visitors.

There is an important requirement that a copy of the Rules should be made available to any inmate who requests it.

Scotland

Regulations covering the young offenders institutions in Scotland (the Young Offenders (Scotland) Rules 1965) are similar, but include a provision allowing inmates to be deprived of their mattress for up to 15 days. This seems a humiliating sanction which should not be applied.[102]

Northern Ireland

As indicated above, the Training School Rules 1952 still permit corporal punishment, but it has not been used for some time. The law in Northern Ireland is under review.[103]

Attendance centres

There are 110 attendance centres in England and Wales, mixed and male-only junior centres (age range 10 - 17 inclusive) and senior centres (males aged 16 - 20). They are governed by the Attendance Centre Rules 1958 as amended by the Attendance Centre (Amendment) Rules 1978.[104] A section on "discipline" states that

"the discipline of a centre shall be maintained by the personal influence of the officer in charge and staff", and that *"persons shall while attending at a centre conduct themselves in an orderly manner and shall obey any order given or instruction issued by the officer in charge or any member of the staff"*.

Any person breaching the Rules can be required to leave a centre. Otherwise, breaches of the Rules can be dealt with

"in either or both of the following ways:

(a) by separating him from other persons attending the centre;

(b) by giving him a less attractive form of occupation".

The rules are under review, and new rules are likely to be implemented in 1993.

Recommendations

1.1 Protecting children's physical and personal integrity

1 Laws concerning the upbringing of children in England and Wales, Scotland and Northern Ireland should be prefaced by a statement of positive principles for caring, addressed to parents, others with parental responsibility and all those having care and control of children.

These principles, which would, as appropriate, provide parents and others with parental responsibility with corresponding rights, should include the following:

Children are entitled to care, security and a good upbringing.

Safeguarding and promoting the welfare of the child shall be a primary consideration in all matters concerning the child.

Caring for the child shall be based on respect for his or her person and individuality, and for the child's evolving capacity to make decisions for him/herself.

The child's views regarding any major decision shall be ascertained and given due consideration having regard to the child's age and understanding.

The child shall not be subjected to corporal punishment or any other humiliating or degrading treatment or punishment (corporal punishment shall be defined as in the Education (No 2) Act 1986).

(An alternative approach would be to include in legislation a "Parenthood Code" including these and other similar principles which all those with parental responsibility and others caring for children would be required to pay due regard to.)

2 Section 1 of the Children and Young Persons Act 1933, barring cruelty (and similar acts affecting Scotland and Northern Ireland), must be amended to remove the current implied justification of "necessary" suffering or injury to health caused by assault, ill-treatment or neglect of children.

(Section 1 currently begins:

"If any person who has attained the age of 16 and has the custody, charge or care of any child or young person under that age, wilfully assaults, ill-treats, neglects, abandons or exposes him, or causes or procures him to be assaulted, ill-treated, neglected, abandoned or exposed, in a manner likely to cause him unnecessary suffering or injury to health...that person shall be guilty of a misdemeanour...")

Section 1(7) of the Act, which confirms the common law freedom of parents and other carers to use "reasonable" physical punishment, and similar provisions in the law affecting Scotland and Northern Ireland, must be repealed.

3 The current common law defence of "reasonable chastisement", in so far as it justifies corporal punishment or other humiliating treatment or punishment should **either** be explicitly removed for the purposes of both criminal and civil proceedings, or it should be removed for the purposes of civil proceedings, and in the criminal law the defence should be limited along similar lines to those proposed by the Scottish Law Commission.

We favour removing the concept of "reasonable chastisement" altogether, as inappropriate and anachronistic, in the context of developing concepts of parental responsibility and respect for children's rights. It should be replaced by parental duties to guide and safeguard their children according to their evolving capacity.

4 Definitions of physical and sexual child abuse used in child protection should be based clearly on the child's right to physical and personal integrity, and should not condone any level of physical or mental violence to children. This should be emphasised in inter-departmental guidance, and local procedural handbooks.

5 We emphasise that the purpose of these reforms is to change attitudes and practice, not to increase prosecution of parents or intervention in family life, which are unlikely to benefit children. We therefore recommend that the Government should use all appropriate channels to clearly discourage physical punishment and other humiliating treatment of children, and provide and/or support information campaigns aimed at encouraging positive non-violent child-rearing.

6 In addition to the general prohibition on physical punishment and other humiliating treatment and punishment proposed above which would apply to all carers, legislation applying to all institutional and other formal placements - day and residential, including foster care, childminding etc - should include a section prohibiting other specified sanctions. The Children's Homes Regulations 1991 issued under the Children Act for England and Wales (SI 1991 No 1506) contain an appropriate list for all residential institutions (see page 38): this could be amended for application to day institutions including schools, and to foster care, daycare etc.

It should be emphasised and made explicit in regulations and guidance that prohibited sanctions are no more acceptable if they form part of a behaviour modification programme, or are described as "treatment" rather than punishment.

7 Where temporary or permanent exclusion from a day or boarding institution (whether state-maintained, voluntary or private) is a permitted sanction, the right to exclude must be limited by appropriate criteria, and excluded children must have a right to appeal to an appropriate tribunal operating on principles of natural justice.

8 The legislation applying to all institutional and quasi-institutional settings must ensure that children and young people are not involved in the administration of sanctions against other children and young people (see also section 1.2 on bullying, page 70).

9 All institutions should be required to ensure as far as possible that all children and young people, their parents/guardians etc and all those working in the institution are aware of the positive principles of care outlined above, of the legislation protecting children from physical punishment and other humiliating treatment, and from other specific prohibited sanctions. They should be encouraged to involve children and young people directly in reviewing behaviour and discipline policies.

10 All "formal" carers (eg those working with children in institutions, and those whom the state is involved in registering or regulating, including eg foster carers, childminders etc) should be required in legislation to sign an agreement to indicate that they are aware of and will respect the legal provisions to protect children from ill-treatment and abuse, and also the positive principles of care outlined above.

11 Sufficient evidence of any breach of the legal provisions to protect children from ill-treatment and abuse should provide justification for dismissal for breach of contract, whether or not a prosecution and conviction follows. Serious breaches should be grounds for preventing the perpetrator from gaining further employment giving access to children (see also section 2.3, page 132). Hopefully, such issues can be built into codes of conduct for those professions which are able to regulate their members who are caring for children and young people (eg see the proposal for a General Social Services Council, supported in section 2.3, page 152).

Proof of such a breach should provide the employer with a defence against any claim for unfair dismissal. Information about any such breach should, after the worker has been given an opportunity to see and challenge it, be forwarded to an appropriately-constituted professional committee (similar to the "three wise men" procedure which adjudicates in relation to certain misconduct by doctors). This Committee would decide whether the information should be forwarded to the office or departments maintaining lists of people considered unsuitable for work involving substantial access to children (see section 2.3).

Gross or repetitive breaches of the provisions, whether or not they lead to any prosecution or conviction, must be regarded as providing evidence of unsuitability to work with children.

12 Codes of practice or guidance should be issued to all those working with children in institutional settings, day and boarding, on positive methods of encouraging acceptable behaviour. Guidance should also be issued to appropriate institutions on responding to challenging behaviour, and the minimum use of force in restraining children and young people who are a danger to themselves or others. This guidance should emphasise that "control" should be based on positive relationships between carers and children and young people, and that carers should aim to encourage acceptable behaviour through example, encouragement and reward rather than by punishment. Where rules of conduct are necessary, they should be clearly explained in ways that are readily understandable to the children and young people concerned. Enforcement of any sanctions should be subject to appeal and principles of natural justice. (The draft guidance on "permissible forms of control in children's residential care", issued by the Department of Health, and the draft guidance from the Social Work Services Inspectorate for Scotland, both issued in 1992, provide a valuable start.)

13 The Department of Health should be designated the lead government department with overall responsibility for all aspects of child protection, charged with co-ordinating policy and action across government. The Scottish, Welsh and Northern Ireland Offices should designate lead departments for co-ordination of policy.

14 Children's law in Northern Ireland and Scotland should allow the development of "refuges" similar to those covered by section 51 of the Children Act 1989 in England and Wales.

1.2 Protection from bullying by children/young people

Bullying is a common occurrence in institutions for children and young people (and indeed in less formal settings). Ill-treatment and humiliation by adults - parents, teachers, residential workers and others - may amount to bullying. But bullying by other children and young people is a distinct issue which demands appropriate action. When children and young people have been asked to identify their concerns about institutional life, bullying has been identified as a very major issue, which has only received serious attention in the last few years. A valuable bibliography listing recent literature including research reports and resources was published in 1992, and demonstrates the upsurge of concern about bullying.[105]

The summary below looks briefly at reports which have drawn attention to bullying and proposed some solutions, mostly in schools. It is clear that the problem exists in all categories of institution (as it does of course in life outside institutions). Our recommendations propose that all institutional settings should be required to have a policy on protection from and prevention of bullying, and that children and young people should be actively involved in drafting, implementing and monitoring it. We also emphasise that children and young people should never be involved in the administration of sanctions imposed on other children and young people.

Schools

Concern about the level of bullying in schools has led to detailed research (including a major project on the development of intervention strategies funded by the Department of Education and Science at the University of Sheffield, due for completion in August 1993), and to reports and proposals for action by local education authorities, governors, teachers and parents. A voluntary group - ABC: the Anti-Bullying Campaign - was set up by a mother following the death of her 13 year-old son in 1985 (Mark had been the victim of bullying for several months and was cycling away from boys at a regular ambush point when he was knocked down by a van and killed).[106] Kidscape, the national campaign for children's safety, has run training conferences and produced materials for schools.[107] An anti-bullying pack was distributed to every school in the UK by the Gulbenkian Foundation and British Telecom in 1992.[108]

In 1990, ChildLine, the national helpline for children, opened a special "Bullying Line", funded by the Gulbenkian Foundation. Over a three month period 2,054 children were counselled. From January to June 1991, ChildLine ran another special helpline for children in boarding schools, funded by the Department of Education and Science and the Independent Schools Joint Council. Calls on this line showed bullying to be a very common problem.

An analysis of the calls received by the Bullying Line and also calls about bullying received by the Boarding School Line shows that children consider a wide range of behaviour to be bullying, from teasing to serious physical harm.[109] Nearly a quarter of the children reported bullying involving violent assault. Others reported theft of money or possessions or extortion. Over three quarters of the bullying occurred in school, with the remainder on the way to or from school, or in the neighbourhood. In boarding schools, nine per cent of the children reporting bullying indicated that it happened in dormitories, at night or at weekends.

The report's conclusion stated:

"The children's implicit definition of bullying is broad and inclusive; it does not attempt to distinguish between 'real' bullying and any other kind of bullying. They most emphatically do not regard bullying as an inevitable part of growing up, but want it to be stopped. Children frequently doubt adults' ability to stop the bullying, and with good reason; many adults do not know what to do when faced with a child being bullied".

A report to the Department of Education and Science on the Boarding School Line emphasises:

"A special difficulty for children in boarding schools is that they cannot escape from those who bully them, by going home after school. While reports were rarely specific about where the bullying took place, in 17 cases it was noted that the bullying took place in dormitories. In more than one case, monitors or prefects came into a dormitory of younger children to bully and hit them. One report concerning a 13 year-old and his friend of the same age noted: 'They dread the nights...Bullying in dormitories is particularly distressing since it leaves the victims feeling they have no safe place to be'."[110]

Bullying often involves elements of racism. In 1984 HM Inspectorate of schools published the results of discussions at meetings in five local education authorities, *Race Relations in Schools*; it commented on the widespread nature of racial harassment and the need for whole-school policies supported by local and central government. The then Secretary of State for Education, Sir Keith Joseph, in a speech on "Racist bullying in schools", said that effective learning could only take place when pupils had a feeling of self-confidence, well-being and security flourishing in conditions conducive to equality of opportunity, mutual respect and co-operation.[111] The Commission for Racial Equality, in a report on a survey of racial abuse and violence in education commented:

"Racial harassment is widespread and persistent - and in most areas little is done about it. Young people in schools and colleges suffer no less than men and women on the streets and in their own homes on housing estates..." [112]

The Elton Report *Discipline in Schools* stated:

"Misbehaviour is usually defined as behaviour which causes concern to teachers. But there are also some serious forms of bad behaviour which only or mainly affect pupils. Bullying and racial harassment are cases in point. Bullying includes both physical and psychological intimidation. Recent studies of bullying in schools suggest that the problem is widespread and tends to be ignored by teachers...

"Research suggests that bullying not only causes considerable suffering to individual pupils but also has a damaging effect on school atmosphere. This is perhaps even more true of racial harassment. The Commission for Racial Equality expressed concern to us about accounts of racist name-calling, graffiti and physical attacks in schools. We consider that sexual harassment is also an aspect of bullying, and are concerned that this was given very little attention in the evidence put before us. It is hard to see how a school can win the confidence of its pupils if it fails to deal with behaviour which so seriously damages the quality of their lives". [113]

The report recommended that head teachers and staff should be alert to signs of bullying and racial harassment, should

"deal firmly with all such behaviour and take action based on clear rules which are backed by appropriate sanctions and systems to protect and support victims".

Schools "behaviour policies" should make it clear that pupils have a responsibility to share knowledge of bullying and racial harassment with staff in confidence.

The Elton Report also emphasised the importance of ascertaining pupils' views, giving pupils every opportunity to take responsibilities and to make a full contribution to improving behaviour in schools, and actively involving pupils in shaping and reviewing schools' behaviour policies: this is reflected in the recommendations in this report.

In May 1992, Schools Minister Eric Forth set out the Government's position on bullying in schools:

"Schools should be in no doubt about the importance the Government attaches to the eradication of bullying, wherever and whenever it appears. Bullying is a very unpleasant practice which schools must deal with firmly. It puts the personal well-being and the educational attainment of victims at risk..." [114]

Mr Forth quoted the Elton Report and commended its advice:

"The report recommended that head teachers and staff should be alert to signs of bullying and should deal firmly with such behaviour. Action should be based on clear rules backed by appropriate sanctions and systems to protect and support victims".

In July 1992 Mr Forth announced that the Government was distributing to all schools in England a pack on bullying prepared by the Scottish Council for Research in Education.[115] The pack, which was created and tested by teachers, head teachers, educational psychologists and advisers had already been distributed to schools in Scotland earlier in 1992. The pack emphasises that the single most important thing a school can do to prevent bullying is to have a clear policy to which staff, pupils and parents are committed.

While the first aim of intervention must be to protect children from being bullied, there is a growing emphasis on non-punitive responses to bullying. Strategies involving "bully courts" and public identification of bullies (one school made bullies wear an "I am a bully" badge for a period) are themselves humiliating and potentially dangerous. There is also an awareness that pupils' experience of physical punishment and other violent and humiliating treatment at home is frequently linked to bullying others at school. As the Association of Educational Psychologists summarised it in their response to a consultation on school corporal punishment in 1977: "Children who are beaten tend in their turn to beat and to bully".[116]

A "no blame" approach to bullying has been developed by two educational psychologists in Avon:

"When bullying is discovered or reported teachers generally investigate the incident, punish the bullies and urge the victims to take preventive or avoidance action. Our evidence from talking to teachers and young people is that these actions are both ineffective and unjustified on philosophical grounds".[117]

The "no blame" approach has been promoted at training courses for teachers and well received.

There is currently no specific legislation to promote local action to protect children and young people from bullying in schools or any other setting. ChildLine and other organisations have suggested that all schools should be obliged to have a written policy on identifying and dealing with bullying; this is supported in our recommendations (see page 72). A bullying policy adopted in Norway is reported to have reduced the incidence of bullying by up to 50 per cent. A national survey of 140,000 Norwegian junior and senior high school pupils indicated that 15 per cent were involved in bullying - six per cent as bullies and nine per cent as victims.[118] Research in the UK suggests that the problem is at least as serious here. For example, a large sample of fourth and fifth year pupils at 16 secondary schools in the London Borough of Newham were questioned in 1987: 39 per cent in the fourth year and 35 per cent in the fifth year reported being bullied. Of the pupils reporting bullying, 56 per cent felt teachers did not do their best to stop the bullying.[119]

Other institutions

Although not documented to the same degree, it seems clear that bullying occurs in all categories of institution for children and young people.

Recently, two reports on residential care have drawn attention to the issue. Sir William Utting's *Children in the Public Care* states:

"Children may need protection from children as well as adults. Verbal or physical violence should always be taken seriously and dealt with under local child protection procedures".[120]

The Scottish review *Another Kind of Home* makes one of the fundamental principles which should underpin residential child care that

"Young people and children should feel safe and secure in any residential home or school".

In draft guidance on "care sanctions and constraints", the review states:

"...young people in residence also look to staff not to allow them to be bullied, terrified or abused by potentially violent residents. They need to see that staff are vigilant and very professional in their response to the violence of young people; that they do not get caught up in the anger and violence, but have a carefully planned strategy which is safe for all the young people and staff".

The report also emphasises that using labels such as "bully, thug or violent" will exacerbate the problem, and that "It is the behaviour which is unacceptable, not the child".[121]

Where bullying involves assault or the threat of assault, it may amount to a criminal offence, and children or adults acting on behalf of children may involve the police in investigation, and consider the involvement of other child protection agencies. The Children Act guidance on residential care, for example, states:

"When a child in a children's home abuses another child, a very clear distinction will need to be made between, on the one hand, behaviour which amounts to physical assault, intimidation and sexual assault which requires external child protection intervention and possibly criminal investigation, and, on the other hand, normal childhood behaviour or sexual exploration which should be dealt with by care staff".[122]

Reports on detention centres and young offender institutions by the Chief Inspector of Prisons and Boards of Visitors have drawn attention to bullying, harassment and intimidation of inmates, particularly in dormitories. At Whatton in 1989 bullying was

"a dominant feature of the male 14-17 year-old bracket and the Board is concerned at its impact on the life of the institution".

At Onley YOI, bullying and intimidation were described as being "intrinsic to the pattern of institutional life in the units". An inspection report on Hewell Grange in 1989 expressed concern about dormitory accommodation "because of the ease of bullying and intimidation", and observed that on his arrival "the new Governor had noted a high number of trainees with black eyes".[123]

Control and discipline by other children and young people in institutions

In some institutional settings, in particular boarding schools, there is a tradition of involving older children and young people in the discipline and control of younger children and young people. There is a delicate balance here between encouraging a sense of participation in the running of an institution and giving positive responsibilities to children and young people, and providing opportunities for exploitation and formalised bullying. Involvement of older young people in positive disciplinary procedures does not carry with it the same dangers as does involving them in administering sanctions. The Children Act guidance on independent schools states very emphatically that "prefects" must not be allowed to administer corporal punishment, and it emphasises that

"where senior pupils have a degree of authority over others, it must be clear that there is no exploitation of one pupil by another".[124]

The case of Castle Hill School, whose proprietor was sentenced to 12 years imprisonment in 1991 for offences against young people including physical assault, indecent assault and buggery, emphasises the potential dangers of involving pupils in control:

"Ralph Morris's management style was totalitarian with ultimate control being vested in him. There was a subculture within the school involving himself and the boys. He operated a hierarchical system whereby some older and more senior boys were afforded special privileges...These favoured pupils presented as a fearful and vindictive corps and were used to control those who dared to go beyond the clearly defined limits. There are many examples of boys being assaulted by members of this elite task force at Ralph Morris's instigation. This group was referred to, by Mr Justice Fennell at the trial, as Ralph Morris's "Republican Guard". Assaults carried out by this group were both physical and sexual...

"The power structure previously referred to involved a strong pecking order (of pupils) headed by Ralph Morris through a system of sinecures and bullying. The young men were therefore reluctant to complain or substantiate other complainants due to fear of physical retribution or loss of position within the school. Furthermore, our inquiries have revealed abuse of other pupils by senior boys which made these young men feel as responsible as Ralph Morris and as liable to prosecution".[125]

The report on the Boarding School Line run by ChildLine in 1991 suggested that serious consideration should be given to how the exercise of authority in boarding schools might contribute to their problems with bullying.[126]

The rules applying to young offender institutions in Scotland state positively that: "No inmate shall be employed in any disciplinary capacity".[127]

Recommendations

1.2 Protection from bullying by children/ young people

1 All institutional settings for children and young people, both day and boarding, should be required in relevant legislation to have a policy on protecting children and young people in them from bullying and preventing bullying, which should be defined broadly to include physical assault and intimidation, theft and extortion, verbal abuse including teasing, racial and sexual harassment, harassment on grounds of religion, gender, sexuality etc.

2 Policies must cover:

arrangements to ensure that everyone in the institution is aware of the importance of reporting bullying and the importance of ensuring that those bullied are not blamed in any way;

specific strategies for preventing bullying;

provision of appropriate protection and support for those who are bullied;

appropriate responses to those who bully (with a strong emphasis on non-stigmatising and non-punitive approaches);

arrangements for responding to those forms of bullying that appear to involve criminal offences.

(see also recommendations in section 2.1, page 125 on access to confidential advice and counselling).

3 Children themselves should be actively consulted and involved in the drafting, implementation (but see 6 below) and monitoring of the policies.

For schools, we commend the Elton Report's general emphasis on ascertaining pupils' views, and on ensuring pupils' active participation and involvement in schools and in the formulation and review of behaviour policies. The curriculum should also appropriately reflect the need to value and respect others, human rights, anti-discrimination perspectives etc. A sensitivity to the issue should also be built into training for teaching and non-teaching staff.

4 The policy should be made available to all those in the institution including children, in a form they can understand.

5 Those responsible for inspecting the institution should be obliged to review the operation of the anti-bullying policy.

6 Children and young people should never be involved in the administration of sanctions for other children and young people: this should be forbidden in legislation on discipline and sanctions applying to all institutional settings.

1.3 Protection against arbitrary and/or unlawful restriction of liberty

The right to liberty is an inalienable human right for everyone including children. This is confirmed in Article 5 of the European Convention on Human Rights: "Everyone has the right to liberty and security of person..." It goes on to list certain very limited exceptions allowing restriction of liberty "in accordance with a procedure prescribed by law".

The UN Convention on the Rights of the Child states:

"No child shall be deprived of his or her liberty unlawfully or arbitrarily. The arrest, detention or imprisonment of a child shall be in conformity with the law and shall be used only as a measure of last resort and for the shortest appropriate period of time;

"Every child deprived of liberty shall be treated with humanity and respect for the inherent dignity of the human person, and in a manner which takes into account the needs of persons of their age. In particular every child deprived of liberty shall be separated from adults unless it is considered in the child's best interests not to do so and shall have the right to maintain contact with his or her family through correspondence and visits, save in exceptional circumstances..." (Article 37)

Another European Convention which the UK has ratified is intended to protect those whose liberty is restricted. Under the European Convention for the Prevention of Torture and Inhuman or Degrading Treatment or Punishment a Committee has been established which will

"by means of visits, examine the treatment of persons deprived of their liberty with a view to strengthening, if necessary, the protection of such persons from torture and from inhuman or degrading treatment or punishment".

States which ratify must allow the Committee unlimited access

"to any place where persons are deprived of their liberty, including the right to move inside such places without restriction"

and to interview in private anyone deprived of their liberty.

There has as yet been little discussion of the restriction of children's liberty by parents and other carers in domestic settings. Clearly there are safety justifications for some restriction of the liberty of young children, wherever they are. But there have been instances in which parents have locked children in rooms or cupboards for significant periods: it is now accepted that any such isolation or separation should be very stringently controlled in the child care system. Parents' and other carers' rights to restrict liberty appear to derive from the concept of "reasonable chastisement", discussed in section 1.1 (page 18).

The summary below (page 83) indicates the lack of case law or even official guidance defining acceptable restriction of liberty by parents and other "informal" carers. "Time out" and "grounding" are very common methods of discipline which can involve varying degrees of restriction of liberty; our recommendations propose clearer limits, governed by children's welfare and other principles in the UN Convention, as well as more positive advice for all carers. Current (1992) proposals from the Law Commission (see page 83) on the offence of unlawful detention do not deal satisfactorily with this issue. It is of particular importance given the tendency of recent criminal justice legislation to place more responsibility for children's and young people's behaviour on parents (eg parents' duty to enforce night restriction orders, made under the Criminal Justice Act 1991, and the power of courts to bind parents over to be responsible for their children's behaviour).

Large numbers of young people have their liberty restricted in penal institutions following arrest and remand or conviction for criminal offences (in 1989 a higher proportion of the total prison population was under 21 than in any other European country apart from Ireland).[128] The criteria limiting custodial sentencing have been progressively tightened in successive Criminal Justice Acts, and there has been a substantial reduction in the use of custody. The most recent 1991 Act, which came into force in October 1992 stipulates that a court must not pass a custodial sentence on an offender unless it is of the opinion

"(a) that the offence, or the combination of the offence and one other offence associated with it, was so serious that only such a sentence can be justified for the offence; or

(b) where the offence is a violent or sexual offence, that only such a sentence would be adequate to protect the public from serious harm from him".

The Act defines a violent offence as

"an offence which leads, or is intended to lead, to a person's death or to physical injury to a person",

including offences of arson. It defines "serious harm" as "death or serious personal injury, whether physical or psychological" (section 31).

Sentencing policy is outside the scope of this report, but it should be noted that the UN Convention, quoted above, emphasises that the

"arrest, detention and imprisonment of a child...shall be used only as a measure of last resort, and for the shortest appropriate period of time".

Despite Government ratification of the Convention and the acceptance of these principles, and the progressive tightening of criteria for custodial sentencing outlined above, the Home Secretary indicated at the end of 1992 that he was considering introducing new and additional custodial sentences for young persistent offenders from the age of 14. In March 1993 he announced that new "secure training centres" would be commissioned from public, voluntary and private bodies to provide detention for up to two years for 12 - 15 year-old boys.[129]

In addition, a small number of babies are detained in prison establishments to avoid separation from their mothers. The UN Convention states in Article 3 that the best interests of the child must be a primary consideration in all actions concerning children, including presumably sentencing of their parents. Article 2 insists that

"States Parties shall take all appropriate measures to ensure that the child is protected against all forms of discrimination or punishment on the basis of the status, activities, expressed opinions, or beliefs of the child's parents, legal guardians, or family members".

Outside the penal system, there are various types of formal detention of children and young people: a small number are detained under sections of the Mental Health Act, a few under immigration legislation, and about 250 have their liberty restricted in approved "secure accommodation" in the child care system in England, Wales and Scotland, some in NHS and private health institutions, some in education and a smaller number in training schools in Northern Ireland.

It is only in the last few years that concern about formal restriction of children's liberty outside the penal system has led to legislative safeguards. Until 1983, there was no legislation in force to limit the restriction of liberty of children in care, who could be locked up in secure units for indefinite periods following decisions by social workers, with no right of appeal. This situation, clearly in breach of the European Convention on Human Rights, was highlighted in reports commissioned by the then Department of Health and Social Security, and in campaigns by the Children's Legal Centre and other organisations.[130] Legislation including criteria to limit placement in secure accommodation, and obliging social services to seek the permission of a court for any restriction of liberty lasting more than 72 hours, was included in the Criminal Justice Act 1982, and came into effect in 1983. In Scotland similar legislation, but involving the Children's Hearings system, was introduced in 1984 (in the Health and Social Services and Social Security Adjudications Act 1983). This legislation allows a maximum period of a week before a hearing (the child or parent can seek one earlier). We recommend that a maximum period of 72 hours should apply consistently throughout the UK.

In 1986, a report from the NHS Health Advisory Service on services for disturbed adolescents recommended:

"The restriction of liberty of disturbed adolescents can only be justified where they can be shown to be an immediate danger to themselves or others, and no other method of containment appears appropriate and possible. Relevant legal provisions should be reviewed to ensure that all young people who may be detained have a right to speedy judicial review of their detention. Staff of institutions should take steps to define which of their practices do in fact constitute restriction of liberty...Any use of solitary confinement should be subject to approval by the Secretary of State (as is the case already within the child care system) and to stringent limitations and safeguards".

The report indicated that HAS team members came across

"a few examples in health service, social services and a private establishment where young people's movement was being clearly restricted for significant periods without the application of legal safeguards".[131]

The report of a major study on *Children in Custody* was published in 1987.[132] The study was the first attempt to establish how many children and young people are deprived of their liberty in the UK (the report also covered the Republic of Ireland). It concluded:

"It seems extraordinary that given the high value put on freedom by the four jurisdictions...we do not know, nor have any routine or simple way of discovering, how many young people are deprived of their liberty".

The study found

"in the four jurisdictions some 450 different and independent authorities...having some direct responsibility for the care of children in custody or the administration of the institutions in which they were held".

It commented:

"...it is our belief that the deprivation of liberty is such a major intervention on behalf of the state that the state must be publicly accountable for its actions. To ensure public accountability, regular, accurate information must be collected and published enumerating the number of children, their age, sex, age, ethnic identity, and legal status, the institutions in which they are held, and the length of time they are held in custody. This is the minimum

information. We would like much more detail, which would allow some assessment to be made of the way in which the state is discharging its duty to its dependent but difficult citizens".

It is still the case, in 1993, that there is no information available on restriction of liberty of children outside the penal system, apart from information on children admitted to secure units in the child care system. We recommend that information should be collected and published centrally on restriction of liberty of children wherever it is permitted.

In January 1993, a report of an official Department of Health and Home Office Working Group on Services for People with Special Needs recommended research to establish the national prevalence of children and adolescents requiring secure or related specialised services.[133]

Children in Custody indicated that an individual's freedom of movement can be restricted by

"physical restraint, special clothing, purposely designed rooms or, ultimately, secure institutions".

It also referred to use of drugs to restrict liberty, but excluded this issue from consideration in the study. The scope of the study was also limited to the age range seven to 16,

"to those children where specific state intervention precipitated by the child's personal behaviour or actions had led to placement in custody. This does not mean that other children are never, rightly or wrongly, legally or illegally, locked up by parents, guardians, teachers, nurses or residential social workers but that to uncover that informal practice is hardly feasible and if uncovered only identifies individual malpractice rather than state responsibility about which action can be taken in the form of legislative reform".

The report concluded that the lack of any definition of custody for children

"endangers the liberty and rights of a number of children and young people each year".

The study attempted to produce data on what it termed "hidden custody":

"unofficially secure settings where children are prevented from leaving, but their position is not registered in any national returns, nor are they protected by any special regulations".

It found substantial numbers of children whose liberty was restricted in "open" children's homes and in mental illness and mental handicap hospitals and units.

Following publication of the reports referred to above, and some publicised cases involving restriction of liberty of children without legal safeguards in a variety of institutions, the legislation in the Criminal Justice Act 1982 was re-enacted and extended in the Children Act 1989 (covering England and Wales). As the detailed summary below (page 83) indicates, this extends the legislation, including criteria for restriction of liberty and the obligation to seek a court's permission for restriction lasting more than 72 hours, to cover not only children being looked after by social services, but any whose liberty is restricted while they are "accommodated" by health and local education authorities, or in residential care homes and private health institutions (nursing homes and mental nursing homes). In addition, regulations issued under the Act break new ground by prohibiting for the first time the restriction of liberty of children in certain institutions: voluntary and registered (private) children's homes.[134] (But in March 1993 the Home Secretary announced that the regulations would be amended to enable private and voluntary bodies to tender to provide new "secure training centres".)

But the protection against restriction of liberty, and safeguards for children whose liberty is restricted, remain as the summary below shows extremely inconsistent, both between different services and categories of institution, and between different jurisdictions within the UK. Certain detailed safeguards for the children who are detained are still only applicable to restriction of liberty in secure accommodation in the child care system. In England, the Government-administered secure youth treatment centres are less regulated than community homes. And while private children's homes in England and Wales are prohibited from restricting children's liberty, private health institutions are allowed to do so with some legal safeguards applying, and the legislation is silent on private education institutions (except that independent boarding schools with less than 51 boarders are obliged to register as children's homes and as such are prohibited from restricting liberty; proposals in the current (February 1993) Education Bill are likely to limit the schools which have to register as homes - see page 57).

The Pindown affair has highlighted again how children's liberty can be restricted by staff presence and other means short of locking doors:

"There was no satisfactory evidence before the Inquiry that doors were actually locked when children were in a Pindown room, although we accept that on at least one occasion at 245 Hartshill Road a door handle was probably removed and placed in an office drawer overnight. We are quite satisfied however that saucepans and other objects were put on door handles as a warning signal; that staff remained and slept outside rooms in order to deter children from coming out; and very many children simply accepted that their liberty was restricted in that they had to knock on the door and make a request to leave the room".[135]

The Official Solicitor and others who gave evidence to the Pindown Inquiry believed that Pindown constituted *"placing children in accommodation provided for the restriction of their liberty"*.

The report recommended that

"the law regarding the 'control and discipline' of children in residential establishments is amended so that definitions of the circumstances which amount to the restriction of a child's liberty appear in legislative provisions and are not left to the language of guidance in circulars".[136]

One particular indirect method of restricting children's liberty, found in Staffordshire and much used in the child care system and in some health and education settings, was referred to in *Children in Custody*:

"to place a young person who is a (persistent) absconder into pyjamas or nightdress, and to remove all day clothes and shoes to a locked office. There may be no physical barrier, in the form of locks, to their further absconding, but such a child is obviously constrained both by social embarrassment and/ or by immediate identification".[137]

The Children's Homes Regulations, issued under the Children Act, forbid "any requirement that a child wear distinctive or inappropriate clothes".[138]

But no such prohibition applies to health or education settings, or to any residential setting in Scotland or Northern Ireland. The Scottish review of residential child care surveyed sanctions used in children's homes and found 13 homes (11 per cent of those which responded) used withholding of normal clothing as a sanction. The report's draft guidance on "care sanctions and restraints" proposed:

"Outdoor clothing may be withheld to reduce the likelihood of absconding. No young person, however, should be deprived of normal indoor clothing, or be required to wear alternative dress either as a form of punishment, or in order to prevent absconding".[139]

Children in Custody refers to a "reliable report" of a

"15 year-old mentally handicapped and apparently very difficult girl being bound by her ankles and wrists to a hospital bed to stop her self-injury and disruptive activity".[140]

In the last five years organisations have reported cases in which children's liberty has been deliberately restricted by the use of bandages, by tying to a chair, hanging from a coathook and even in one case by nailing a boy's shoes to the floor.[141]

Tranquillising drugs can be used to restrict liberty, and have at times been widely used on children and young people. In England and Wales, the *Gillick* principle, and over 16 year-olds' statutory rights to consent under the Family Law Reform Act should limit parents' and other carers' ability to authorise the use of sedative drugs for children and young people (although a recent Appeal Court judgment appears to weaken these independent consent rights of children and young people in exceptional circumstances[142]). In Scotland the Age of Legal Capacity (Scotland) Act now provides that young people under the age of 16 have the right to consent

"where in the opinion of a qualified medical practitioner attending him, he is capable of understanding the nature and possible consequences of the procedure or treatment" (section 2(4)).

As with other forms of restriction of liberty, legislative limits and guidance on the use of sedative drugs as a form of control only cover certain settings: the Children's Homes Regulations forbid the use of medication as a "disciplinary measure", and the accompanying guidance goes further in "totally forbidding in all circumstances" the use of medication for discipline or control (see page 87).[143] The fact that prescription of tranquillising medication comes within the clinical discretion of medical practitioners has probably inhibited its detailed regulation in all settings, although the professional medical bodies have become more concerned with safeguards . The report of the Health Advisory Service referred to above emphasised:

"Liberty may be restricted by medication...any institution which might consider using such a form of control must formulate clear procedures with the medical practitioners involved" .[144]

Sir William Utting's report *Children in the Public Care* reviewed the safeguards on use of secure accommodation, including those introduced by the Children Act:

"These are important provisions, as the restricting of liberty deprives a person of a fundamental right. So it is essential that in relation to children the safeguards are sufficient and satisfactory.

"Sometimes the line between control of a child's behaviour and the restriction of his or her liberty is finely drawn. The Pindown approach clearly incorporated the deliberate - and illegal - restriction of liberty. Practices where children are confined to locked rooms, sometimes referred to as 'time out', are equally culpable...Placement in secure accommodation should never be used as a form of punishment" .

The report goes on to conclude that

"all secure accommodation in health care premises, whether NHS or private - or indeed in educational settings - should be approved by the Secretary of State before it is used for accommodating children" .[145]

Both in "open" institutions, day and boarding, and within secure institutions, temporary restriction of liberty (described variously as time out, seclusion and separation) is widely used. Some schools, health institutions and secure units as well as penal institutions have specially-designed single cells. *Children in Custody* described, for example,

"Time out room: This is normally a single room with little, if any furnishings, restricted outward visibility, protected electric light fittings and possibly strengthened doors. No substantive security features are built in.

"Single separation room: This facility differs from a time out room in that it has been designed to withstand deliberate damage and attempts to escape and has viewing facilities for staff".[146]

In other institutions, ordinary rooms (often bedrooms in residential institutions) or even cupboards are used to restrict children's liberty. A newspaper report in December 1992 described how a 12 year-old was shut in a cupboard-sized "referral room" for six hours because his head teacher judged his hairstyle to be unacceptable.[147]

It is only in children's homes that attempts have been made to rigorously control such practices, in legislation and guidance (see page 86): any use of solitary confinement, if permitted at all, must clearly be subject to the most rigorous controls.

Professional bodies have attempted to define more clearly various practices involving restriction of liberty. For example a report from the Royal College of Psychiatrists, approved by its Council in 1989 distinguished "time out" from aversion , punishment, seclusion and restraint:

"Time out, used correctly, is a brief removal, normally of less than five minutes, from the reinforcing stimuli which maintain an undesirable behaviour. Such removal may occasionally require a degree of persuasion or even physical pressure, but if any struggle ensues the object of time out is in any case defeated.

"The term is frequently misunderstood and misused. It is essential that correct procedures are used. Minimum requirements include:

(i) a written protocol outlining the procedure to be followed;

(ii) appropriate monitoring and follow-up;

(iii) supervision by a responsible senior person, experienced in behavioural treatments.

"Time out should not be confused with aversion or punishment. It must be carefully distinguished from 'seclusion' and 'restraint', which are controls on behaviour whose purpose is to protect the patient from himself and others or others from the patient".[148]

Guidance from the Royal College of Nursing in 1992 on seclusion, control and restraint emphasises that

"Seclusion is not a procedure that is specifically regulated by statute. It should be used as little as possible and for the shortest possible time. Seclusion should not be used as a punitive measure or to enforce good behaviour...Seclusion is a last resort where all reasonable steps have been taken to avoid its use..." [149]

The summary below of existing safeguards against unlawful or arbitrary restriction of liberty of children underlines their inadequacy and inconsistency. Our recommendations (page 97) propose a clearer definition of restriction of liberty, stricter limits on its use in all settings (and extended prohibition of its use in private sector institutions), and consistent safeguards for all those whose liberty is restricted, as well as detailed recording and centralised reporting. As in section 1.1 we also call for more positive and detailed advice for all carers on the avoidance of restriction of liberty, and on the use of physical restraint where justified.

Summary of current law and safeguards against arbitrary and unlawful restriction of liberty

Children and young people at home

Case law suggests that parents and others caring for children have some rights to restrict their children's liberty as a form of control or punishment, provided their actions are "reasonable". A Court of Appeal judgment in 1985 stated that the sort of restriction imposed by parents on children was usually well within the realms of reasonable parental discipline and that parents would seldom be guilty of false imprisonment. The Lord Chief Justice stated:

"It hardly needs saying that a parent will very seldom be guilty of that offence in relation to his or her own child. The sort of restriction imposed upon children is usually well within the realms of reasonable parental discipline and is therefore not unlawful".

It was held that where a parent restrained a child's freedom of movement, that would only be false imprisonment if the restraint was unlawful; that unlawfulness was not restricted to cases where a parent acted in contravention of a court order or against the other parent's wishes, but included cases where the detention was for such a period or in such circumstances as to take it out of the realms of reasonable parental discipline.[150]

There have been very few cases to define "reasonableness" in this context: is a parent allowed to lock a child in his or her bedroom, or in a cupboard? If so, for how long, and at what age? Detaining a child in a separate room is prohibited in open children's homes, and tightly controlled in secure units and penal institutions (see pages 86 and 95).

The Law Commission is currently reviewing the law on offences against the person, including detention and abduction, as part of a larger project to codify the criminal law for England and Wales. Its proposals follow those of the Criminal Law Revision Committee.[151] A draft Bill prepared by the Law Commission makes a person guilty of unlawful detention

"if, without lawful justification or excuse, he intentionally or recklessly takes or detains another without that other's consent".

But it specifically excludes detention of under 16 year-olds by anyone having "lawful control":

"A person does not commit an offence under this section if the person taken or detained is, or he believes him to be, a child under the age of 16 and -

(a) he has, or believes he has, lawful control of the child; or

(b) he has, or believes he has, the consent of a person who has, or whom he believes to have, lawful control of the child, or he believes that he would have that consent if the person were aware of all the relevant circumstances".[152]

Parents' rights to authorise a degree of restriction of liberty of their children by, for example, admitting them to a hospital are already limited by the *Gillick* principle, that once a child is judged to have "sufficient understanding" he or she can consent or withhold consent to medical treatment in their own right, and by the statutory right of those aged 16 and over to consent under the Family Law Reform Act 1969. In certain circumstances however the child's or young person's right to consent or refuse consent to treatment may be subject to veto by the court or those holding parental responsibility, following a recent Court of Appeal decision.[153] In Scotland the *Gillick* principle has been confirmed in statute in the Age of Legal Capacity (Scotland) Act 1991.

Further confirmation of children's rights to control admission to hospital were given in the Code of Practice on the Mental Health Act 1983 (currently - February 1993 - under review):

"Parents or guardians may arrange for the admission of children under the age of 16 to hospital as informal patients. Where a doctor concludes, however, that a child under the age of 16 has the capacity to make such a decision for himself, there is no right to admit him to hospital against his will".[154]

A child who is admitted to a NHS or private health institution in England and Wales as an informal patient on the authority of a parent, and has their liberty restricted, eg in a locked ward, is now covered by the legal safeguards under the Children Act (see page 90).

Children being looked after by a local authority

Until 1983 there was no legislation in force limiting the restriction of liberty of children in care. Since then, care authorities in England and Wales have been precluded from restricting the liberty of children they are looking after unless certain criteria are met, and they must seek the authority of a court to keep a child in secure accommodation for more than 72 hours.

The Children Act 1989 re-enacted and extended this legislation covering England and Wales (section 25). The Act gave local authorities a new duty to take reasonable steps to avoid the need to place children in their area in secure accommodation (schedule 2 para 7(c)). If a child who is being looked after by an authority, but is not in care, is placed in secure accommodation, parents must consent to the placement, and anyone with parental responsibility for the child may remove him or her at any time.

The Act provides criteria to limit any placement of a child

"in accommodation provided for the purpose of restricting liberty ('secure accommodation')".

A child may not be placed or kept in secure accommodation:

"unless it appears -

(a) that -

> *(i) he has a history of absconding and is likely to abscond from any other description of accommodation; and*

> *(ii) if he absconds, he is likely to suffer significant harm; or*

(b) that if he is kept in any other description of accommodation he is likely to injure himself or other people".

The criteria are modified for remanded children, and children detained under the Police and Criminal Evidence Act 1984 in the Children (Secure Accommodation) Regulations.

These regulations issued under the Children Act define in detail the period a child may be kept in secure accommodation without court authority (generally an aggregate of 72 hours in any period of 28 days), and the maximum periods that a court can authorise (initially three months). They also set out duties to inform parents and others of the placement, and duties to review the placement.[155]

The Act does not define restriction of liberty. But the specific reference in section 25 to *"accommodation provided for the purpose of* restricting liberty" (our italics) appears to limit its scope.

Guidance issued under the Act states that the definition of restriction of liberty is ultimately a matter for the courts:

"However, it is important to recognise that any practice or measure which prevents a child from leaving a room or building of his own free will may be deemed by the court to constitute 'restriction of liberty'. For example, while it is clear that the locking of a child in a room, or part of a building, to prevent him from leaving voluntarily is caught by the statutory definition, other practices which place restrictions on freedom of mobility (for example, creating a human barrier) are not so clear cut. In the latter case, the views of the authority's legal department should be sought in the first instance as to the legality of the practice or measure. The views of the Social Services Inspectorate might also be sought".

The guidance also indicates that the use of accommodation to physically restrict the liberty of any child is

"totally prohibited in community homes except in premises approved by the Secretary of State for use as secure accommodation and under criteria set down in section 25...However, locking external doors and windows at night time, in line with normal domestic security, is not excluded. Responsible authorities should give clear, written guidance to staff about the extent to which the home, or any part of it, may be locked as a security measure. Similarly, refusal of permission to go out (eg 'gating' in schools) short of measures which would constitute restriction of liberty, is not forbidden..." [156]

Solitary confinement

A handbook of guidance on the use of secure accommodation, issued by the Social Services Inspectorate in 1986, gave criteria for the use of a "single separation room" as secure accommodation. At that time the criteria formed

"part of the Secretary of State's approval...for the use of a separation room as secure accommodation".

This handbook is currently under review, and an updated version is at final draft stage (February 1993). The criteria in the 1986 handbook are stringent:

"1 The separation room shall be used solely by children already accommodated within the secure unit.

2 Placement in a separation room is an extreme measure which may be taken only when other appropriate methods of control have been tried and failed.

3 No child shall be placed in a separation room as punishment.

4 A child may be placed in a separation room only if

a) he is a severe risk to himself or others; or

b) his continued presence in the group is likely to have an unacceptably deleterious effect on them; and

c) his behaviour is such that placement in his own room is likely to create unacceptable stress for other children or cause serious damage to property.

...

6 A child placed in a separation room must be observed at intervals not exceeding 15 minutes.

7 A child placed in a separation room shall be released from the room as soon as the disturbance in the child's behaviour which led to his placement has diminished.

8 In any case, no child shall be held in a separation room unaccompanied by a member of staff for a continuous period longer than 3 hours in any period of 24 hours, save that where this period expires after the unit's normal bedtime and the child is asleep, the child may be held in the separation room until he awakens the next morning".[157]

According to the Department of Health, early in 1993 there were only two approved separation rooms within secure units in community homes in England. But in other institutions both day and boarding where restriction of liberty is permitted, it appears there is no legislation or official guidance limiting the use of "single separation rooms", or other accommodation or practices used to place children in solitary confinement. Similar criteria should clearly apply to placement of a child in solitary confinement in any setting where it remains a permitted practice.

Sedation

The Children's Homes Regulations issued under the Children Act for England and Wales set out among a list of disciplinary measures that are not permitted: "the use or withholding of medication or medical or dental treatment".

But the regulation also states that nothing in it shall prohibit:

"(a) the taking of any action by, or in accordance with the instructions of, a registered medical or dental practitioner which is necessary to protect the health of a child;

(b) the taking of any action immediately necessary to prevent injury to any person or serious damage to property..."[158]

Guidance on the regulations appears to ignore these provisions, emphasising that the use or withholding of medication

"would be a dangerous and utterly unacceptable practice and is accordingly totally forbidden in all circumstances, whether as a disciplinary measure or otherwise to control the child".

Guidance on the regulations also emphasises the importance of having clear policies and procedures in relation to consent to treatment:

"Where the child is of sufficient understanding medical treatment may only be given with his consent. When the child is not of sufficient understanding, the consent of the parent, including a person who has parental responsibility, is required. Doctors can of course administer treatment or medication in emergencies without consent if this is medically necessary but firm guidelines should be laid down by responsible authorities about the procedure which should operate for emergency medication".[159]

Previous to implementation of the Children Act, detailed guidance (replaced by the guidance issued under the Act) had been issued by the Department of Health on "Use of Tranquillising Medication" for children placed in secure accommodation. This followed revelations of forced drugging of young people in a London secure unit. The guidance emphasised that

"as a general principle tranquillising medication should be administered to a child in secure accommodation only on clinical or therapeutic grounds".

In emergency the use of tranquillising drugs were only to be considered:

"(a) where all other appropriate responses have failed to resolve a clinical situation in which a child is at imminent risk of serious self-harm or of harming others, and

(b) if after full joint assessment by care and medical staff it is considered that the likelihood of this situation arising is such as to justify medication to avert it". Administration by injection must be by a medical practitioner or qualified nurse". [160]

Scotland

The legislation on restriction of liberty of children by social work departments in Scotland is broadly similar to that for England and Wales, but involves the children's hearing system in authorising and reviewing placements in approved secure accommodation (Social Work (Scotland) Act 1968, sections 58A and 58B and regulations). [161] In Scotland, a child may not be placed in secure accommodation for more than seven days (or a total of seven days in any 28 day period) without authorisation by either a children's hearing or a sheriff (the child or parent can seek an earlier hearing). The period of seven days contrasts with a period of only 72 hours before a court hearing under the legislation for England and Wales.

There does not appear to have been any guidance on use of sedation for children in Scottish institutions. The Scottish review of residential child care suggested in draft guidance that "withholding or use of medication should not be used as a sanction".

The review found that "isolation" was being used as a sanction in 24 of the homes which responded to a survey (in nine with the presence of staff). This represented 20 per cent of the sample which responded. The draft guidance on "care sanctions and constraints" suggests:

"A child or young person may be separated from the group to a room on her or his own, as a means of enabling him or her to regain self-control. The door to the room must never be locked, and staff must monitor or accompany the child or young person throughout any period of separation".

The review report also emphasised that

"bedroom doors should only be lockable from the outside and also be able to be opened from the inside (except for secure accommodation)".[162]

Northern Ireland

There is as yet no legislation controlling restriction of liberty of children in care and in other institutions outside the prison system in Northern Ireland (the law in Northern Ireland is under review - February 1993).

Of the four Training Schools in Northern Ireland (which include children and young people convicted of offences) one, Lisnevin, operates within a secure campus. Two others have limited secure facilities. These schools are governed by the Children and Young Persons (Northern Ireland) Act 1968 as amended, and the Training School Rules, made in 1952. According to information from the Northern Ireland Office, the Rules allow for "separation" or "time out" as a disciplinary measure:

"It is employed when necessary (for example to control a particularly violent pupil) but is carefully monitored and is always for the minimum period needed. A legal opinion dated November 7 1989 stated that temporary solitary confinement used to restrain a violent pupil would not constitute inhuman treatment".

Rathgael Centre for Children and Young Persons, and St Patrick's Training School have limited secure facilities

"in which to place particularly disturbed or difficult young persons. There are house units in which a number of young people reside. The young people are placed there after full consideration has been given to their problems and needs by professional staff (including social workers and psychologists) within the school...If a boy proves to be totally unmanageable, an application may be made by the managers of the school to the Secretary of State to transfer him to the secure unit at Lisnevin. The fullest consideration is given to the request and a transfer may only take place with Departmental approval. If a boy is placed in Lisnevin his case is reviewed regularly and the possibility exists that he could return to the open setting if his behaviour improves".[163]

Thus restriction of liberty of children and young people in these institutions is not subject to any judicial appeal or fair hearing, which would appear to breach Article 5 of the European Convention on Human Rights, as well as Article 37 of the UN Convention on the Rights of the Child.

There is no legislation limiting or preventing restriction of liberty of children in other institutions in Northern Ireland.

Sedation is not used in the four training schools, according to information from the Northern Ireland Office. There does not appear to have been further advice on use of sedation in institutions.

Restriction of liberty by education and health authorities, and in private health institutions and residential care homes

The statutory safeguards in section 25 of the Children Act have been extended by the Children (Secure Accommodation) Regulations 1991 to apply to any restriction of liberty of children who are "accommodated" by education authorities and health authorities including NHS Trusts in England and Wales.

They have also been extended to apply to private health institutions (nursing homes and mental nursing homes) and to residential care homes.[164]

In all these cases, the criteria in section 25 (see page 84) must apply to children before and while their liberty is restricted for any period, however short (so that the criteria must be applied to practices such as "time out" if they involve restriction of liberty); their liberty must not be restricted for more than 72 hours unless a successful application has been made to court.

Those with parental responsibility have the right to remove their children from these settings (unless the children are in care). But parents do not have to consent to the restriction of liberty, as they do in the case of children being looked after by social services departments in a voluntary capacity (nor is there an obligation to immediately inform parents of the restriction of liberty - see below).

Certain safeguards included in the Children Act and the regulations for children placed in secure accommodation in community homes do not apply to children whose liberty is restricted in other settings. The accommodation does not have to be approved by the Secretary of State, and the following provisions do not apply:

prohibition on the placement of children under 13 in secure accommodation without the Secretary of State's approval; obligation to inform parents etc of placement;

obligation to review placement;

obligation to keep records (regulations 14-17).

The guidance issued under the Act on the extension of section 25 indicates that *"an authority is 'accommodating' a child if it is either accommodating him in a directly provided establishment, or has responsibility for placing a child in accommodation provided by some other body or organisation under a contractual arrangement (eg through the payment of fees)".*[165]

Section 25 does not apply to children who are being detained under the Mental Health Act, or under section 53 of the Children and Young Persons Act 1933 or under certain other provisions.[166]

Children and young people who have been sentenced under section 53 of the Children and Young Persons Act 1933 form a substantial proportion of those detained in secure accommodation in the child care system. The regulations applying to others in secure accommodation do not apply to them (except those on record-keeping in the Children (Secure Accommodation) Regulations). Guidance issued under the Children Act states that:

"Where a child is sentenced to detention under section 53...and a local authority agrees to detain him in secure accommodation in a community home, the local authority will receive detailed instructions and guidance from the Department of Health (or)...Welsh Office".[167]

The Home Office has issued guidance on "mobility" of young people detained under section 53, which emphasises that the primary concern is protection of the public.[168]

Thus section 25 now covers any restriction of liberty by education authorities in maintained boarding schools, including special schools and hostels, and non-maintained special schools and independent boarding schools where the authority is paying the fees.

In the health service, it covers any restriction of liberty of children "accommodated" by a health authority or NHS Trust. The Gardener Unit at Prestwich Hospital in Manchester is the only NHS secure facility designed for mentally disordered adolescents; most are admitted to the Unit under child care legislation, a minority under mental health legislation. The secure Special Hospitals occasionally take under 18 year-olds (the Firs Ward at Ashworth Hospital, Liverpool). *Children in Custody* found it particularly difficult to estimate the numbers of children whose liberty is restricted in health settings, but concluded that there was substantial detention of children in mental illness and mental handicap hospitals, adolescent units etc.[169]

A number of private health institutions have provided accommodation for restricting the liberty of children and young people (some under mental health legislation, some under child care orders and some apparently admitted by parents). Langton House, a mental nursing home in Dorset owned by AMI Healthcare, closed in 1991 following concerns about restriction of liberty including the use of sedation.[170]

No information is available centrally on the numbers of court applications made under section 25 by education and health authorities or residential care homes and private health institutions. We recommend that such information, and details of the children detained, length of detention etc, should be collected centrally and published regularly.

Sedation

There is further guidance issued under the Children Act on possible use of sedation for children detained in institutions other than children's homes: guidance on safeguarding the welfare of children being provided with accommodation by any health or education authority, or in residential care homes, nursing homes or mental nursing homes states:

"Where local authority social services departments are considering placing children in a psychiatric unit, hospital or registered mental nursing home on a Children Act secure order it is particularly important to ensure that consent by the children to any treatment, including the administration of drugs, is given following full agreement by, and with the full understanding of, the child. Treatment and consent to treatment may then only be given in line with Part IV of the Mental Health Act and staff practice informed by the Code of Practice of the Mental Health Act. Unless treatment with sedative drugs is clearly needed for a child's medical condition, SSDs should take into account an establishment's practice in this respect when making placements. SSDs should be cautious about exposing a child to a regime where sedation is used to control behaviour in any case and should be very cautious where major tranquillisers (eg Largactil) are involved. In such cases it may be appropriate to consider whether formal admission under the Mental Health Act would be a more appropriate way of protecting the child's interests. This would require the strict criteria laid down in the Mental Health Act to be met".[171]

A Code of Practice for residential care homes, *Home Life*, states that

"Medication must never be administered for purposes of social control or punishment".[172]

Restriction of liberty in other settings

Youth treatment centres

As noted in section 1.1 the two existing youth treatment centres in England are largely secure, and are the responsibility of the Secretary of State (see page 45). Section 25 of the Children Act and parts of the Secure Accommodation Regulations relating to the court process apply to children placed in them, but not those regulations specifically applying to restriction of liberty in a community home: the lower age limit of 13, duties to inform of placement and review placement and record-keeping duties. No other regulations apply.

The Department of Health has suggested that the Secretary of State cannot make regulations for the conduct of institutions for which s/he is directly responsible. If this is the case, it suggests that a new statutory basis for these centres is needed, which permits proper regulation (this is after all achieved for prisons and young offender institutions).

In 1988, a Social Services Inspectorate report on the two youth treatment centres highlighted concerns about the treatment model and lack of rights for children at St Charles.[173]

In 1991, following complaints by a young woman about her treatment in St Charles Youth Treatment Centre during 1989 and 1990, the Department of Health commissioned an independent team of external professionals to investigate them. A summary of the results of the investigation was published.[174]

The young woman complained about being injected with sedative drugs against her will and by force, every two days during her last seven weeks at St Charles. The team found evidence to substantiate this complaint:

"they found evidence that intra-muscular medication was used on 14 occasions, of which eight were reportedly administered under restraint. They found that documents at the Centre giving written guidance on the use of sedative medication were out of date, and took no account of developments in the mental health field on guidance relating to treatment of mentally disordered patients without consent. They found that the policy that did exist at the Centre on crisis sedation was clearly breached..."

The young woman also complained that she was held in a "separation" room for seven weeks continuously: again, the team found evidence to substantiate the complaint, that she was held in "single separation" for the majority of the time between 11 November and 28 December 1990. They found "considerable confusion" about procedures to be followed on separation, that placement did not meet the criteria for separation, and the team

"expressed great concern at the general nature of the environment in both the Separation Room and Observation Room. Both were bare and without any furniture and decoration, other than a mattress on the floor, and afforded little privacy from outside the house".

From February to May 1991, the Social Services Inspectorate also investigated practice and procedures at St Charles, in the light of the complaints, *"to establish whether there were concerns that needed addressing more widely than just with regard to this one individual"*.

They found evidence to suggest:

"use of separation rooms against the criteria, and under-reporting to the Department of Health;

use of tranquillising medication without consent and in breach of guidelines;

use of physical and psychological coercion to attend group treatment meetings and to reveal 'secrets' at the meeting;

restriction and censorship of telephone calls, letters and contact with parents and the outside world;

deficiencies in the operation of the complaints procedure;

inadequate training in the use of physical restraint techniques rendering staff and young people unacceptably liable to injury;

use of repeated interrogation of young people in single separation to obtain information under duress or to effect collaboration, including, routinely, the use of separation to debrief young people returning from absconding;

an incident where a young person's liberty had been unlawfully restricted".[175]

Foster care

Fostered children in care in England and Wales whose liberty is restricted will be covered by section 25 and the regulations. There are no provisions limiting restriction of liberty of children in private foster care: the legal situation is presumably the same as that applying to parents (see page 83).

Voluntary homes and registered (private) homes

The use of "accommodation for the purpose of restricting the liberty of children" in voluntary homes and registered children's homes in England and Wales is prohibited under the Children (Secure Accommodation) Regulations 1991.[176] Contravention of this regulation without reasonable excuse is an offence. (But in March 1993 the Home Office indicated that this limitation may be removed.)

Non-maintained special schools

Although run by voluntary organisations, non-maintained special schools are not defined as voluntary homes, so there is no prohibition of restriction of liberty in them. If a local education authority is responsible for placing a child in a non-maintained special school, then section 25 applies to any restriction of liberty.

Independent schools

There are no provisions in the Act on restriction of liberty in independent schools. Those boarding schools registered as children's homes (see page 57) as such are barred from restricting liberty. Those registered as residential care homes (see page 57) will be covered by the legislation outlined above (page 94). Local education authorities could place a child in an independent school in which case section 25 applies to any restriction of liberty.

Guidance issued under the Act states:

"restricting the liberty of a child means locking that child in any room, including his own bedroom, and/or a 'time out' room, or part of the school premises with the intention of preventing the child leaving voluntarily. Restricting the liberty of a child is a serious step. It should never be used because of inadequacies in staffing, because a child is simply being a nuisance or disruptive, or as a form of punishment. Its use is unlikely to be appropriate within the setting of an independent school.

"Section 25 of the Children Act 1989, and the accompanying Secure Accommodation Regulations 1991 set out the legal framework governing the restriction of liberty of children being looked after by a local authority and other specified categories of children including those placed by local education authorities and health authorities...

"Proprietors will wish to be alert to the possibility that in the absence of specific legal authority to restrict liberty such action may render them open to civil action".[177]

A Department of Education Circular issued on the Education (Special Educational Needs) (Approval of Independent Schools) Regulations 1991 states inaccurately (in the context of a section on discipline):

"It is furthermore illegal to lock up children who are in the care of a local authority. Section 25 of the Children Act governs the use of secure accommodation".[178]

There are no provisions on restriction of liberty in independent schools in Scotland or Northern Ireland.

Penal institutions

The rules governing treatment of young offenders within penal institutions in England and Wales limit further separation or isolation.[179] An inmate who is "refractory or violent" may be confined in a special cell or room,

"but an inmate shall not be so confined as a punishment, or after he has ceased to be refractory or violent".

These cells or rooms must be specially certified by an officer of the Secretary of State to ensure that they are suitable, and enable the inmate to communicate at any time with an officer.

Inmates can also be removed from association with others, either generally or in relation to particular activities,

"where it appears desirable for the maintenance of good order or discipline, or in his own interests".

Inmates must not be removed from association for more than 24 hours without the authority of a member of the Board of Visitors or of the Secretary of State; maximum periods are set but may be renewed; the governor can allow the inmate to resume association at any point and must do so if the medical officer advises it on medical grounds.

Only inmates aged 17 or over may be put under restraint

"where this is necessary to prevent the inmate from injuring himself or others, damaging property or creating a disturbance".

Medical officers, and a member of the Board of Visitors must confirm the action. The rule does however allow restraint in certain other circumstances - for safe custody during removal and on medical grounds by direction of the medical officer - even it appears for younger inmates. Restraint must not be used as a punishment.

Scotland

Rules governing Scottish young offender institutions allow inmates to be confined to their room for up to 14 days (more for extreme offences) and to be deprived of their mattress for up to 15 days; but these punishments must not be awarded unless the medical officer has certified that the inmate is in "a fit condition of health to sustain it".[180] Restraints may not be used except on medical grounds by direction of the medical officer. Confinement of "refractory or violent" inmates to special rooms or cells is governed by the same conditions as in England and Wales, but the medical officer must certify that the inmate "is in a fit condition of health to be so confined".

Recommendations

1.3 Legal protection against arbitrary and/or unlawful restriction of liberty

1 Restriction of a child's liberty by a parent or other informal carer should be lawful only in so far as it is necessary for the safety and welfare of the child, and in line with the child's evolving capacities. Parents and other informal carers should be warned that, for example, locking a child in a room or space alone, even for short periods, is dangerous and could render them liable to prosecution for cruelty and/or false imprisonment. Punitive practices which involve formal restriction of liberty of children in their homes should be clearly unlawful. (This is an additional argument for removing the current defence of "reasonable chastisement": see section 1.1 page 62). It implies revision of the law on unlawful detention.

2 As in section 1.1 (page 61) we recommend that positive advice should be available to all those caring for children to limit unnecessary and unlawful restriction of liberty. In particular there should be further guidance on permissible forms of restraint in institutional settings.

Some children and young people with complex and multiple disabilities and challenging behaviour may occasionally pose major risks to themselves or others without some form of restraint. Parents and other informal carers may be very isolated when attempting to care for such children and may, without support, use inappropriate methods. Such situations must be acknowledged and appropriate support and advice must be provided.

3 Legislation providing appropriate safeguards for children and young people whose liberty is restricted outside the penal system in Northern Ireland should be introduced without delay.

4 The statutory definition of "restriction of liberty" in section 25 of the Children Act 1989 (and in similar statutes applying to Scotland) should be revised to remove the implication that the provisions and safeguards only apply when a child is placed or kept in "accommodation provided for the purpose of restricting liberty". It should be made clear that any forced detention of a child is covered by the provisions, whether by locking doors, perimeter fences, physical restraints, staff presence or other means. Guidance should be expanded to reinforce the wider definition.

5 The prohibition on restriction of liberty of children in voluntary and registered (private) children's homes under the Children Act should be extended to apply to all voluntary and private institutions throughout the UK, including eg independent schools, non-maintained special schools, residential care homes and nursing homes and mental nursing homes (in these last two categories of private institutions, the detention of children and young people under the Mental Health Act should also cease).

6 The extension of section 25 of the Children Act to apply to children accommodated by a local education authority (under regulation 7 of the Children (Secure Accommodation) Regulations 1991) should be repealed. We can see no grounds for allowing formal restriction of liberty of children in boarding schools, and local education authorities should thus be prohibited from restricting the liberty of children they are "accommodating".

7 Wherever restriction of liberty under section 25 of the Children Act (and similar provisions for Scotland) is permitted, the safeguards in the Children (Secure Accommodation) Regulations 1991 should apply. Currently certain safeguards only apply when the restriction of liberty is in secure accommodation in a community home, including the requirement that the accommodation must be approved by the Secretary of State; the minimum age limit of 13 without prior approval of Secretary of State; and arrangements for review and record-keeping. The statutory basis for the provision of youth treatment centres should be changed to ensure that such institutions can be properly regulated and the regulations enforced. The maximum period for restriction of liberty of a child covered by these provisions before a court hearing should be 72 hours.

8 The criteria for restriction of liberty in section 25 of the Children Act (and similar provisions for Scotland) should be carefully reviewed and tightened to ensure compliance with the UN Convention on the Rights of the Child and the European Convention on Human Rights.

The current criteria (see page 85) include absconding which renders a child "likely to suffer significant harm". Evidence of absconding would be relevant to proving that the above criteria applied to a particular child - but only where the risk was extreme.

9 Legislation should make clear that any restriction of liberty of children in day settings which falls within the definition under recommendation 4 above must not be used as a measure of punishment or treatment, but only as a reasonable measure of safety, whose use should be for the shortest possible time and should be recorded.

10 The placing of children in solitary confinement (eg use of "separation" or "seclusion") should be explicitly forbidden in all open institutions. In any secure institutions in which it is permitted, its use must be limited by strict criteria and detailed safeguards, similar to those applied to the use of "single sep-aration rooms" in secure units in the child care system in England and Wales.

11 There should be an obligation to record restriction of liberty of children in all institutional settings; statistics including all applications to court for permission to restrict liberty, full details of the children involved, length of detention etc should be collected centrally and published regularly.

12 The *Gillick* principle, that children judged to have "sufficient understanding" have a right to consent or withhold consent to medical treatment (and thus, for example, to control their admission to and discharge from hospital) should be included in primary legislation, as it is already in Scotland, with a presumption that a child who has reached the age of 12 has sufficient understanding.

13 Medication or withholding of medication must not be used as punishment. The prohibition on the use or withholding of medication as a measure of control in children's homes, except in extreme circumstances, in regulations issued under the Children Act, should be extended to cover all placements.

14 Rules applying to young offender institutions throughout the UK should ensure that no inmate is placed in isolation without the express approval of the medical officer and for the shortest possible time.

Part Two

Three suspended 1,000 school
over sedation of boarders tell
girls at care home of bullying
HEAD LOCKS UP and abuse
HAIRCUT BOY HUNDREDS ABUSED IN CARE
Spot checks to fight children's home abuse
Children Disturbed child
at special centre to close
school after drug ban
'forced to
eat vomit' Children force-fed
Child care in and beaten in home
Britain 'an illusion' Children's
Up to 2000 children locked up
Troubled home for home was
children to close 'repressive'
'SCHOOL OF CRUELTY' CONDEMNED
The care Child-care staff 'must be
nightmare vetted for crime record

Strategies for positive and preventive protection of children and young people

The second part of the report highlights certain key issues for protection:

2.1 access by children and young people to advice and counselling, advocacy and effective complaints procedures;

2.2 access to independent people;

2.3 arrangements to prevent people who may threaten children's welfare gaining inappropriate access to them;

2.4 arrangements for monitoring and reviewing placement and treatment of children; and

2.5 arrangements for inspection.

This is not of course a comprehensive list of strategies for positive and preventive protection. But they are strategies which are relevant wherever children are living, and the summary in each section demonstrates how inconsistent and inadequate the patchy reforms have been which have followed various scandals.

Recent major reports have covered other issues, but only in relation to residential child care, including selection and recruitment of those working with children and young people, and their training, status, pay and conditions and management.

2.1 Access to advice and counselling, advocacy and effective complaints procedures

Over the last few years there has been increasing recognition of the need for children, particularly those in residential settings, to have ready access to complaints procedures with appropriate support and advocacy. Cases of serious abuse in children's homes, independent schools and other institutions have been the main impetus for reform.

The purpose of complaints procedures is two-fold: the resolution for the individual or group of the particular matter complained of, and improvement of services. As Department of Health guidance on inspections states:

"The number and content of complaints are important indicators of the quality of care provided and the quality of life experienced by service users".[1]

Within services for children and young people in particular, there needs to be a culture which makes it easy for children to complain, and welcomes complaints for the positive contribution they can make to the development of services.

Investigated cases of serious ill-treatment of children have frequently shown that the child did not or could not complain about the treatment, or that complaints were ignored or not taken sufficiently seriously. Some children, because they are very young, or because of serious disability, may be unable to complain on their own behalf. In other cases there has been no obvious and/or independent person to complain to.

The two inquiry reports published in February 1993 following the conviction of Frank Beck for physical and sexual assault on children in Leicestershire children's homes provide the most recent demonstrations of disbelief of children's complaints, and inadequate investigation. The Kirkwood Report referred to

"a general disposition not to believe children. There was an assumption that children either had an ulterior motive for complaint or would be likely, for whatever reason, to fabricate".

It also identified fundamental failures in investigation in the care branch of social services:

"In almost every case there was a failure to talk to those children who would be likely to be able to speak specifically or generally of the complaint...There was failure to recognise the hopeless inadequacy of an investigation confined, or largely confined, to obtaining, and accepting the account of the person complained about".[2]

An inquiry supervised by the Police Complaints Authority into the police investigations in Leicestershire also found that

"some officers showed their disbelief and even openly expressed it. This attitude was confirmed in the fact that they did nothing about the complaint. It is hardly surprising that as a result those children were discouraged from saying more".

An overview of the 29 cases investigated raised various concerns:

"They range from a failure to identify complaints and to record them, to a failure to investigate complaints properly. At a different, but nevertheless significant, level interviews were undertaken in circumstances which markedly inhibited the children who were complaining".

In some cases "investigation" merely amounted to returning children to the home and causing the child to repeat the allegation to a social worker.

"The mistakes occurred through a combination of incompetence, negligence and prejudice compounded by a lack of understanding about child abuse...Had these mistakes and failures not occurred we have no doubt that Beck's criminal activities would have been exposed before 1990".[3]

Given the current status of children in the UK, although they may recognise that the way they are being treated is unfair, unlawful or inappropriate, they may not feel able or ready to use a formal complaints procedure, even if it is well-publicised and access to it is made easy for them. This is no argument against providing effective procedures, but it does mean that children should know how to contact independent adults who will listen to their concerns. There has been increasing acknowledgement of the need for children to have access to confidential advice and counselling, which involves in institutions being able to use a telephone in private.

Sir William Utting comments in *Children in the Public Care,*

"Complaints procedures are necessary but, for a child in residential care, they are not sufficient. The child will know only that he or she has a very serious problem which he or she needs to talk to someone about, however difficult that may be...

"In every residential home there should be a culture which encourages and supports staff in listening to children, taking on their distress and acting to resolve it. I am concerned that under the (Children) Act a child needs to

formulate what has happened as a complaint and to know of the existence of a complaints procedure as well as how to activate it..." [4]

The report of the Warner Inquiry, *Choosing with Care*, also underlined

"the right of children to have concerns and complaints fairly and impartially considered and investigated (as) integral to the proper management of children's homes". [5]

The Children Act 1989 provides (for England and Wales) the first detailed statutory obligation in the UK to develop a complaints procedure designed primarily for use by children and young people (see page 115). All services except education appear to have accepted the need for well-publicised procedures which are readily accessible to children.

Our recommendations seek to ensure that children and young people in all settings have access to confidential advice and counselling, advocacy when needed, and to well-publicised local complaints procedures with an independent element. Children and young people themselves should be consulted about all aspects of the procedures. Their use should be subject to ethnic and other appropriate monitoring to enable action to be taken to counter any discrimination.

Throughout, special consideration must be given to safeguarding disabled children. Sir William Utting stresses that the vulnerability of children living in residential care is compounded for children with disabilities:

"A child lacking mobility may be totally dependent on those providing physical care and may be unable to ward off physical or sexual abuse. Such a child may not be able to communicate except through a trusted and skilled intermediary. A child with a learning disability may have no understanding of the significance of being abused save the personal distress experienced. Because children with a disability may be prone to injury, or may have an atypical developmental pattern, the detection of abuse becomes much more difficult. Furthermore, physical signs which could appear to be signs of abuse may have a benign explanation.

"These special vulnerabilities, and the necessarily intimate relationship between the child with disabilities and the staff in these homes imply an extra burden of responsibility and place on staff an extra vulnerability to accusations of abuse...It may be hard for a child with disabilities to obtain effective access to a complaints procedure. Using telephone helplines may be difficult..." [6]

Staff need to be able to report concerns or suspicions without fear of reprisals. The history of residential institutions includes many incidents in which staff have risked, and sometimes suffered, dismissal in order to ensure action on some major injustice or abuse of children. Whistle-blowing to protect children's welfare is still sometimes necessary when "normal channels" fail: our recommendations address this issue.

And if staff are to support children's easy access to complaints procedures, they must have confidence in the procedures themselves. The Warner Inquiry Report indicated that many staff felt

"excessively vulnerable to unjustified complaints about their actions. It is essential to the good management of homes that staff are treated fairly - and seen to be treated fairly - when complaints are made against them. We believe that this can be achieved if the child's right to complain is balanced by a parallel right of staff to receive support independent of line management when under pressure as a result of a complaint, and by adherence to written procedures for investigating complaints that avoid unfair damage to the reputations of staff".[7]

Further avenues of complaint must be available where local resolution fails. We propose either a new children's ombudsperson service with appropriate powers, or extending the role of the Commissioners for Local Administration.

As Sir William Utting points out, the Commissioner for Local Administration is able to examine allegations of maladministration in relation to the handling of a complaint, but current powers may not allow the Commissioner to consider the substance of a complaint. He proposes that the local authority associations consider offering a service of independent adjudication in cases of intractable dispute between a child and his or her care authority.[8]

The proposal for a statutory "Children's Rights Commissioner", published in 1991, which has gained wide support in the children's field suggested that the Commissioner should have the power to review children's use of complaints procedures, to press for their extension and improvement, to issue a code of good practice, and to advise on new procedures. These are essential and on-going tasks to ensure that all children have effective means of redress, and that the content of children's complaints is used as a tool for central and local policy development for children.[9]

In Scotland, the *Review of Child Care Law* suggested that the Secretary of State for Scotland should commission an examination of the case for and feasibility of a Child Welfare Commission in Scotland. Among tasks for such a Commission would be

"to advise children on their legal rights, on agency complaints and appeals procedures and on how to initiate judicial reviews or appeals".[10]

Beyond complaints procedures, we recommend that children should have clear rights of access to the courts, with necessary legal aid for representation. As the Scottish Law Commission stated in relation to children's rights to apply to court for an order relating to their upbringing: "No-one has a greater interest".[11]

Summary of existing access to advice and counselling, advocacy and complaints procedures

Advice and counselling

There are as yet no statutory obligations to ensure that children are aware of confidential advice and counselling services, and few obligations to ensure that in institutions they have access to a phone in private. But services have expanded, with ChildLine now providing a national free helpline, and other local phone lines and drop-in advice centres. Some of these may be prepared to mediate with parents or other carers on a child's behalf, with his or her permission. All institutions, day and boarding, as well as other services for children and public places frequented by children should advertise helplines.

The Children's Homes Regulations require all children's homes in England and Wales to

"ensure that a pay telephone is available for children accommodated in the home in a setting where it is possible to make and receive telephone calls in private".[12]

Guidance emphasises that

"this facility should be available for ordinary everyday use and not restricted or treated as being available as if it were a privilege".[13]

Sir William Utting underlines the importance of displaying the telephone numbers of child care helplines, independent visitors, the social services department, the police etc.[14] And the Warner Inquiry Report emphasises that

"employers should ensure that all children in residential care have access to a telephone helpline on which they can raise concerns without being overheard..."[15]

The Scottish review of residential child care also proposes that

"young people and children should be able to make and receive telephone calls in private".[16]

Guidance from the Social Services Inspectorate on inspection of independent boarding schools by social services states:

"It is not satisfactory for boarders to have to ask permission to use a staff phone nor for the telephone to be placed in a busy corridor or in such a position that pupils have to queue alongside. There is a difficulty with young boarders who have not yet learnt to use a telephone, but this is a skill which

ought to be taught within the school. It is not appropriate that schools should prevent even young boarders from telephoning home from school in the belief that this will exacerbate home sickness. Where there is close and warm support for boarders and plenty of activities this is rarely a long-lasting problem and all boarders must have the freedom and privacy to make phone calls".

Helplines such as ChildLine should be advertised and explained to boarders and those with parental responsibility.[17]

It is important to remember that there are far more children and young people living away from home in boarding schools than in child care institutions. Only those independent schools required to register as children's homes are required under the regulations to provide private access to a telephone.

As emphasised earlier there must be special consideration of disabled children. Sir William Utting stated:

"Using telephone helplines may be difficult because of problems with oral communication and the limitations on privacy imposed by severe immobility".

This leads him to propose that such children may require independent visitors (see page 129).[18]

Advocacy

There are no statutory obligations to provide independent advocates or representatives for children and young people in any setting, although there are now several large-scale voluntary initiatives. The only relevant legislation is that in the Children Act obliging authorities in England and Wales to appoint "independent visitors" for certain children (and unimplemented provisions in Scottish legislation - see page 129). But the role of advocate or independent representative is different to that of independent visitor, and guidance specifically advises that independent visitors are not expected to act as advocates (see page 130). The role is also quite distinct from that of guardian ad litem (curator ad litem in Scotland) appointed by the court to investigate and represent the interests (but not necessarily the views and wishes) of children in care and allied proceedings.

The Wagner Report, *Residential Care: a positive choice*, proposed that children in all forms of residential care should have access to an independent advocate.[19] And more recently the Scottish review, *Another Kind of Home*, noted:

"A child has a right to her or his childhood, a young person a right to her or

his youth. They must not, therefore, be given all the responsibilities of adulthood and at times should be able to call on someone to act as their advocate.

The report encourages the appointment of children's rights officers:

"Children's rights officers in social work departments can provide a useful background for children's rights and promote good practice in residential child care. They also provide an appropriate way of handling the vast majority of complaints and concerns".

But lack of independence of the department may be seen as a problem.[20] The Warner Inquiry Report also believes that children's rights services are important:

"Such a service will provide another valuable check on the conduct of children's homes; and further means by which children are able to have their concerns voiced".

The report recommends that children in children's homes should

"have the support of their own advocates when pursuing serious complaints against staff".[21]

Recently three organisations, A Voice for the Child in Care (VCC), Independent Representation for Children in Need (IRCHIN) and ChildLine have come together to establish an independent service of advice, advocacy and representation for children. ASC - Advice, Advocacy and Representation Service for Children - aims to provide an independent and confidential service for children and young people who receive services from local authorities and voluntary organisations. Its objectives are

"to enable and empower disadvantaged children and young people to use the services offered to them by welfare agencies in ways which ensure maximum benefit to their self-esteem and overall development".

ASC aims to:

"1 seek to ensure that all children are involved in the plans being made about their lives;

2 respond to children who are questioning the legal and administrative decisions being made about their future care and well-being by welfare agencies;

3 relate to children in need, as defined by the Children Act 1989;

4 enable children being cared for by local authorities and voluntary agen- cies to effectively use the complaints mechanisms established by the Children Act 1989 by providing support, advice and the use of advocacy techniques, where they have identified a failure in the service being offered to them".

Local authorities and voluntary organisations obtain the services of ASC by paying a fee for coverage of children and young people in their area. All children who are potential users receive a leaflet, with a freepost contact card. Children can also contact the service via a freephone number which connects them to a ChildLine counsellor. The child's relationship with the service is confidential

"unless serious harm may occur to the young person or to a third party if information is not disclosed. This would only be done as far as possible where the young person can agree to the action taken".

The limits to confidentiality are explained at the outset of the contact.

A report issued in July 1992 stated:

"ASC believes that young people need an advice and advocacy service before making a formal representation or complaint; whilst such a representation/complaint is being considered or investigated (to support and advice the young person through the process) and even beyond the decision of the authority, after consideration of the recommendation of the Panel..."

The report refers to the

"depressing increase in inquiries into abuse in residential care - for example Kincora in Northern Ireland, the Melanie Klein House in Greenwich, the Leeways and Spyways inquiries and more recently major criminal investigations into widespread sexual abuse in children's homes in Leicestershire, Clwyd and Gwynedd...etc"[22]

Since 1979, IRCHIN has been providing independent reports and recruiting, training and accrediting children's advocates.[23] VCC has worked on improvement of complaints procedures and provided "independent representatives" to children in secure accommodation. Some are attached to individual secure units which they visit regularly; there are also "pool" independent representatives who can work with individual children as requested. They are volunteers who work independently of the institution and the authorities involved. VCC suggests that children and young people are more able to confide in and seek help from someone who is familiar to them. A "link person" is attached to each establishment who explains the scheme to the staff and keeps in touch with them; VCC has found that the introduction of an advocate at a time of crisis can result in a hostile reaction from some staff members.[24]

The advice from the Social Services Inspectorate on inspection of boarding schools, referred to above (page 107) also outlines a role for what it terms "independent listeners", similar in some respects to independent visitors (see section 2.2, page 128), but with an advocacy role:

"...wherever possible the school should have adults to whom a boarder can

turn in privacy. These adults, independent of the school, have a role as independent listeners or counsellors and in the complaints procedures. There is a delicate balance to be struck; they should not be complete strangers to the boarders yet they must be seen to be divorced as much as possible from the school hierarchy. Finding people who fulfil both parts of the specification is likely to be difficult and a degree of flexibility will be needed to identify who best can do the job. It may be possible for a chaplain, a school nurse or a school doctor to fulfil this role, or for interested parents or other persons who have a professional interest in counselling or pastoral work. In all instances those fulfilling the role will need to be checked before appointment through DES, for England and Wales, in accordance with the procedures for appointing staff. SSDs should satisfy themselves that whoever is appointed is made aware of the action they should take when any serious allegation, or one which concerns the proprietor or senior staff of the school, is made to them".[25]

A survey of children's homes, reported in *Choosing with Care*, the report of the Warner Inquiry, showed the current very patchy availability of advocates for children in homes:

"When asked whether systems are in place whereby children can have advocates of their choice external to the social services department, 23 per cent responded with a clear 'yes' and 17 per cent with a clear 'no'. 61 per cent of authorities responded 'to some extent', and several comments indicated that such systems tend to be at development stages and are not yet felt to be complete or satisfactory. Some authorities have forged relationships with voluntary organisations to support advocacy arrangements. Voluntary and assisted community homes and private sector homes both gave a higher proportion (over a third in each case) of clear 'yes' responses. This may indicate relative ease in establishing such systems in single home organisations, or, as stated earlier, a tendency to apply less strict criteria in responding".[26]

An addition to the Asylum Bill, currently (March 1993) before Parliament, would require the Home Secretary to establish a panel of advisers or advocates for young people arriving alone in the UK seeking asylum. These unaccompanied refugee children and young people have been identified as a very vulnerable group requiring advocacy.

Whistle-blowing

In a number of cases over the last few decades, adults working with children have tried to raise concerns about abuse or treatment with appropriate authorities within and outside the institution, and in the face of denial or inaction have decided to take their concerns to outside bodies or the media. Some, who were clearly working to safeguard the welfare of particular children, have suffered suspension or even dismissal for their actions.

The Warner Inquiry Report stated:

"We have had our attention drawn to several cases where a member of staff has felt that they had to resign before they could express their concerns about their experiences".

The survey commissioned by the Inquiry found that over two-thirds of employers gave care staff guidance on the circumstances in which they should make a formal complaint.

"We consider that this should be done everywhere. It is also reassuring that our survey reveals that the proportion of local authorities in which care officers can make complaints to more senior officers outside the home and outside the line management structure is 80 per cent and 65 per cent respectively. In addition, care officers have access to private and confidential counselling support outside the line management structure in about two thirds of authorities, and in private homes this proportion is over 80 per cent. These are very encouraging developments in producing a climate of legitimate whistle-blowing by staff when they see children being mistreated or abused".

The report recommends:

"Employers should accept that staff in residential homes for children should be able to raise significant concerns outside their normal line management when they consider the line manager has been unresponsive or is the subject of concern; they should enable staff to make use of complaints procedures established by legislation".[27]

Such proposals are clearly relevant to all institutions and services for children.

A recent report from the National Consumer Council on a consumer focus in the health service emphasised that

"the upholding of professional standards relies on members regulating themselves and one another...Individual members of staff willing to risk their careers about abuse in long-stay hospitals brought scandals to light and made an important contribution to the protection of vulnerable patients. However, in practice 'whistle-blowers' have often experienced extreme personal hostility and difficulty at work from colleagues and managers".[28]

These statements equally apply to whistle-blowers in relation to abuse of children in residential care and schools.

Particular concerns were voiced at the Royal College of Nursing's 1992 conference, after some NHS Trusts included "no speaking-out" clauses in staff contracts. As a result the Department of Health issued draft guidance on "Freedom of Speech for NHS staff" in October 1992. This initially emphasises that the key principle is that the interests of patients are of "paramount importance", and that all NHS employing authorities and Trusts must draw up policies and procedures to ensure that any concerns raised by staff are properly investigated and dealt with, where necessary at the highest level. Where contracts contain express confidentiality provisions,

"they should be expressed in a manner which does not in any way conflict with the principles set out in this guidance".

But the guidance also emphasises that staff have a duty of confidentiality to patients, and that any unauthorised disclosure of personal information about any patient

"will be regarded as a most serious matter and will always warrant disciplinary action".

Employees also have a duty of "confidence and fidelity" to their employer.

The guidance considers a situation in which an employee has exhausted all locally-established procedures without satisfaction, and

"may as a last resort contemplate the possibility of disclosing to the media a matter of genuine concern".

But this, it emphasises, could be seen as a potentially serious breach of contract.[29]

The guidance as drafted falls short of clearly upholding the right of staff to take exceptional steps when normal procedures fail to safeguard a patient's welfare. It is essential that contracts and terms of employment for those working with or for children do not limit their right to inform appropriate authorities and seek outside help, in order to safeguard and promote children's welfare.

Complaints procedures

Children at home

The rights of children living at home to complain about ill-treatment or other matters are not formalised. They could of course complain about serious ill-treatment to the police, or to a local social services department. Social services have duties to investigate if they receive information suggesting that

"a child who lives, or is found, in their area is suffering, or is likely to suffer, significant harm".

They must

"make or cause to be made, such enquiries as they consider necessary to enable them to decide what action they should take to safeguard or promote the child's welfare" (section 47, Children Act 1989).

The inter-departmental guide to arrangements for inter-agency co-operation for the protection of children from abuse in England and Wales, *Working Together*, states that the statutory duties of social services departments apply to all children

"whether the child is living at home with parents, in residential care in either a children's home or a residential school, or living with another carer (who may be a local authority foster carer)".

Similarly the police are obliged to investigate potential crimes. As *Working Together* indicates,

"Police involvement in cases of child abuse stems from their primary responsibilities to protect the community and bring offenders to justice. Their overriding consideration is the welfare of the child. In the spirit of Working Together, *the police focus will be to determine whether a criminal offence has been committed, to identify the person or persons responsible and to secure the best possible evidence in order that appropriate consideration can be given as to whether criminal proceedings should be instituted...The decision whether or not criminal proceedings should be instituted will be based on three main factors: whether or not there is sufficient substantial evidence to prosecute; whether it is in the public interest that proceedings should be instigated against a particular offender; and whether or not it is in the interests of the child victim that proceedings should be instituted. Although police may instigate proceedings it is the responsibility of the Crown Prosecution Service to review and, where appropriate, conduct all criminal proceedings instigated on behalf of a police service".*[30]

Children in England and Wales who are in care but placed at home with parents, and other children who come within the Children Act's definition of "in need" (section 17(10)) can use the new statutory complaints procedure to complain about the discharge of any of the local authority social services department's functions in relation to them, including arrangements for their placement (but not, it appears, to complain about aspects of their treatment at home).

The Children Act also allows children to seek to make applications to court for an order concerning any aspect of their upbringing (section 8 of the Act defines four types of order: contact orders, prohibited steps orders, residence orders and specific issue orders). Children in care can only apply for residence orders. But in every case, the court retains discretion as to whether to allow the child to make an application.

In its 1992 *Report on Family Law*, the Scottish Law Commission proposed that in Scotland children's rights to apply for an order relating to parental rights or responsibilities should be spelt out in legislation for the avoidance of doubt. At present under section 3 of the Law Reform (Parent and Child) (Scotland) Act 1986 anyone "claiming an interest" can apply for an order relating to parental rights, "and the court shall make such order as it thinks fit".[31]

Organisations providing advocacy find that there is a lack of any guidance for children and young people on legal options available to them. As IRCHIN comments:

"Access to accurate information is one of the factors which helps to equate the unequal balance of power between children and powerful adults".[32]

Children Act complaints procedure, England and Wales

The Children Act obliges authorities in England and Wales to set up procedures to consider "representations including any complaints" from children they are looking after and any other children who are "in need" (section 26). The Act's definition of "in need" includes children who are unlikely to achieve or maintain a reasonable standard of health or development, or whose health and development is likely to be significantly impaired, without local authority help, as well as those who are "disabled" (section 17).

Voluntary organisations and registered - private - children's homes are also obliged to set up procedures for those children they are accommodating who are not being looked after by a local authority. In order to ensure an independent complaints procedure, National Children's Home has used a seconded staff member from Barnardos to organise and oversee its complaints procedure and provide a clients' rights service for children and families with whom NCH works. The Warner Inquiry Report supports a proposal from the Children's Legal Centre that children in voluntary and private homes should also be able to use the complaints procedures established by both their placing authority, and the authority in whose area the home is situated.[33]

Complaints and representations may also be made by parents and others with parental responsibility, foster carers, and anyone whom the responsible body considers has sufficient interest in the welfare of the child. Regulations (Representations Procedure (Children) Regulations 1991) set out a framework for the procedures.[34] Guidance issued under the Act states:

"The Act requires that responsible authorities establish a procedure which provides an accessible and effective means of representation or complaint where problems cannot be otherwise resolved...The procedure will involve independent persons in responsible authorities' considerations and should ensure that the child, his parents and others significantly involved with the

child have confidence in their ability to make their views known and to influence decisions made about the child's welfare. The responsible authority should aim to develop a procedure which is understood and accepted by all involved..." [35]

The procedure requires that an independent person (neither a member nor an officer of the authority) is involved once informal attempts to resolve a complaint have failed, and a formal complaint is registered with the designated complaints officer. The responsible authority which receives a complaint must consider it with the independent person and respond within 28 days. The experience of A Voice for the Child in Care suggests that 28 days is too short a period to allow for proper investigation and a solution; community care legislation allows for an extension of up to three months. If the complainant remains dissatisfied and requests within 28 days that the complaint be reviewed, a panel including at least one independent person (who may be the same independent person involved earlier) must meet to consider the complaint within 28 days of the authority receiving the request. The responsible authority must "have due regard to the findings" of the panel, and consider them together with the independent person on the panel. It must inform the complainant of the decision and reasons for it, and where appropriate provide advice on other avenues for complaint or appeal.

While these procedures do contain an independent element, they are administered by the authority being complained against, the panel may include a majority of authority representatives, and its recommendations are not binding on the authority: the authority must consider them in the light of its overall welfare duty towards the child. The role of the independent person involved at the first stage is impartial - not that of an advocate for the child. The independent person has an investigative role and is part of the process of seeking a resolution. If they are recruited by and solely responsible to a local authority, their independence is questionable. We concur with the view of VCC that the independent element in complaints procedures should be provided by a voluntary organisation. This should include training, accreditation and support (at present VCC, National Children's Home and the Children's Society provide such services).[36] It is not appropriate for independent advocates also to act as the independent element involved in investigation and resolution of complaints, at least in relation to the same authority, service or institution.

The guidance points out that the handling of a complaint may be concurrent with action under disciplinary procedures, or child protection action:

"The need to protect a child has to be the first priority, and where the complaint is made by a child, the need for child protection action should be considered". [37]

Responsible bodies had to set up procedures by October 1991 when the Act was implemented. Authorities are obliged to monitor their operation and effectiveness, and produce an annual report. A survey of children's homes commissioned by the Warner Inquiry revealed some information about how authorities inform children of their complaints procedure:

"In nearly two thirds of (responding) authorities...children are made aware of complaints procedures through their use of leaflets either before or on arrival (in a children's home). In the other (voluntary and private) sectors the proportions are lower, this practice taking place in around 50 per cent of cases. In around a quarter of authorities, verbal methods are used to inform children of complaints procedures, usually before or on arrival in the home. As would be expected given the relatively higher absence of leaflets in the other sectors, their use of verbal methods is higher than in local authorities".

The survey also showed that 84 per cent of authorities reported that children can make complaints privately,

"eg by the use of freephone facilities, tear-off slips to the Director, or direct access to the Chief Inspector or Children's Rights Officer". [38]

The report of the Warner Inquiry and others have emphasised the particular importance of informing children of complaints procedures in a form that they can readily understand, and enabling children to make a complaint initially in confidence:

"Employers should provide children with easily understood guidance on how children can raise concerns and complaints and in particular how this may be done initially without the knowledge and involvement of the person complained of". [39]

Community care complaints

Local authority social services departments have been obliged since April 1 1991 to have similar complaints procedures to hear complaints about social services functions in providing community care (National Health Service and Community Care Act 1990, section 50).

Secretary of State's default powers

Children and young people can complain direct to the Secretary of State if they believe that a local authority is not fulfilling a statutory duty (eg, its welfare duty towards the child). The Children Act (section 84) gives the Secretary of State the power to make enforceable orders when satisfied that a local authority has without reasonable excuse failed to comply with any of its duties under the Act. The Secretary of State has similar powers in relation to local authority duties under the National Health Service and Community Care Act 1990 (section 50).

Scotland

Social work and community care complaints

Under the National Health Service and Community Care Act 1990, Scottish authorities were obliged to establish complaints procedures in respect of all their social work functions (by 1 April 1991). A circular gives advice to authorities; complainants who are dissatisfied with resolution of a complaint must be able to have it considered by a review committee including independent people. Leaflets explaining the complaints procedure should be widely available, and attention should be given to the information needs of special groups, including children.[40]

A Scottish Office report *The Introduction of Local Authority Complaints Procedures* was circulated by the Social Work Services Inspectorate in June 1992. It indicated that three Scottish authorities either had or intended to develop specific support for children using complaints procedures:

"a member of the social work staff seeks to act as an advocate for all children in receipt of social work services and may be involved in either the formulation or investigation of complaints".

One Scottish authority, Lothian, has adopted a "Lothian Children's Family Charter": the Departments of Education and Social Work and the Health Board have together adopted a charter of entitlements for children, and also a complaints procedure:

"Any child or young person who lives in Lothian Region and feels that his or her entitlements under the Charter have not been met, or have been infringed, should have ready access to a clear structure which will ensure that these complaints are addressed and resolved at the earliest possible stage".

Each of the Departments and the Health Board has established an internal system for dealing with complaints. If unresolved, they can be taken to an independent adjudicator. While appointed by Lothian Regional Council, the adjudicator works completely independently of any department.[41]

The review of residential child care in Scotland emphasises:

"Young people need to be able to make their complaints in confidence, and to make them to someone independent from the residential home...Young people and children in residential care should be able to raise complaints entirely confidentially to someone who is not involved in the management of the home. Managers will always have to deal with a number of complaints, but they are under a range of different pressures, some of which may militate against thorough investigation and resolution of complaints. They, as well as the young people, should have the capacity to refer particular complaints on

to a more independent agent. Additional arrangements should be made to monitor the quality of provision for children and young people who are not able to complain on their own behalf, due to communication or language differences".

The review also emphasises:

"The use of formal complaints procedures is bound to remain very limited. In any field formal complaints are a very small percentage of total complaints and faults. Informal complaints, therefore, need to be carefully listened to and passed on to the person who has the authority to deal with it. Allegations of physical or sexual abuse by staff, whether made as formal complaints or not, should always be handled by staff outwith the home. They should not be handled by the officer-in-charge. This is because such a procedure would enable matters to be covered over too easily, whether intentionally or not...

"It is essential that young people, children and their parents should have a clear route to having complaints considered independently of the home and its managers. In the majority of cases they will not wish to follow that route, and will prefer a very quick and straightforward resolution of their grievance, at a very local level. But their access to independent assessment of serious complaints must never be blocked..."

The review also mentions another relevant right

"which is rarely covered in statements or procedures is the right to consult a general practitioner, and to be able to do so without informing care staff or others, and without having to explain the reason for the consultation. This right should be clearly spelled out for young people and children in residential care".[42]

Northern Ireland

Residential care

In Northern Ireland, following the Kincora affair, a consultative paper on a complaints procedure for children in residential care and their parents was circulated for comment. Then in 1985 a circular was issued by the Department of Health and Social Services in Belfast. This outlined the information to be circulated and procedure to be introduced by Northern Ireland Health and Social Services Boards and by voluntary organisations which run residential facilities for children and young people in care. The proposed arrangements did not involve any independent element in investigation or resolution of complaints.[43]

In the secure Training School at Lisnevin the Northern Ireland Association for the Care and Resettlement of Offenders (NIACRO) after successfully operating a pilot independent representation scheme is now expanding the scheme in that school. Plans were well advanced (December 1992) to set up a scheme in another of the Training Schools at Rathgael, while in St Patrick's Training School independent volunteers have already been recruited to perform this function.

The independent representatives will see any young people who wish to talk to them, inform them of their rights, discuss possible action and take up matters including complaints on their behalf, but there are no formal complaints procedures in the four Training Schools. Serious complaints are referred to the Department responsible for the Training Schools.[44]

Commissioners for local administration

The Commissioners (separate offices exist for England, Wales, Scotland and Northern Ireland) can investigate complaints of injustice arising from maladministration by local authorities and certain other local bodies, from children and others. In a number of recent cases they have investigated complaints by children in care, in some instances from groups of young people. They are barred currently from investigating internal school matters.

Other child care settings

England

Youth treatment centres

There is no statutory obligation to provide a complaints procedure for residents in the two Department of Health administered youth treatment centres in England. The Department has indicated that both Centres do in fact have procedures, and the "Policy and Management Specification" for the Youth Treatment Service includes among functions of the service

"operating an effective complaints procedure which ensures that young people's concerns are dealt with fairly and speedily".[45]

Residential care homes

These homes must

"inform every resident in writing of the person to whom and the manner in which any request or complaint relating to the home may be made and the person registered shall ensure that any complaint so made by a resident or a person acting on his behalf is fully investigated".

Residents must also be informed of the name and address of the registering authority to which complaints about the home may be made (Residential Care Homes Regulations 1984).[46]

Health and mental health settings

There are detailed procedures to enable patients including children to complain about hospital care, including clinical judgment, and about health care in the community. Directions issued to health authorities under section 17 of the National Health Service Act 1977, following the Hospital Complaints Act 1985, provide a formal framework for complaints about hospital services, care or treatment. There are similar provisions for Scotland in the National Health Service (Scotland) Act 1978. In Northern Ireland there are non-statutory complaints procedures relating to health services.

Complaints by patients detained under the Mental Health Act must be investigated by the Mental Health Act Commission (in Scotland and Northern Ireland there are separate Commissions).

The Commission has sought to have its powers extended to cover "informal" child patients, admitted by their parents.[47]

There is no obligation on private health institutions - nursing homes and mental nursing homes - to operate a complaints procedure (but young patients placed in them by local authorities in England and Wales have a right to use the Children Act local authority complaints procedures referred to above).

Education

Maintained schools

Local education authorities in England and Wales are obliged to set up arrangements for the consideration of complaints under the Education Reform Act (section 23) - but only about specified actions of LEAs and governing bodies relating to the curriculum and religious worship in schools. There is no obligation on schools or local authorities to establish procedures for hearing complaints about any other matters. Similar arrangements apply to the Education and Library Boards in Northern Ireland.

Complaints can be made to the Secretary of State for Education about breaches of duty or "unreasonable" conduct of LEAs and governing bodies of schools by pupils and anyone else affected. The Secretary of State has powers to intervene under sections 68 and 99 of the Education Act 1944 (England and Wales). The Secretary of State for Scotland has similar powers under the Education (Scotland) Act 1980.

There are no other formal channels of complaint for pupils in maintained schools, day or boarding. The Commissioner for Local Administration is specifically barred from investigating complaints concerning internal school matters such as discipline (the Commissioner has sought to have this limitation on powers of investigation removed), and from investigating actions of governors of voluntary aided and grant-maintained schools.

In October 1992 the National Consumer Council published a report, recommending that the Government should require LEAs and grant-maintained schools to establish well-publicised complaints procedures on all school matters. But it curiously proposes that such procedures should be aimed primarily at parents, with no access for young people under the age of 16 (it does propose that the Department for Education should encourage local experiments

"aimed at finding out what sort of procedures would enable school students aged under 16 to complain effectively").[48]

Some individual local education authorities have set up schemes to allow pupils to complain about school issues. Shortly before it was disbanded the Inner London Education Authority established a pilot "education ombudsman" service in certain divisions. In Lothian (see page 118) in 1992, an independent adjudicator was appointed following adoption of a charter of rights for children and young people served by the social work and education departments and the health authority. Complaints about schooling have to go first to individual teachers and head teachers, but can be referred to the independent adjudicator if there is no satisfactory resolution at school level. Birmingham local education authority has appointed an education rights officer.

Independent day schools

There are no obligations to provide complaints procedures in independent day schools.

Independent boarding schools

The Children Act provides new protection for children and young people in independent boarding schools in England and Wales. Independent schools with less than 51 boarding pupils are obliged to register as children's homes (unless they are registered as residential care homes or approved under the Education Act 1981 to take children with statements of special educational needs). As children's homes, these schools are required to have a complaints procedure for any pupils they are accommodating who are not being looked after by a local authority (but the Department for Education is proposing to use the Education Bill currently before Parliament - February 1993 - to drastically limit those independent schools obliged to register as children's homes - see page 57). The very few independent schools which are registered as residential care homes are obliged to inform residents how to make complaints and to ensure that any complaints are fully investigated (see page 57). The proprietors of other boarding independent schools in England and Wales are placed under a general duty to safeguard and promote pupils' welfare, and guidance issued under the Children Act suggests that *"it is important that there should be clear and accessible avenues for children to alert an appropriate adult to situations which are causing them distress. This has been demonstrated in a number of instances where disadvantage has been aggravated because a child did not know whom to approach. The normal recourse for a child with a complaint which he cannot deal with informally is his parents. However children in boarding do not have the same daily access to their families as day pupils, and it is important that every boarding school has an effective means by which children's concerns or complaints can be heard. Such a procedure cannot and should not replace the school's normal daily mechanisms for dealing with minor problems; the aim should always be to identify and resolve issues before formal action becomes necessary.*

"It is also necessary to take into account the ages of the children when considering what arrangements might be appropriate. For all children however a clear and simple procedure should be available to enable them to raise concerns which cannot be dealt with informally. Information in writing or in an appropriate permanent form about it should be given to all children as well as to those with parental responsibility. It is important that provision is made for contact with an adult outside the school's structure including telephone Help Lines where appropriate for those situations where an additional element of confidentiality or independence is needed".[49]

A *Practice Guide on the Welfare of Children in Boarding Schools* for social services inspection of independent schools from the Social Services Inspectorate underlines the importance of all boarding schools having an established routine for investigating formal complaints:

"Such procedures should have been made clear to the boarder on joining the school and to parents or those with parental responsibility. The system needs to be well understood by pupils and should explain how boarders may seek confidential advice and raise matters of serious personal concern such as bullying and abuse. It is important that the arrangements should allow for complaints to be made on behalf of the boarders by parents or staff".

The guidance suggests that the procedures should allow a boarder to be accompanied by a friend, and for there to be recourse to someone who is independent of the school if the boarder so wishes:

"Having an informal friend or advocate present is important in promoting a fair hearing".

Complaints should be dealt with speedily, with a time limit for written acknowledgement.

The guidance also underlines the importance of boarders being able to use a phone in the school in privacy (see page 108), and outlines a role for what it terms "independent listeners", similar in some respects to independent visitors, but with an advocacy role.[50]

Non-maintained special schools

These schools are run by voluntary organisations, and where they take boarders, the voluntary organisation is obliged to set up a complaints procedure under the Children Act and the Representations Procedure (Children) Regulations 1991 (see page 115), to hear complaints from or about children who do not come within the scope of the local authority complaints procedure.[51]

Penal institutions

There are formal procedures for young people detained in young offender institutions and those detained in prisons to make complaints. There are a series of levels of complaint: to member of staff in charge of "wing"; application to governor; application to Board of Visitors; application to see Visiting Officer of the Secretary of State; petition to Secretary of State.[52] Concerns have been raised about a lack of confidentiality and fear of reprisals.

There are similar procedures for young offender institutions in Scotland (The Young Offenders (Scotland) Rules 1965.[53]

Recommendations

2.1 Access to advice and counselling, advocacy and effective complaints procedures

1 Current law, policy and practice should be reviewed to ensure that children in all settings have ready and well-publicised access to:

(a) confidential advice and counselling (including confidential access to their GP);

(b) help from an independent advocate or representative (distinct from independent visitors - see section 2.2);

(c) complaints procedures with an independent element;

(d) ultimate access when necessary to the courts.

In all cases, special provision should be made for disabled children and young people (see also section 2.2), and to enable representations to be made on behalf of disabled children and very young children.

(a) Confidential advice and counselling

All institutions and services for or used by children and young people should be required to display readily understandable details of confidential helplines, and ensure that children/young people are able to use a telephone in private (with special arrangements for those with special needs).

(b) Independent advocates or representatives

Children and young people in all settings should be told how they can contact an independent advocate or representative, who can advise them on important matters in confidence, and help them to seek redress for any wrongs they are suffering by guiding them through complaints procedures, and where appropriate representing them. In particular, information on how to contact an independent advocate or representative should be available through helplines for children, and in information about any complaints procedures they may use.

(c) Complaints procedures

All guidance on complaints procedures should emphasise that complaints and representations from children are to be welcomed for the contribution they can make to improving the quality of a service or an institution.

Children and young people themselves should always be adequately and continuously consulted about the design, implementation, dissemination of information about, and operation of complaints procedures.

All complaints procedures which may be used by children and young people should allow complaints by groups of children as well as individuals, and by others on behalf of children (if a child is of "sufficient understanding", complaints made on their behalf should only be considered with their consent; this does not of course prevent relatives or friends making complaints on their own behalf about eg the level of contact allowed with a young person).

(i) "Local" complaints procedures:
There should be clear procedures to encourage informal resolution of complaints whenever possible.

Children and young people in all settings must have ready access to well-publicised complaints procedures which include elements independent of the setting in which they are living or in which they are being provided with a service. Local authorities providing complaints procedures should use independent people recruited, trained and supported by a separate body. It is essential that children should not at the first stage have to complain **to** or through someone they are complaining **about**.

Short time limits, compatible with effective resolution of complaints and extendable in exceptional circumstances, should be set.

If a complainant is not satisfied with the resolution of a complaint locally he or she should always be informed how else to pursue it.

Fulfilling this recommendation will require reviewing existing complaints procedures as outlined above, and providing legal duties to ensure appropriate procedures are available in, for example, the education service and all private and voluntary institutions (and, for example, extending the role of the Mental Health Act Commission to cover "informal" child patients in NHS and other health provision).

The content and resolution of complaints must be monitored in order to take account of implications for policy and service development. Any complaints procedure should also be monitored to see whether children and young people know about it, and have confidence in it.

(ii) When local resolution of complaints fails:
Where complaints are not resolved to the satisfaction of the complainant at service or institution level, there needs to be a further avenue of complaint for children. This could be provided by:

a new UK-wide children's ombudsperson service, with regional offices and powers of investigation etc similar to those of the Commissioner for Local Administration, and covering local authority, voluntary and private services and institutions used by children and young people;

widening the powers of the Commissioners for Local Administration appropriately to cover services and institutions for children.

(d) Access to the courts

All children and young people, including those in care, should have the same rights as adult parties to have applications about aspects of their upbringing considered by the courts: this will require amendments to the Children Act (which currently gives courts discretion whether or not to hear applications from children, and specifically excludes applications from children in care) and to relevant legislation for Scotland (following the proposals for clarification of the Scottish Law Commission) and Northern Ireland.

2 All those involved in providing confidential advice and counselling to children, any independent advocates available to children, and those involved in complaints procedures should be subject to special recruitment and vetting procedures if their work involves significant unsupervised access to children and young people (see section 2.3).

3 Social services departments, the NSPCC and the police should be advised to ensure that children and young people are provided with readily understandable information on child protection procedures: on how children can approach these agencies, and on likely action that may follow a complaint of ill-treatment by a child or young person.

4 Conditions of employment and contracts for all those working with or for children should not limit in any way their right to inform appropriate authorities, to seek appropriate help and to take any other necessary action to safeguard and promote the welfare of children they are working with or for. Necessary whistle-blowing in children's services should be clearly protected.

2.2 Access to independent people

The previous section has underlined the need for children in all settings to have access to confidential advice and counselling, and to an independent advocate or representative who can advise them and where necessary provide representation during informal resolution of problems, or through formal complaints procedures.

But in addition to these services, some children, in particular those who are out of touch with their parents and close relatives, or are formally detained, need to be offered visits by adults who are independent of the institution and of any local authority which is responsible for them.

Child care legislation in England and Wales already recognises the need for some children in residential settings to have "independent visitors" appointed for them, to visit, advise and befriend, and there is a similar provision, as yet unimplemented, in Scottish legislation. The independent visitor has a longer-term role than that of advocate: to befriend and provide support for children who are out of touch with parents and others with parental responsibility.

In relation to the particular concern of this report, protection from ill-treatment and abuse, it is vital that all children living away from home should have regular access to adults who are entirely independent of the setting. Our recommendations, as in other sections, are intended to ensure consistency: that an independent visitor is appointed whenever the child's isolation or particular situation justifies it.

The Children Act for England and Wales re-enacts and extends the obligation on local authorities to appoint independent visitors in limited circumstances. There is a duty to appoint an independent visitor for any child the local authority is looking after (ie children in care and other children provided with accommodation by the local authority) if the authority believes it would be in a child's best interests and certain conditions are satisfied (Children Act schedule 2 para 17). Guidance suggests that the need for such an appointment arises where communication between the child and his/her parent or person with parental responsibility has been infrequent, or where s/he has not visited or been visited by parents or others with parental responsibility during the previous 12 months. Guidance stresses that the views of the child are important, and that the local authority

"may not appoint an independent visitor for a child if the child objects to it and the authority are satisfied that he has sufficient understanding to make an informed decision".[54]

Regulations set out the definition of independent visitor (Definition of Independent Visitors (Children) Regulations 1991).[55] Additionally, the regulations on reviews (Review of Children's Cases Regulations) require the review to consider whether an independent visitor should be appointed.[56]

These are the only statutory duties to consider appointment of independent visitors for individual children in institutions in England and Wales. In Scotland, the Social Work Scotland Act 1968 allows for regulations to be issued to set up a visitor system for residential establishments (section 60(1)(c)). No regulations have been issued, and the *Review of Child Care Law in Scotland* makes no proposals for independent visitors; nor does the Scottish review of residential child care.[57]

The Children Act provisions do not extend to children who are not being looked after by a local authority but are accommodated by health or education authorities or in residential care homes, nursing homes or mental nursing homes, who may be just as isolated. Under the Children Act there is an obligation to inform appropriate local authorities of any child who is accommodated for three months or more by a health or education authority or in a residential care home or a nursing home or mental nursing home (sections 85 and 86). This legislation could be extended to oblige local authorities to consider the appointment of independent visitors for these children in appropriate cases (with corresponding duties on the relevant authorities and institutions to allow proper access etc).

Some children in residential institutions will be unable, because of disability, to use conventional complaints procedures, and to contact helplines: in our view they too need the additional support of an independent visitor. This is also advocated in Sir William Utting's report *Children in the Public Care*:

"It may be hard for a child with disabilities to obtain effective access to a complaints procedure. Using telephone helplines may be difficult because of problems with oral communication and the limitations on privacy imposed by severe immobility. I consider therefore that consideration should be given, in the light of the operation of the new complaints procedure, to extending the appointment of independent visitors to children with disabilities. Such visitors, who would need appropriate communication skills, would play a particular role in relation to protection from abuse and access to representation and complaints procedures".

Sir William also suggests that consideration should be given to extending the role of independent visitor in relation to all children in residential care.[58]

Our recommendations also cover certain exceptional situations in which the normal criteria for appointment of an independent visitor may not apply, but where we believe there are strong grounds for such an appointment. There are instances where children's emotional or behavioural difficulties or disability may cause a serious risk of self-harm or harm to others without some use of restraint. Wherever the child is living (and subject as above to the child's consent in appropriate cases) an independent visitor provides some safeguard against inappropriate restraint, and support for children in difficult circumstances.

Guidance on the role of independent visitors issued under the Children Act suggests that they are not expected to act as advocates.[59] But the "Independent Representative Service" set up by A Voice for the Child in Care and now used by most secure units in England and Wales (see page 110) appears successfully to combine aspects of the role of independent visitor and advocate, as VCC has found it important that children in an institution should be able to confide in and if necessary seek help from someone who is familiar to them. The independent representatives are volunteers who are attached to a particular institution and visit regularly. We propose that such a service should be available for all those whose liberty is restricted (and that consideration should be given to making the availability of such a service a requirement for all residential institutions). The independent team which was appointed by the Department of Health to inquire into complaints about treatment of a young woman at St Charles Youth Treatment Centre (see page 93) recommended that all young people held in secure conditions should have independent visitors appointed.[60]

Arrangements for inspection will generally involve opportunities for children and young people to talk to inspectors who are independent of the institution - local authority-appointed inspectors, the social services inspectorate, schools inspectors, Boards of Visitors and inspectors of penal institutions etc. Our recommendations on inspections (page 190) emphasise the importance of ensuring there is always an opportunity for children and young people as well as staff to talk to those inspecting in confidence.

Recommendations

2.2 Access to independent people

1 In addition to the current obligation in legislation applying to England and Wales to consider the appointment of an independent visitor for certain children and young people, there should be (in legislation applying throughout the UK):

(a) an obligation to consider the appointment of an independent visitor for any child whose accommodation by an education or health authority, or in a residential care home or nursing home or mental nursing home for three months or more is notified to a local authority;

(b) a requirement to appoint an independent visitor or representative for any child placed in secure accommodation, or in other accommodation to restrict liberty falling within section 25 of the Children Act (and similar provisions for Scotland and Northern Ireland), together with an obligation to ensure that the child is visited within two weeks of the placement and thereafter at regular intervals;

(c) a requirement to appoint an independent visitor for those children and young people who are judged unable to use the complaints procedures available to other children and young people in an institution;

(d) a requirement to appoint an independent visitor for any child or young person in need, wherever placed, if the authority has reasonable cause to believe that the child's emotional or behavioural difficulties or disability may cause the child at times to be at serious risk of harming self or others without some use of restraint;

(e) All these requirements should be subject to the child's consent, where judged to have "sufficient understanding".

2 Consideration should also be given to requiring all residential institutions to ensure the availability to children of independent representatives.

3 Consideration should be given to similar requirements in relation to institutional placements in Scotland and Northern Ireland.

2.3 Arrangements to prevent people who threaten children's welfare gaining inappropriate access to them

Reforms in arrangements for recruiting and checking the backgrounds of those who apply to work in situations which give them substantial access to children were considered following the conviction of Colin Evans in 1984 for the murder of Marie Payne. It was revealed that despite an existing record of offences against children, Evans was able to use voluntary work as a means of gaining access to children. In fact he did not meet Marie through his voluntary work, but through a babysitting arrangement.

The tragedy illustrates two points: first, it is yet another example of how child protection arrangements are seldom reviewed without some scandal to trigger the review. Second, while the case led to the conclusion that vetting arrangements should be extended, it is clear that vetting would not in itself have prevented Colin Evans gaining access to Marie and other children.

The report of the inquiry into Pindown in Staffordshire considered issues concerning protection of children in residential establishments. This followed revelations during the inquiry that children in care in homes had been visited by adults who had been convicted of sexual offences against children, and that in one case a young person in care had been placed in lodgings where he was later sexually abused by the landlord.

The report made a series of recommendations concerning vetting of visitors to residential establishments and private sector landlords providing accommodation for children in care and others. It proposed that social services staff should be able to seek information from the police on possible sex offenders who might pose a threat to children. The report also suggested that local authority departments should be informed of convictions for offences against children of people residing or intending to reside in their area, irrespective of where the offence was committed or the nature of the disposal by the court.[61]

More recently, the conviction in 1991 of Frank Beck, a residential care worker, for numerous sexual and other offences against children in a local authority children's home, triggered further ministerial action: an inquiry into selection and recruitment of staff for children's homes was announced by the Secretary of State for Health. Its terms of reference were:

"To examine selection and recruitment methods and criteria for staff working in children's homes and recommend practicable improvements; to make such further examination as the Committee may consider justified of management and other issues relevant to the protection of children and young people and to the support and guidance of staff in such homes; and to report with recommendations to the Secretary of State for Health".

The Committee of Inquiry was chaired by Norman Warner, former Director of Social Services for Kent, and its report, *Choosing with Care*, was published in December 1992. Limiting the inquiry to the staffing of children's homes was yet another example of a narrow response to a particular scandal. As the report itself acknowledges, its recommendations may have implications for other residential institutions for children and young people.[62]

The Inquiry Report considers recruitment, selection, appointment and management of staff for children's homes, including staff development, training and qualifications. The report's recommendations are relevant to all those employing people who will have substantial access to children, and should form the basis for the development of comprehensive codes of practice.

None of the arrangements for checking on possible criminal backgrounds of those applying to work with children is mandatory. The arrangements are set out in circulars, not in legislation. (But it has been suggested that an authority which did not carry out any vetting of an employee with substantial access to children, who subsequently harmed a child in the authority's care, could be liable.)

Signs that the Government has accepted the case for obligatory checks came in September 1992 when the Department for Education consulted on new proposals to put some statutory pressure on proprietors of independent schools to institute proper checks. The proposals, likely to be implemented in the Education Bill currently (February 1993) before Parliament, would allow the Secretary of State for Education to "de-register" an independent school if it is found without reasonable excuse to be employing a person barred from working in a maintained school; the powers would also cover instances in which a barred person applies to register an independent school, or acquires an existing school.

This policy of making checks obligatory will be further encouraged by the Warner Inquiry Report, which proposes that employers should be required by regulation to consult the lists of unsuitable people maintained by the Department of Health and the Department for Education (see pages 142 and 143) in respect of anyone they intend to appoint to a children's home.[63]

But there is no consistency in current Government policy. A circular issued by the Department of Health on daycare in January 1993 emphasises that criminal record checks should be carried out on all childminders and on staff working in local authority day nurseries, but there should not be checks in relation to staff of private and voluntary playgroups, day nurseries, out of school clubs or holiday playschemes (although access to children is just as substantial in these settings).[64]

The summary below shows that evaluations of vetting procedures have emphasised that use of police checks must not be regarded as a panacea, and that other recruitment and employment procedures may be more significant for child protection. But while stricter limits on who should be checked have been proposed, there has been no proposal following these evaluations to stop checks. Given this, it appears not only illogical but dangerous to children to limit checks on resource grounds.

Our aim in this section is to review current arrangements for checking the backgrounds of all those recruited to positions giving them substantial access to children, and to make recommendations (see page 154) to ensure that proper recruitment procedures, including police checks, are used in all appropriate cases. We propose that all relevant employers should be required to follow codes of practice on recruitment and employment of those having substantial access to children; these codes would include arrangements for police checks where justified. The increased mobility of workers within Europe and beyond makes it essential that there should be reciprocal arrangements for police checks between countries, with appropriate safeguards for the individuals concerned. It appears that current arrangements vary enormously from country to country.

We also propose that detailed guidance on child protection should be available to all those working with children, with special guidance for those working with very young children, and with disabled children. There should be a particular emphasis on the importance of enabling children to protect themselves (though not of course as an alternative to the responsibilities of adults to provide protection). Inspectors of institutions should monitor compliance with the codes, and also knowledge of and compliance with the guidance on child protection.

It is important to give a special emphasis to the protection of disabled children and young people. The degree of intimate care which may be required by many of them, and the inability of some to complain directly, highlighted in section 2.1 (page 104) raise particular issues for those recruiting and supervising carers.

Detailed proposals for a General Social Services Council, published in a report in January 1993, suggest ways in which a new statutory professional body covering the whole of the UK could help to raise and regulate standards of social services, including services to children, operating in similar ways to medical professional bodies. The proposal if accepted will take up to 10 years to become fully operational. The report suggests that the first stage of registration should include all social work and social care staff working in residential child care. The proposal could clearly make a major contribution to protection of children, and would replace the need for police checks of those registered by individual employers. The plan is summarised below (page 152).[65]

Summary of arrangements for police checks

Checks by local authority and health authority employers

In July 1986, after acceptance by the Government of the recommendations of the review which followed the Colin Evans case, joint circulars were issued setting out new arrangements for checks to be made by local authority employers with local police forces on the possible criminal background of those - both paid employees and volunteers - who apply or move to work with children. These circulars were revised and re-issued in December 1988.[66] Another circular was issued in March 1988, setting out similar arrangements for checks on staff and volunteers within the National Health Service.[67]

The circulars suggest that checks as to whether a person has a criminal record, and the content of any record, should be made after selection but before appointment to a position "giving substantial access to children". "Children" are defined as anyone up to 16, but the definition

"does not exclude those with access to older children in local authority care, with mental or physical handicap, or who continue at school".

There should also be checks when someone already employed moves to work involving extensive access to children. Otherwise, the circular advises, checks should not in general be made on existing employees:

"If, exceptionally, serious allegations are made against a person already working with children, or previously unrevealed information comes to light, a check may however be made. This must not be done without the knowledge of the individual concerned who must be given an opportunity to discuss the information supplied..."

The circular lists the main groups of people for whom checks should be considered where a person is being appointed, approved or registered:

(a) prospective long-term and short-term foster parents (including private foster parents), and other adults in their households;

(b) prospective adoptive parents (including those adopting through private agencies) and other adults in their households;

(c) applicants for custodianship orders, and other adults in their households (no longer applicable following implementation of the Children Act 1989);

(d) childminders on registration, and other adults in their households;

(e) staff of local authority provided day nurseries and similar local authority facilities such as playgroups;

(f) managers and staff in community (children's) homes provided by local authorities, and controlled community homes;

(g) local authority social services staff (including social work staff and those involved with intermediate treatment) who have substantial opportunity for access to children;

(h) school teachers in schools maintained by local education authorities;

(i) other staff in education departments who have substantial opportunity for access to children (eg education welfare officers, educational psychologists, para-medical staff, school caretakers);

(j) full or part-time youth and/or community workers employed by local authorities;

(k) probation officers and other probation service staff who have substantial opportunity for access to children.

The revised circulars also include a list of posts for which a check "would normally be undertaken", and guidelines on the definition of "substantial access to children":

*"**Does the position involve one-to-one contact?** If it does and such contact is likely to be away from the child's home, or separate from other adults or children, then access should be regarded as substantial;*

***Is the position supervised?** It is possible for a person to spend considerable amounts of time with children, but under close supervision. This should not normally be regarded as substantial access;*

***Is the situation an isolated one?** There is greater risk to a child who is living away from home, eg in residential care, perhaps for lengthy periods, and the risks may increase the further the child is from the parental home, or where parental visits are infrequent. A similar situation could arise where there is opportunity to take children singly, or in a group, away from the family surroundings (for example on holiday);*

***Is there regular contact?** The more regular contact a person has with the same child or group of children, the greater the opportunity to put the child at risk. This is especially so if the contact is unsupervised, or occurs away from other children. Intermittent contact, for example parent helpers for school trips, would not normally be regarded as having substantial access for the purpose of requesting checks (although there may be exceptional instances of parent helpers in schools whose access to children might be* *judged substantial in terms of these guidelines). Checks should not be carried out simply because an individual works at, or visits, schools or other local authority establishments where children are present, as part of their duties, unless those duties would normally bring them into unsupervised direct contact with children. In view of this, delivery men or swimming pool attendants would not normally be subject to checking;*

Are the children particularly vulnerable? *It may be considered that younger children are more vulnerable than older children and generally less able to protect themselves, but the nature of the risk must also be considered. Younger children may be more at risk of sexual abuse; older children from drugs. More particularly, children with a physical or mental handicap, or who have social or behavioural problems, are likely to be more vulnerable than those whose health is sound and/or come from a stable home background".*

The circulars emphasise that checks must not take the place of "normal recruitment procedures":

"References should be required and taken up in the case of all new appointments, with unexplained gaps in employment being satisfactorily accounted for".

The request for a check goes to the Chief Constable for the area in which the applicant has applied to work: if necessary information is sought from other police forces in whose area the applicant has lived. In any cases in which a police check is likely to be required, employers are advised to require applicants to list, as part of the recruitment procedures, any convictions, bind-over orders or cautions. The Rehabilitation of Offenders Act 1974 (Exceptions) Order 1975, as amended by the Rehabilitation of Offenders Act 1974 (Exceptions) (Amendment) Order 1986 allows convictions that are spent under the terms of the Act to be disclosed by the police and taken into account in deciding whether to employ someone. So in relation to jobs involving substantial access to children,the applicant may properly be requested to list all convictions and cautions. If applicants fail to disclose convictions when requested, they can be excluded from consideration for the job, and if deception comes to light they can be dismissed and may be liable to criminal charges (the Theft Act section 16(1) makes it an offence for a person to obtain by deception "pecuniary advantage", which includes obtaining remuneration, or greater remuneration, through employment).

The applicant must give permission before a police check goes ahead, and should be told that refusal could prevent further consideration of their application. The police will reply to a request either showing that they have no record, or if they have giving full details. This will include details of convictions, cautions and bind-over orders, and "other relevant information" which the circulars suggest

"would include factual information which the police would be prepared to present as evidence in court, or details of acquittals or decisions not to prosecute where the circumstances of the case would give cause for concern".

The circulars emphasise that the fact that a person has a criminal record does not automatically render him or her unsuitable for work with children:

"A person's suitability should be looked at as a whole in the light of all the information available".

If the information given by the police is different to that given by the applicant, the discrepancy must be discussed with the applicant before reaching a decision on whether to appoint. Where there is disagreement, the person should have the opportunity to see the information provided by the police. A person who believes the information is incorrect and who wishes to make representations to the police should be told how to do so.

Checks by voluntary sector employers

In 1989, pilot schemes were set up to extend vetting arrangements to some voluntary sector employers, through the Voluntary Organisations Consultancy Service (VOCS), which is administered by the National Council for Voluntary Child Care Organisations (NCVCCO).[68]

In December 1992, a Home Office Circular announced the extension of the voluntary sector scheme.[69] It accepted proposals made in an evaluation report (see page 151) for limiting the scope of vetting:

"In future checks will only be made on people applying to work with children:

(i) who are in a highly vulnerable or isolated setting where supervision or control of the adult is not possible; or

(ii) who for continuous, extended periods have no meaningful, regular contact with other adults independent of that setting".

The circular states:

"Given the diversity of the voluntary sector, it would be impracticable and probably undesirable to try to list here all the posts which should or should not attract a check under these arrangements but they might include for example prospective adoptive or foster parents; persons providing short but frequent spells of respite care for children; telephone counsellors speaking to distressed children; and people applying to work with children in residential care".

In addition, the Home Office is to circulate a Code of Practice for safeguarding the welfare of children in voluntary organisations (provisionally entitled *Safe from Harm*) emphasising good management policies and practice in preventing abuse, providing a set of principles and brief guidelines. The Code will not impose any statutory duties, but will support and reinforce existing legislation.

The scheme for police checks is only available to certain national voluntary organisations, although requests from other national organisations to be admitted will be considered. But if the need for police checks is accepted as government policy in relation to some employment involving substantial unsupervised access to children, then it must be dangerous as well as inconsistent to limit the availability of checks in the voluntary and private sectors. This is very strongly felt by the NCVCCO and other organisations. We recommend the logical extension of availability of checks.

Checks by independent schools

In 1987, a circular letter was sent to proprietors of all independent schools by the Department of Education and Science, setting out arrangements to enable them to check the possible criminal backgrounds of potential employees.

New powers for the Secretary of State for Education to "de-register" schools which are found to be employing barred people are likely to be included in the Education Bill currently before Parliament (February 1993). The powers would also cover instances in which a barred person applies to register a school, or acquires an existing school.

A consultative letter from the Department for Education stated:

"Proprietors have been strongly advised on several occasions to check the list of barred persons (DFE List 99) when making any new appointments to posts involving substantial access to children, either through the Department for Education or through an authorised holder of the list. However our monitoring of the frequency of requests for checks suggests that, while many schools regularly make enquiries, far too many appointments are still being made without recourse to a List 99 check. The safety of children is clearly at risk while this continues".

The letter emphasises that under the new proposed powers

"the onus will be on proprietors assiduously to conduct checks, keeping appropriate records that they have done so. It is, of course, a criminal offence to operate an unregistered independent school".[70]

A report on the Castle Hill School case revealed that the proprietor, Ralph Morris, used false qualifications in promoting the school. The report suggests among "more rigorous checks and balances" the confirmation and validation of staff qualifications and backgrounds.[71]

Scotland

In Scotland, the revised system for checking is centred on the Scottish Criminal Records Office within Strathclyde Police Headquarters in Glasgow, where a record of convictions is stored in a new computer linked to all Scottish police forces. Arrangements for checking, similar to those set out above, are described in circulars.[72]

The existence of the General Teaching Council for Scotland (GTC) provides a distinctive system for deciding whether an individual is a fit person to teach. The GTC requests checks on all those who are to be accepted on to its register, and will therefore be eligible for employment in local authority schools in Scotland. Details of convictions which appear to render a person unsuitable to be employed in the education service are passed to the GTC by the Scottish Criminal Records Office. The GTC arrangements do not cover non-teaching employees, for whom vetting is carried out by the local authority employer with the Criminal Records Office.

The Scottish Office Education Department also keeps a list of "unsuitable" teachers (see page 144).

Other vetting systems

The Department for Education and the Department of Health in England and Wales, the Scottish Social Work Services Group and the Northern Ireland Department of Health and Social Services operate systems designed to help protect children, by collecting information on people who may be unsuitable to work in positions giving substantial access to children. The police provide information to the Departments on relevant convictions, and local authorities and some other employers are under a legal obligation to provide information on employees in certain circumstances (see below).

Inter-departmental guidance on inter-agency co-operation on child protection, *Working Together*, suggests that some local authorities and "other agencies" have found it useful to maintain a list of all offenders in the area who have been convicted of relevant offences.

"Such a list has its limitations because it is difficult to keep it up to date. Although the prison service, through the probation service, notifies local authority social services departments of the discharges of Schedule 1 offenders, such people are often highly mobile".

The guidance also states ambiguously that

"Care should be taken with case records which contain information about adults suspected but not convicted of offences against children and a list of such people should not be held. The confidentiality of such records must be safeguarded and should not be shared except for child protection purposes... Where there is information about an abuser they must be informed and told of the possibility of questioning the details or making representations about the entry".[73]

The Department of Health Consultancy Service

The Department of Health (DH) Consultancy Service is available to any employer in the child care field, whether local authority, voluntary or private. The service notes convictions against those who (at the time of conviction) are or were in child care work; it also notes the names of people formerly in such work who have been dismissed or who have resigned

"in circumstances which might suggest that children would be put at risk if the person were again appointed to a position involving responsibility for children's welfare".

There need not be police proceedings for such reports to be made. When information is received, it is considered within the Department of Health by administrative and Social Services Inspectorate staff, and others if necessary, against a set of criteria: primarily, whether children would be at risk if the person was to be employed in child care; the gravity of the offence; and any previous history. Then, if it is considered appropriate, the name and information is added to the register. The person concerned is notified and told of the use to which the information may be put. He or she has the opportunity to confirm, correct or contest it, or generally to make representations to the DH.

When a local authority or voluntary organisation is considering an applicant for a post involving substantial contact with children, it can use the consultancy service to check whether information is held. The DH will either respond "no observations", or will take a decision on the validity and relevance of the information held, and if necessary contact the local authority or voluntary organisation. Normally the DH does not provide the information it holds about convictions, but suggests that a reference is taken up from the applicant's previous employer.

The DH also holds a regularly updated copy of the Department for Education List 99 (see below), so that those who consult the service have automatic access to this additional list of "unsuitable" individuals. However, the DH Consultancy Service list is currently kept on file cards and it is therefore not practicable to provide a copy for the DFE.

According to the Warner Inquiry Report, use of the DH Consultancy Service has increased between four- and five-fold during the 1980s. Around 52,000 checks were made in 1990 - but only six "positives" were found. The report comments:

"Thus these lists are hardly rooting out large numbers of would-be abusers for employers in the residential child care sector, although the greater publicity around their existence may deter abusers from applying for jobs with children".

A survey commissioned by the Warner Inquiry and carried out by Price Waterhouse in 1992 found that about half of employers in the local authority and voluntary sectors use the DH Consultancy Service, but less than one third of private children's homes. There is some use of the Department for Education's List 99 (see below), "but users are heavily outnumbered by non-users", the report of the survey comments.

"Clearly the Government guidance is not being followed by large numbers of employers. We therefore recommend that the requirement on employers to consult both the Consultancy Service and List 99 be put on a statutory basis, by incorporating it in regulations. This will help also to reinforce the importance of notifying Government departments of adverse information on staff".[74]

Department for Education List 99

The Secretary of State for Education has power under regulation 10 of the Education (Teachers) Regulations 1989 (SI 1989/1319) to bar "unsuitable persons" from "relevant employment", defined as employment by local education authorities or other bodies in schools and further education establishments of people

"whose work bring him regularly into contact with children or young persons who have not attained the age of 19".

The Department keeps a list (List 99) of both teachers and non-teaching staff who are considered unsuitable. The circulars on disclosure of criminal backgrounds of those with access to children advise LEAs and other employers in education to consult List 99 before using the new checking procedures. If the checking procedures reveal additional information on relevant convictions, the DFE should be informed in order to "tie the new procedure in with List 99 procedures".

Those placed on List 99 are informed and are able to challenge the information recorded.[75]

Scotland

In Scotland, as described earlier (page 141) the procedure for police checks is centralised on the Scottish Criminal Record Office. The Scottish Social Work Services Group also maintain a list, whose operation is described in a circular.[76] If in the course of their operations local police forces become aware that a person already employed in a residential establishment for children or registered as a childminder has convictions which cast doubt on his or her suitability for such employment, they report this to the Scottish Office, who consider whether it is appropriate to inform the employer. Local authorities and voluntary bodies in Scotland can check potential employees against the list (to check potential employees from elsewhere in the United Kingdom, employers are put in touch with the Department of Health or the appropriate Northern Ireland Department (see below)). The circular suggests that these arrangements

"are scarcely ever used by local authorities and their usefulness will be reviewed in the light of the extended scope of police checks".

The Scottish Office Education Department maintains a list of those considered unsuitable to work with or have access to children in a teaching capacity. This is circulated with List 99, and there are similar arrangements for compiling the list. Returns required from independent schools in Scotland of all teaching staff are checked against the lists.[77]

Northern Ireland

In Northern Ireland, the Pre-employment Consultancy Service run by the DHSS in Belfast covers employment of those having substantial access to both children and "mentally handicapped people". It covers those employed or volunteering in both child care and health settings, and the service is offered to voluntary organisations and other organisations working with children.

The police in Northern Ireland inform Health and Social Services Boards and professional bodies of relevant convictions of people working with children (or the Child Care Branch of the DHSS is informed if there is any doubt about identity).[78]

Duties to report "unsuitable" people

The Children's Homes Regulations 1991 issued under the Children Act 1989 to apply to all local authority, voluntary and private (registered) children's homes in England and Wales place an obligation on the appropriate authority (local authority, voluntary organisation, or person carrying on a registered home) to report to the Secretary of State for Education

"any conduct on the part of a member of staff of the home which is or may be such, in the opinion of the responsible authority, that he is not, or as the case may be would not be, a suitable person to be employed in work involving children".[79]

Strangely, there does not appear to be any similar duty in relation to carers who are not members of staff of a children's home, eg foster parents, daycare staff etc.

An inquiry report into the death of a child in foster care emphasised the importance of reporting any concerns about particular foster parents:

"The decision of individual workers not to place a child with a particular foster parent is an inadequate response to concern over their suitability... Complaints both from within and outside the (social services) department should be investigated immediately".

The report also proposed that prospective foster parents who apply for approval outside their local authority area should, as a precautionary measure, be asked their reasons for doing so.[80]

The survey commissioned by the Warner Inquiry into recruitment practice in children's homes suggests that it is not consistent practice to alert other prospective employers about staff leaving who have given rise to concern:

"Only around half local authority respondents (and a slightly higher proportion of respondents from voluntary and private homes) claim 'always' or 'usually' to alert other potential employers about staff leaving their employment about whom there may be concerns".

The Inquiry Report recommends that employers should

"retain records of disciplinary offences or concerns that enable them to be passed on to a potential employer when requested in connection with a job which involves working with children".

It also suggests that the Department of Health should issue guidance

"pointing out the responsibility of all employers to pass on information about unacceptable behaviour; making it clear to all employers the types and characteristics of behaviour which are deemed unacceptable and therefore notifiable; and clarifying the format in which this information should be passed on".[81]

A Home Office circular issued in December 1992, announcing the extension of the scheme enabling voluntary sector organisations to check prospective employees (see page 139) also reminds voluntary organisations of the need to continue to inform the Department of Health Consultancy Service about members of staff or volunteers who are dismissed or resign

"in circumstances where the welfare of the child would be put at risk if they were engaged again in working with children".[82]

Local education authorities and other education employers are required to make misconduct reports to the DFE in respect of workers with children and young people, including teachers. Following the scandal of child abuse at an independent school, Crookham Court, in 1990, certain safeguards for pupils in independent boarding schools were included in the Children Act (see page 55). The arrangements to prevent unsuitable people being employed in private schools were also strengthened. Proprietors of independent schools are required to report instances in which any person - not just teachers - is dismissed from employment on grounds of misconduct, or resigns in circumstances where dismissal would be considered (Education (Particulars of Independent Schools) (Amendment) Regulations 1991).[83] The schools are also now required to give full details of all staff, not just teaching staff, on application for registration and annually.

Current arrangements to ensure that evidence of unsuitability for work with children is recorded and available to potential employers (with appropriate safeguards for the subjects of the information) are clearly incomplete: our recommendations make proposals to remedy this.

Arrangements under the Children Act for disqualification from caring for children

Regulations issued under the Children Act enable individuals to be disqualified from private fostering, from being involved in any way with a voluntary or registered (private) children's home, providing daycare or working as a childminder. The Disqualification for Caring for Children Regulations 1991 apply to England and Wales, and as far as they relate to childminding and daycare, to Scotland too. The arrangements replace those in the Nurseries and Childminders Regulation Act 1948 and the Foster Children Act 1980. A person who is disqualified from one of the activities, is also disqualified from the others. Grounds for disqualification include:

having had a child who has been the subject of a care order, or where an order has been made to remove a child from the person's care, or preventing the child from living with the person;

having been convicted of various offences listed in a schedule to the regulations (including sexual offences, "any offence involving injury or threat of injury to another person", and others);

having been involved in a voluntary or private children's home which has been removed from the register, or having been refused registration of a home;

having been prohibited from being a private foster parent, or refused registration as a provider of daycare or a childminder, or having had registration cancelled.

A person who is disqualified who wishes to be involved in registration of a private children's home, or in providing daycare or being a childminder, must disclose their disqualification to the relevant local authority, and obtain their written permission.[84] Authorities have the discretion to give permission, but guidance suggests that they should do so "only in the most exceptional circumstances".[85] In the case of applications concerning voluntary homes, disqualification must be revealed to the Secretary of State, who retains discretion over waiving disqualification. In each case, there are appeal rights for the disqualified individual.

Surprisingly, these provisions on disqualification do not apply to children's homes, foster care or daycare provided by, or paid for by local authorities. The guidance suggests that children in local authority provision

"should similarly be protected from those who might wish to harm them or are otherwise unfit to care for them".

It suggests that local authorities "will wish to" have regard to the regulations on disqualification and the guidance when considering the appointment and suitability of staff.

Assessing the effectiveness of vetting

As with other issues of protection for children, there appears to have been little attempt to look comprehensively at how to use recruitment and vetting procedures effectively to seek to safeguard children from ill-treatment and abuse by people working with or for them. Even the most recent inquiry chaired by Norman Warner had narrow terms of reference, limiting its scope to selection and recruitment of staff working in children's homes (see page 133).

Discussion of safeguards has tended to be dominated by the issue of checking on criminal records and related information, yet it is only very recently that there has been any attempt to evaluate the process of vetting. The results emphasise that vetting is no panacea, and that there is a danger of it giving employers a false sense of security. Other recruitment and employment procedures, including arrangements for supervision and inspection are of more importance in providing protection.

Various reports have considered vetting arrangements recently: none advocates discontinuing the process altogether, but all advocate stricter limits on its use. As the Warner Report states:

"Although checking whether a candidate has a criminal record is a useful safeguard for posts in children's homes, it is important to recognise their limitations in terms of child protection. Home Office statistics suggest that only an estimated four per cent of all offences committed result in a criminal conviction, so police checks are going to reveal only a very small proportion of child abusers".[86]

Current moves to centralise criminal records into a single computerised system available on line to police forces, the courts and other criminal justice agencies will certainly simplify and speed up the process of vetting (as has already been the case in Scotland).

In 1991 the Home Office published the report of an efficiency scrutiny on *The National Collection of Criminal Records*. This proposes that there should be no change in vetting procedures, or the scope of vetting, until after computerisation. At that stage - expected in the mid-1990s - vetting should continue to be available for posts involving substantial access to children, but "substantial access" should be more closely defined (the report also proposes that vetting should be available for those applying to work with other vulnerable groups - the elderly and people with disabilities and learning difficulties).[87]

The report proposes that a central agency - part of the main criminal records agency - should handle all vetting, and that it should be financially self-supporting. It would prescribe procedures for handling the information disclosed, and should publish codes of practice from time to time setting out key factors on using the vetting process. The criminal record should generally pass through the hands of the data subject on its way to the employer, to provide a chance for the subject to challenge the information. Safeguards would be introduced to make it difficult to amend or forge records. Employers should not be allowed to copy or retain the document shown to them by the applicant.

In a section on vetting the report emphasises:

"Vetting is no panacea. There will always be a significant risk that some users would place excessive weight on the results of vetting, and would pay too little attention to the other elements of their recruitment, which in aggregate are far more important. There is no objective evidence to show us to what extent vetting may reduce crime".

Yet the report rejects the case for reducing or ending vetting: vetting may help to deter potential offenders from seeking jobs which give them easy access to children. And where vulnerable individuals are placed in the care of others,

"we have no doubt that the public would regard it as reasonable to take the additional precaution of vetting alongside other measures, to protect them as far as possible from risks to which they are especially prone. This applies with particular force to the risk of sexual and violent assaults upon children, and a limited intrusion into the privacy of those who have a criminal record seems to be a reasonable price to pay, for these cases in particular".

The report proposes that procedures should be extended to cover all posts in the private and voluntary sector giving substantial access to children,

"but that in order to minimise the range of posts subject to vetting, the characteristics of the posts where it is required should be more clearly defined.

"The principle underlying this approach is that vetting should be available only where the risk of danger to the child cannot be reduced to a satisfactory level by other means. There are, for example, many reasons apart from the risk of sexual abuse why groups of young children need to be supervised by more than one adult. If criminal acts would require collusion by two or more adults, that in itself will often substantially reduce the risks, perhaps even to the point where vetting may become unnecessary. Circumstances tending to strengthen the case for vetting would include those where the task of the adult was to form a relationship with the child; where the relationship would be on a one-to-one basis (which certainly includes the exceptional risks associated with adoption and fostering); and where the child's circumstances - perhaps because he or she was already disadvantaged or injured in some way - created exceptional vulnerability".

The report suggests that disclosure of convictions in relation to work with children should include "spent offences" and cautions:

"The basis of this recommendation is that the history of some offenders against children suggests that the urges to commit such offences may persist for a very long time, and that a clear period of 10 or 15 years may not be an adequate safeguard".

The report also considers the disclosure of other information than convictions:

"This is intended to cover instances where, to take an extreme and obvious example, a man seeking a post involving access to children is known to the police to have been charged with indecent assault on a child, but was acquitted (or the prosecution did not proceed) solely because the only witness was the very young victim of the offence".

The scrutiny found that in some forces it was a well-established unofficial practice for junior officers to read over extracts of intelligence files to trusted contacts in local authority departments. The report recommends that chief officers should give instructions to stop such practices. But it does nevertheless propose that

"it should be open to the Crown Prosecution Service, following an acquittal or decision to discontinue proceedings for any charge involving serious violence or sexual assault on a person less than 16 years old, to recommend that the fact of the charge or acquittal or abandonment of proceedings should be retained on the record, instead of the record of pending proceedings being removed (and the whole record being removed where there were no previous convictions)".

Such recommendations would be made when the Crown Prosecution Service felt, on the balance of probabilities and the evidence available, that a person's behaviour suggested that he could be a threat to the safety of children. Where such information was recorded, the person concerned would be notified that it would not be cited in court, would not be required to be disclosed as a conviction in a job application, but that it would be disclosed by the vetting authority in cases where "special disclosure" applied, including work involving substantial access to children.

The Warner Report supports this proposal, that the Crown Prosecution Service

"should make available to the police information suggesting that individuals should not work with children, who in turn could inform employing authorities through the medium of police checks".[88]

The inquiry into police investigation of abuse in Leicestershire children's homes was concerned at the lack of information passed from police to social services,

"when at the conclusion of a criminal investigation insufficient evidence is available to justify criminal proceedings but nevertheless an individual's conduct gives rise for serious concern".

The inquiry report indicated that at present social services would only be told that there was insufficient evidence for criminal proceedings:

"There would be no reference to any concerns...or to the facts giving rise to those concerns. As a result a suspected child abuser could remain in post...This inquiry believes the police must be allowed to disclose their concerns and the facts giving rise to them to enable the management of the agency to take whatever action they deem necessary".

The report proposes that the Home Office should urgently review the position and provide adequate protection and safeguards for the police, who are currently reluctant to make disclosures which might lead to civil litigation or contravene the Police Discipline Regulations.[89]

The Government has indicated that a consultation paper on proposals for new disclosure arrangements following computerisation will be circulated "in due course".

Further doubts on the significance of vetting in child protection have been voiced by the Monitoring and Evaluation Committee appointed by the National Steering Committee for the Voluntary Sector which was set up to oversee the pilot schemes for vetting in the voluntary sector (see page 139).

Dr Judith Unell was appointed to carry out an independent evaluation of the schemes for the Home Office. Her report was published early in 1992.[90] The Monitoring and Evaluation Committee welcomed her report as a major contribution to the debate on the use of criminal records for vetting purposes. Key findings included a considerable mis-match between the individuals checked and the population of sex offenders; the heavy costs; the weakness of other recruitment procedures practised by some voluntary organisations; misuse of the scheme even under tight controls; doubts about the value of the additional information revealed by the check, and the possibility that checking might have a deterrent effect on volunteering.

The Committee notes that

"only an estimated four per cent of criminal offences result in a conviction or caution, and criminal record checks can be relatively easily subverted by the use of false identities".

The Committee recommends that the Government should publish a Code of Practice on recruitment, supervision and induction for those whose work gives them substantial access to children. It concludes that in some cases effective supervision will not be possible (for example adoption), and that

"some children might be particularly vulnerable because for continuous and extended periods they had little or no access to adults who were independent of the organisation undertaking their care (for example, children in residential care). In those circumstances, the Committee concluded that vetting was a helpful safeguard".

In defining the circumstances in which vetting should be available to voluntary organisations, the Committee mention those having "substantial unsupervised access to children up to the age of 16". As examples the Committee cite children in residential care, with adoptive or foster parents or with daily childminders. Organisations using the service should be required to comply with a code of practice for the selection, training and supervision of paid staff and volunteers working with children.[91] These proposals have been accepted and incorporated in the circular outlining the extension of the voluntary sector scheme (see page 139).

The Committee echoes the proposal of the Efficiency Scrutiny report referred to above, that following centralisation of records, vetting should be available through a new agency which would be able to "enforce" proper recruitment and supervision procedures amongst organisations seeking vetting.

A recent circular from the Department of Health on daycare re-emphasises the Department's view of the limited value of police checks:

"While criminal record checks are a useful tool for excluding undesirable people from working with children, it is still the employer's responsibility to obtain a full employment history, to check all references thoroughly and to make a detailed examination of any inconsistencies and unexplained gaps. It is unsafe to rely on criminal record checks on their own as a means of preventing children being exposed to the risk of abuse. They cannot detect first offenders or repeated offenders who have never been caught. Some of the worst offences of child abuse have been committed by people with no previous convictions..." [92]

Proposal for a General Social Services Council

In 1990 a report from the National Institute for Social Work recommended the establishment of a General Social Services Council. Following publication, an action group was set up which in January 1992 published and presented a detailed proposal to the Secretary of State for Health and Scottish, Welsh and Northern Ireland ministers. Its aim is to

"promote and improve standards of practice, training and conduct in the personal social services. It would achieve this primarily through the registration of those working in the services, and through the regulation of conduct and practice".

The ultimate aim is a register including all those working in the personal social services, but the proposal suggests that first priority should be to register staff with direct responsibilities for the most vulnerable users of services. Thus the first stage of registration would include all social work and social care staff working in residential child care.

Those registered would be expected to abide by a Code of Conduct drawn up by the Council (which would include members appointed by the Secretaries of State, nominations by major interests, election by those registered and co-options). The Council would have powers to investigate complaints, and to impose a range of sanctions (caution, suspension from practice, limited registration, removal from register) following a hearing at which misconduct is proven. In serious cases, by removing someone from the register the Council could effectively prevent alternative employment within the personal social services. The statute setting up the Council and register would provide a right of appeal to an appropriate court.[93]

The report states:

"Recent inquiries, such as that of the Warner Committee, have exposed the lack of an effective, co-ordinated system for excluding from employment those found guilty of serious misconduct and criminal offences. The existence of a register should assist in preventing such cases from recurring".

Recommendations

2.3 Arrangements to prevent people who threaten children's welfare gaining inappropriate access to them

1 We echo the recommendations of other bodies that a code of practice should be drafted as soon as possible (or a series of codes) on the recruitment, induction and supervision of people working or volunteering in situations which give them substantial unsupervised access to children. An inter-departmental group involving representatives from the voluntary and private sectors should be appointed to oversee drafting and should review and monitor implementation. The group could draw on recommendations in *Choosing with Care* and other reports.

Following a short period of consultation, the code(s) should be disseminated very widely to all bodies employing or likely to employ people or use volunteers in positions giving them substantial unsupervised access to children.

2 All employers - local authority, health authority, voluntary and private - of relevant workers/volunteers should be required in primary legislation to follow these codes, which would include appropriate arrangements for police checks.

3 All relevant voluntary and private employers should be enabled to check the possible criminal background of those who apply or move to work in paid or voluntary posts which will give them substantial unsupervised access to children. We are particularly concerned about the need for checks for volunteers who work in a one-to-one situation with children with learning difficulties, and eg guardians appointed for children in boarding schools whose parents are abroad.

4 In relation to private and voluntary organisations, procedures should ensure in certain cases (eg independent schools) that those responsible for employment and supervision have themselves been checked, either when they applied for registration of an institution, or when they first apply to use the checking procedures.

5 We support the proposal of the Home Office Efficiency Scrutiny on collection of criminal records, and other reports, that once criminal records are centralised (as they are already in Scotland), a single agency should take on the task of collecting, storing and providing access in defined circumstances to criminal records and other agreed information relating to potential unsuitability. This agency would take over the roles of government departments (eg the DH Consultancy Service, DFE List 99 etc). It would be responsible for ensuring that no information was provided until the subject of it had had an opportunity to check and if necessary formally challenge it. There is a strong case for central government meeting the cost: it is essential in any case that charges do not become a disincentive to employers to use vetting procedures: thus they should be available free at least to voluntary organisations.

This agency could also take on some responsibility for ensuring that codes of practice on recruitment and employment procedures are implemented.

6 We support the case for a General Social Services Council, which could make a major contribution towards protecting children from people who threaten their welfare.

7 Increasing mobility of workers within Europe and beyond makes it essential that there are reciprocal arrangements for police checks across country boundaries, with appropriate safeguards for the subjects of checks.

8 The obligation on the responsible authority for a children's home to report to the Secretary of State any conduct of a member of staff suggesting that s/he is not or may not be "a suitable person to be employed in work involving children", and the similar duty on proprietors of independent schools to report misconduct should apply to all employers of people who may have substantial unsupervised access to children (such information would eventually be directed to the central agency referred to above). A process of appeal should be built in to ensure that the subject of such reports is shown the information before it is made available to potential employers, and can challenge the information.

9 The necessary review of existing legislation implied by recommendation 8 should also include consideration of the arrangements in the Children Act for disqualification of certain carers. It appears to us either that such arrangements should apply consistently to all forms of employment involving substantial access to children, or the arrangements should be harmonised with those for reporting and recording information about other potentially unsuitable staff.

10 All those working in institutions and quasi-institutional settings with children should receive detailed guidance on protection of children. Particular guidance will be required for those working with very young children and children with learning difficulties.

11 In all advice relating to employment of people in settings with children there should be an emphasis on the importance of enabling children to protect themselves (though this should never be seen as an alternative to the responsibilities of adults to provide protection), on adequate supervision, and on clear procedures in the event of suspicion of inappropriate conduct with children.

12 Those responsible for inspection of institutions and other settings including children and young people should be required to monitor compliance with the codes of practice on employment, and awareness of the guidance on child protection.

2.4 Arrangements for monitoring/reviewing placement and treatment of children

Children and young people who are placed away from their home, either by their parents or through a local authority or health authority or a court decision, are subject to a variety of arrangements for review of their placement and treatment. These vary according to legal status and institution or service involved. As in other sections of this report the summary below reveals extraordinary inconsistency. Those living at home (unless they are in care) are free of formal monitoring and review.

This section looks at the diversity of current arrangements, and ways in which they could be improved to provide better protection for children and young people from ill-treatment and abuse, whatever setting they are in. We propose that the frequency of reviews and arrangements for involvement of the child or young person, and parents when appropriate, and for reporting should be consistently applied to all children living in institutional and quasi-institutional settings throughout the UK. In addition we propose that in every case there should be an "exit interview", at which the child or young person is enabled to comment if s/he wishes on the placement, its successes and any problems. (The 1993 report on police investigations of abuse in Leicestershire children's homes proposed that every child reported missing should be interviewed when traced, to establish why the child went missing, as this could indicate abuse.)

It is beyond the scope of this report to look in detail at the procedures for protecting children once they are judged to be at risk, but this section does cover arrangements intended to ensure identification of children at risk, including the obligation to maintain a child protection register.

The NSPCC has for some time argued that there should be a radical review of child protection procedures to take account of the past 10 years' experience and the findings of various inquiries. Revisions in the detailed advice issued for inter-agency co-operation over child protection have followed consultation but no wide-ranging review. We strongly support the case for a full-scale review or reviews, co-ordinated throughout the UK. Changes in the administration of the education and health services and other local government reorganisation add to the case for full-scale review.

Children living at home with parent(s)/ guardian(s) before school age

Children and young people living at home with parent(s) or guardian(s) are not subject to any compulsory review by outside authorities, unless they are in care to a local authority or in Scotland are under the supervision of a Children's Hearing.

A midwife is required to notify a birth within 36 hours, and there is an obligation on parents to register a birth within six weeks (21 days in Scotland). Every child should thus obtain a National Health Service number, and be invited for appropriate developmental checks. There is no statutory framework for visiting by health visitors nor for developmental checks for babies and children although the intention is that the arrangements should be universal.

In relation to all children, the community at large has a moral duty (but no statutory duties) to protect children from harm. *Working Together* (the inter-departmental circular on "arrangements for inter-agency co-operation for the protection of children from abuse" in England and Wales) states:

"This means that all citizens should remain alert to circumstances in which children may be harmed. Individuals can assist the statutory authorities by bringing cases to their attention. Relatives, friends and neighbours of children are particularly well-placed to do so, but they must know what to do if they are concerned, in addition to providing support for the family and child, which may include help with caring for the child. They must also be confident, because of the difficult and sensitive nature of the situation, that any information they provide will be treated in a confidential way and used only to protect the interest of the child..."[94]

The report of a review of residential child care in Scotland, *Another Kind of Home*, suggests that anyone receiving allegations or suspicions about possible abuse of young people or children in residential care should inform the police without hesitation.[95]

In order to protect any children who may be at risk of ill-treatment or abuse, social services departments are given general investigative duties. The police also have duties to investigate. In England and Wales, the Children Act places social services departments under a statutory duty (section 47) towards any child living or found in their area who "is suffering or is likely to suffer, significant harm". The authority must

"make or cause to be made, such enquiries as they consider necessary to enable them to decide whether they should take any action to safeguard or promote the child's welfare".

Social services departments can call on other authorities - including local education authorities (but it is not clear whether this applies to schools operating outside LEA control), health and housing authorities - to assist them by providing relevant information and advice; the other authorities must do so "unless it would be unreasonable in all the circumstances of the case".

There are various powers to take emergency and longer-term action to protect children who are believed to have suffered or to be at risk of suffering significant harm. In particular, if anyone authorised by social services or the NSPCC is denied access to a child, or denied information about the child's whereabouts, the authority or NSPCC must apply for a court order (emergency protection order, child assessment order, care or supervision order),

"unless they are satisfied that his welfare can be satisfactorily safeguarded without their doing so".

Anyone can apply for an emergency protection order.

If the authority decide not to apply for any order, they must in addition consider whether it would be appropriate to review the case at a later date, and if they decide that it would be, determine the date on which the review should begin (section 47(7)).

Working Together states that in the area of every social services department, a central child protection register must be maintained - listing all children in the area who are considered to be suffering from or likely to suffer significant harm, and for whom there is a child protection plan. It appears, surprisingly, that there is no statutory obligation to have and maintain a register, nor provisions relating to review of children placed on registers. *Working Together* does state that

"if a child's name is placed on the child protection register, a review conference should be held at a time agreed at the initial conference, and the intervening period should be no more than six months. For the first review it will be less, unless the initial conference had before it enough material to assess fully the risk to the child".[96]

Developmental checks and health surveillance from birth to five may work well if they are available and properly promoted, and if parents use them. Where parents for whatever reason avoid them, this may alert appropriate authorities (in particular health visitors) to potential risk for the child.

It is clear that once children reach school age, they are subject to a degree of continuing if informal monitoring by adults outside their family (see below, page 163) and many will attend various forms of daycare before the age of five. Of course in the vast majority of cases parents will be promoting their children's welfare from birth and seeking help and advice as necessary. But neither the moral obligations of the community to promote children's welfare, nor the arrangements for health surveillance and developmental checks, nor the investigative and protective duties of social services, the NSPCC and the police, provide any clear obligation to monitor or review all children living at home with parent(s)/guardian(s) before they start school. This contrasts with the detailed arrangements for reviews including regular health checks for very young children in care or being looked after by local authorities (see page 164). From the child's perspective, does the state not have a more active duty to ensure that children's health and welfare is safeguarded and promoted?

Legal concepts of parental "rights" over their children are being modified and replaced by concepts of parental responsibility. The Scottish Law Commission has proposed that parents should have a statutory responsibility "to safeguard and promote the child's health, development and welfare".[97] The child's right to life and healthy development is enshrined in the UN Convention on the Rights of the Child. Article 6 guarantees the right to life and insists that

"States Parties shall ensure to the maximum extent possible the survival and development of the child".

Article 24 begins:

"States Parties recognise the right of the child to the enjoyment of the highest attainable standard of health and to facilities for the treatment of illness and rehabilitation of health. States Parties shall strive to ensure that no child is deprived of his or her right of access to such health care services..."

But despite the recommendations of the Court Report, there is no statutory basis for monitoring to ensure that these responsibilities are fulfilled to a reasonable degree, at least in the period from birth to school age. The report stated:

*"During the intervening years (**between birth notification and five**) of rapid development when children are particularly vulnerable to adverse physical and social factors, it is much less easy to achieve and maintain effective contact with families".*

The report argued that there should be a statutory medical examination for all children at school entry (this had ceased to be a statutory requirement in 1974). It also argued for legally enforceable medical examinations in certain circumstances: that where surveillance services are not taken up, or where there is suspicion of serious ill-health for which medical help is not being sought, the health visitor should seek access to the child by persuasion; in the event of failure, she should have the right to apply for a legally enforceable medical examination. Head teachers should also have the right, said the report,

"on reasonable grounds for concern, to request the medical examination of a child in their charge, if necessary without the consent of parents".[98]

None of these proposals has been implemented. There is a strong feeling in the relevant professions that policies of partnership with parents are more constructive than additional statutory powers of enforcement.

The Court Report also proposed that:

"In cases of suspected abuse or neglect, local authorities should have the power to seek a legally enforceable medical examination separately from a removal order".

This has now been implemented in England and Wales in the Children Act 1989, which enables courts on application by local authorities, the NSPCC or anyone authorised by the Secretary of State to make "child assessment orders".

The court may make the order if satisfied that:

"(a) the applicant has reasonable cause to suspect that the child is suffering, or is likely to suffer, significant harm;

(b) an assessment of the child's health or development or the way in which he has been treated is necessary to determine whether or not the child is suffering, or likely to suffer, significant harm;

(c) it is unlikely that such an assessment will be made or be satisfactory, in the absence of an order..." (section 43 Children Act 1989)

The order must specify the date by which the assessment is to begin, and have effect for not more than seven days from that date. Any person in a position to produce the child must do so and comply with any directions in the order. (Children judged to have sufficient understanding have a right to refuse consent to any medical or psychiatric assessment under the order.)

Guidance issued under the Children Act suggests that the conditions for a child assessment order are very specific:

"The order is for cases where there are suspicions, but no firm evidence, of actual or likely significant harm in circumstances which do not constitute an emergency; the applicant considers that a decisive step to obtain an assessment is needed to show whether the concern is well-founded or further action is not required, and that informal arrangements to have such an assessment carried out have failed. For example, the parents or other persons looking after the child have resisted attempts to arrange an examination or assessment by agreement or failed to bring the child to see a doctor when arrangements have been made, and have not made suitable

alternative arrangements. The problem may have come to light from contact with the family or child by a health visitor, social worker, doctor, teacher or other professional, or from a concerned relative or friend".

The guidance suggests that an order will be most appropriate usually where the harm to the child is long-term and cumulative rather than sudden and severe:

"The circumstances may be nagging concern about a child who appears to be failing to thrive; or the parents are ignorant of or unwilling to face up to possible harm to the child because of the state of his health or development..."

On the other hand, refusal to allow a child about whom there is serious concern to be seen

"can be a classic sign of a potential emergency, and will require the response of an application for an emergency protection order".

The guidance also emphasises that applications, which represent a "substantial intervention in the upbringing of the child", should be contemplated

"only when there is reason for serious concern for the child. It should not be used for a child whose parents are reluctant to use the normal child health services. There should have been a substantial effort to persuade those caring for the child of the need for an assessment and to persuade them to agree to suitable arrangements voluntarily".[99]

The Court Report proposed that a basic programme of health surveillance should be offered to all children, and additional surveillance arranged for

"those children who need it, particularly for children who are developmentally vulnerable" or *"disadvantaged"*.

As an aid to achieving "whole child population health surveillance", the report proposed that health visitors should be assigned geographically defined communities "with whom they should ensure that the child health services keep in touch"; an effective system should be devised to record a family's "transfer in" or "transfer out" of a defined neighbourhood; parents should be required to notify a change of address when applying for family allowances; and (as noted above), health visitors should have a right to apply for a legally enforceable medical examination of young children whose health and welfare they fear may be jeopardised by the failure of their parents to make use of available child health services.

These and other recommendations in the Court Report indicate that this unique and wide-ranging review of child health services felt that all children should be subject to some health surveillance. The particular concern of this report is protection of all children from ill-treatment and abuse. Developmental checks are a vital preventive strategy in that they form the basis for deciding whether all is going well for the child, and thus the occasions when they are carried out can be used to talk things over with parents, and to raise the alarm if there is serious suspicion that the child is coming to harm, as well as to promote good health.

The ability to seek a Child Assessment Order does provide an ultimate form of compulsory assessment where there is serious concern and partnership with and persuasion of parents has failed. But it is crucial that adequate health services including appropriate developmental checks should be available to all children, as our recommendations emphasise.

School-age children

School attendance implies a degree of consistent monitoring of children and young people by teachers and other staff. Parents are under a duty to ensure that their children receive full-time education, by regular attendance at school or otherwise. The period of compulsory schooling which lasts to 16 starts at the beginning of the term following a child's fifth birthday (in Northern Ireland compulsory schooling for most children now begins earlier, following their fourth birthday). But it is not clear how systematically local education authorities become aware of children approaching or of compulsory school age in their area, unless their parents present them for schooling. Occasionally teenagers come to the attention of the authorities, having never been at school.

There are statutory arrangements for monitoring school attendance, and if a child ceases to attend school without good reason, the education welfare service follows up and visits families and there are legal powers to seek to enforce school attendance. Where parents wish to educate their children otherwise than at school (home education), the local education authority has a duty to ensure that the child is receiving efficient full-time education, generally involving visits by education advisers/inspectors as well as education welfare officers to the home. There does not appear to be any central collection of information on children being educated otherwise than at school. The Children Act has introduced new duties for promoting and monitoring the welfare of children attending independent boarding schools in England and Wales (see page 55).

Schools are under a general duty of care and maintained schools also have duties to provide parents with information on their children's progress.

When children are suspended or excluded from schools, local education authorities retain duties to provide appropriate education, but there is concern that some children get "lost" outside the education system once suspended or expelled.

Health authorities are obliged to provide a school health service which forms part of a wider programme of child health surveillance. But there are no powers to compel routine medical examinations, except that in England and Wales LEAs can direct that all or some pupils at a school and their clothes should be examined for nits and vermin (section 54 Education Act 1944). Education law (section 48 Education Act 1944) specifically allows parents to opt their children out of any school medical (and dental) inspections. In Scotland there is a power to authorise examinations to "ensure cleanliness" (Education (Scotland) Act 1980 (section 58)).

Circulars provide advice to schools, including independent schools, and teachers on recognising child abuse and taking appropriate action. There are no statutory duties placed on schools, teachers or education authorities in relation to suspected child abuse (but there is a duty placed on education and other authorities to assist social services in making enquiries about children at risk: see page 159).

Children who are placed away from home

England and Wales

The Children Act places duties on local authority social services departments to review children who are being looked after or accommodated by them (Children Act sections 26, 59(4) etc and Review of Children's Cases Regulations 1991).[100] These reviewing duties apply to all children and young people in care, wherever placed, and to all those for whom the local authority has arranged accommodation, eg in foster care or an institution.

The National Foster Care Association is concerned that many children in foster homes do not have a designated social worker, and so reviews are not taking place. An inquiry report published following the death of a child in foster care emphasised that

"statutory regulations for reviews, visits and medical examinations of children should be strictly observed. Delays and omissions should be a matter of concern for supervisory staff".[101]

Voluntary organisations and the proprietors of registered (private) children's homes have similar duties towards children who are being accommodated by them, except that the duty to review those that are being accommodated by them on behalf of a local authority rests with the authority, and if a child is being accommodated in a registered children's home on behalf of a voluntary organisation, the duty will rest with the organisation. This reviewing duty will apply to children in certain schools: those independent schools which are obliged to register as children's homes (see page 57), and to non-maintained special schools, which are maintained by voluntary organisations (see page 53).

Under the arrangements, each child's case must first be reviewed by the responsible authority (local authority, voluntary organisation or proprietor of registered children's home) within four weeks of the date when they began to be looked after or provided with accommodation. The second review must take place within three months of the first, and subsequent reviews at not more than six monthly intervals.

Arrangements for reviews must be set out in writing. The child, his/her parents, others with parental responsibility, and anyone else considered to have relevant views must be consulted before the review and involved in it and in any meetings held in connection with it where the responsible authority organising the review consider this appropriate. They must also be informed of the results of the review and any decisions made by or as a result of the review. The responsible authority must make arrangements to implement decisions. The regulations set out elements to be included in the review (schedule 1), which include informing the child of steps that s/he may take, including seeking leave to apply to court (eg for residence, contact or other orders); if in care, his/her right to apply for discharge of the care order and to use the procedure for making representations including complaints which the Act obliges authorities to set up (see page 114).

The regulations also set out considerations which the responsible authority must have regard to, including: if the child is in care, whether the care order should be discharged; whether a change in legal status for the child should be sought; arrangements for contact with parents and others; immediate and long-term arrangements for looking after the child; educational needs, progress and development; any special arrangements that have been made or need to be made, eg carrying out assessments of the child, including assessments of special educational needs under the Education Act 1981 (see below page 170) etc.

Health considerations which reviews must consider are listed separately (schedule 3): the child's health history and state of health, arrangements for medical and dental surveillance and care; possible need for changes of care, treatment or surveillance, and for preventive measures such as vaccination, and immunisation.

The regulations also oblige the responsible authority to make arrangements for the child to be examined by a doctor, and for a written assessment on the child's state of health and need for health care to be made at least once in every period of six months before the child's second birthday, and from then on at least once in every 12 months. Children who have "sufficient understanding" may refuse to submit to such examinations.

Responsible authorities must monitor arrangements for reviews to ensure they fulfil the regulations.[102]

Scotland

Since 1984 Scottish local authorities have had a similar duty to review children in care (under section 20A of the Social Work (Scotland) Act 1968) at no more than six monthly intervals. There has been guidance on reviews but no regulations.[103]

The Review of Child Care Law in Scotland recommended that an initial review should be held within six weeks of reception, with a further review after three months, and then at six monthly intervals. The Review also proposed that

"children aged 12 and over should have a statutory right of attendance at their case reviews; requests from younger children to attend should be considered in the light of their age and capacity to understand; and care authorities should be required to prepare children and young persons for such attendance".[104]

In relation to reviews of children in residential care, the Scottish review *Another Kind of Home* proposed that local authorities should consider introducing procedures to ensure that no review is postponed without consulting the young person concerned and parents, and that they should be able to require that an overdue review be called.[105]

Northern Ireland

There are similar arrangements in Northern Ireland under the Children and Young People (Boarding Out) Regulations (Northern Ireland) 1976. There are however no obligations to consult with parents and those with parental responsibility.

Children in private foster care

England and Wales

The Children Act and regulations issued under it (the Children (Private Arrangements for Fostering) Regulations 1991) set out arrangements for visiting children in private foster care and making reports (see section 2.5, page 178), but there are no obligations specifically to review the children's cases.[106]

Scotland

There are similar arrangements in Scotland for visits, but not formal reviews.

Northern Ireland

There are no formal arrangements for monitoring private foster care in Northern Ireland.

Children in secure accommodation

In addition to the duties outlined above to review children in care and those being looked after by authorities, there are specific additional duties to review children who are placed in secure accommodation in community homes in England and Wales (Children (Secure Accommodation) Regulations 1991).[107] There are similar duties to review children placed in approved secure accommodation in Scotland. The local authority responsible for the child must appoint at least three people, one of whom must not be employed by the authority,

"who shall review the keeping of the child in such accommodation for the purposes of securing his welfare".

There must be a review within one month of placement and then at intervals not exceeding three months for the remainder of the placement. Those undertaking the review must take account of the child's views and those of parents etc. They must satisfy themselves whether the criteria for keeping the child in secure accommodation continue to apply, the placement continues to be necessary, and whether any other accommodation would be appropriate (see also section 1.3, page 84).

These special review duties, like certain other duties in the secure accommodation regulations, do not apply to children placed in secure accommodation in youth treatment centres, or in other accommodation for restricting liberty provided by health or education authorities (see also page 90). In relation to youth treatment centres, the Department of Health indicates that there are quarterly case reviews (no regulations apply; see page 92).

Other institutional placements

England and Wales

Following concerns about children placed away from home in health and education institutions who may become "lost" in the system, new duties on notification of certain placements were introduced in the Children Act 1989. If a child is provided with accommodation by a health authority or education authority for a consecutive period of three months or with the intention of accommodating the child for such a period, the accommodating authority must notify the relevant social services department (this will normally be the department in whose area the child was "ordinarily resident" before placement; otherwise it will be the department in whose area the accommodation is. They must also notify the department when the placement ceases. The social services department must "take such steps as are reasonably practicable" to determine whether the child's welfare is being adequately safeguarded and promoted, and consider whether they should exercise any of their functions under the Children Act in relation to the child (section 85).

Similar duties apply in the case of children accommodated for similar periods in residential care homes (see page 46), and in nursing homes and mental nursing homes (see page 50). In the case of these placements, the social services department is given a right of entry to the homes to establish whether the requirements have been complied with, and intentionally obstructing anyone authorised by the department constitutes an offence (section 86).

These duties provide the relevant social services authority with a continuing duty to satisfy themselves that the welfare of the children concerned is adequately safeguarded and promoted during the placement. But unlike the other review duties set out above, they do not specify that the children must be visited or reviewed regularly.

Social services departments are given similar general duties in relation to children accommodated (ie boarding pupils) in independent schools in their area. The authority

"must take such steps as are reasonably practicable to enable them to determine whether the child's welfare is adequately safeguarded and promoted while he is accommodated by the school" (section 87).

Again, there is no obligation to visit or review the children regularly. But as indicated above, page 165, children being accommodated in some independent schools which are obliged to register as children's homes will be covered by the review duty applying to children in such homes; similarly, children attending non-maintained special schools will be subject to the review duties applying to voluntary organisations. (Following representations from organisations representing independent school interests, the Department of Health consulted in March 1992 on changes in the application of certain regulations issued under the Children Act to some boarding schools. It proposed exempting from the review duties those independent schools obliged to register as children's homes, and non-maintained special schools.)

The Child Care Law Review in Scotland has proposed similar arrangements in relation to safeguarding the welfare of children placed away from home in Scotland.[108]

Review duties in education legislation

Aside from duties in education legislation to provide parents of pupils in maintained schools with information about their progress, the only specific obligation to review is in the law on meeting special educational needs. The Education Act 1981 (which is being largely re-enacted with some changes in the Education Bill currently - February 1993 - before Parliament) places a duty on education authorities to review statements of special educational needs within every 12 months. These reviews do not necessarily involve a full re-assessment, and while there is official guidance on reviewing, there is no legislation concerning the form reviews must take, who should be involved etc.

This duty refers to reviewing not the child, but the statement of special educational needs, which gives details of the authority's assessment of the child's special educational needs and of special educational provision to be made to meet those needs.

In Scotland, education authorities are obliged to review "recorded" children and young people (both the decision to record and the contents of the record) when they think it expedient to do so, or - a year or more after the decision to record or the last review - if requested by the parent or by a recorded young person themselves from the age of 16 (Education (Scotland) Act 1980 section 65A).

Penal institutions

While there are arrangements for penal institutions to be visited frequently by Boards of Visitors, and to be inspected (see page 189) there are no requirements in legislation to regularly review individual children and young people. However Home Office Circular Instructions do emphasise the need for sentence plans and reviews to take account of the inmate's progress or changed circumstances at "regular and specified intervals".[109]

Recommendations

2.4 Arrangements for monitoring/reviewing placement and treatment of children

1 Throughout the UK, health legislation should ensure that there is a clear obligation to make available specified appropriate developmental checks for all children in their area between notification of birth and age of starting school, and (subject to the child's right to consent) at appropriate intervals during the period of compulsory schooling.

2 We support the NSPCC's call for co-ordinated reviews of child protection procedures throughout the UK, which should take as their starting point fundamental principles of children's rights.

3 The obligation to maintain local child protection registers should be set out in legislation. Having a child protection plan should not be a pre-condition of placing a child's name on a register. Regulations should set out an obligation to devise a child protection plan within a short period of placing a child's name on the register (seven days perhaps) and also obligations to review children on the register at appropriate intervals.

4 Arrangements for formal review of placement and treatment of children, involving the children themselves and similar in frequency and scope to those set out in the Review of Children's Cases Regulations 1991, issued under the Children Act 1989, should extend to all children being accommodated in institutions and quasi-institutional settings throughout the UK - eg to those not already covered who are being accommodated by a local education authority or health authority, all those in residential care homes, nursing homes and mental nursing homes, independent schools in the case of children accommodated for substantial parts of holidays in addition to school terms, private foster care etc, and also to young offenders in penal institutions.

In addition to these arrangements, in the case of all placements away from home for a significant period, we propose that there should be an "exit-review", or "leaving interview", at which the child or young person would be invited to comment, if s/he wished, on the placement and its successes, any problems etc.

Reports of all reviews should be made available to the subjects of them, in appropriate cases to parents, and submitted as appropriate to the relevant social services/social work departments (as well as to other appropriate authorities - eg health or education) which should be under a duty to consider them and take any necessary action to ensure that the child's welfare is being adequately safeguarded and promoted. Children should be consulted about such dissemination of information about them, and their views taken account of, in line with Article 12 of the UN Convention.

5 Wherever a child is placed in "secure accommodation" (accommodation provided to restrict the liberty of children - see section 1.3, page 85) there should be an obligation on the appropriate body (but involving an independent element) to review the placement; arrangements should be equivalent in frequency etc to those set out in the Children (Secure Accommodation) Regulations 1991, issued under the Children Act.

2.5 Arrangements for inspection of institutions and quasi-institutional settings

Arrangements for inspection of institutions where children and young people may spend significant periods of their lives vary widely between different services (health, education, social services, penal), and according to their status - maintained, voluntary, private etc. Some institutions are inspected by local authority appointed inspectors, some by government inspectors, eg the Social Services Inspectorate, others by quasi-independent inspectors - Her Majesty's Inspectors of Schools, and the new registered inspectors, and some by all three. It is extraordinary that in the case of some institutions there is still no statutory duty to inspect. The UN Convention on the Rights of the Child (see page 7) insists (Article 3.3):

"States Parties shall ensure that the institutions, services and facilities responsible for the care or protection of children shall conform with the standards established by competent authorities, particularly in the areas of safety, health, in the number and suitability of their staff, as well as competent supervision".

Current arrangements for inspection are inconsistent in many ways: in frequency (in some cases not specified at all); whether reports are publicly available; whether legislation specifies what aspects of the institution and of the children should be inspected; whether inspectors are required to see and talk with children.

The range of scandals involving serious abuse over long periods in all kinds of residential institutions shows how far inspection arrangements (as well as other safeguards) have failed children. Many of the reports following these scandals, and those considering reform of law, policy and practice have made detailed recommendations about inspection, although none has looked across all sectors and services as we attempt to do.

Recently there have been major changes in inspection arrangements, in particular in education, and in the development of inspection units for residential care in local authorities. For England and Wales, the Children Act has given the Secretary of State wide powers to arrange inspections of institutions and premises where children are living.

Independence of the institution/service being inspected is clearly a key issue, and one that has been highlighted in other reports. The Wagner Report on residential care recommended bluntly that:

"To ensure independence and impartiality, no agency should undertake the inspection of its own residential establishments".[110]

The involvement of trained lay members in all inspections, including those who have had direct experience of residential child care, is developing and must be welcomed. A recent Department of Health circular on inspections of children's homes (see page 180) proposed the involvement of young people with experience of residential care in inspection teams, who

"may have much to offer in defining standards and criteria and advising on effective techniques for gathering reliable information".

In a 1992 consultation paper *Inspecting Social Services*, the Department of Health recognises that local inspection units' conclusions

"will not carry weight, or create confidence amongst the public and users, if ...independence is in doubt...On the evidence so far available, much good and effective inspection work has been done from these units but it is too soon to assess fully the extent to which proper separation and independence are being achieved across the country. The introduction of lay people to all inspection teams should provide a further safeguard".

The report indicates that in the longer-term, if the Government considers there are "justifiable anxieties" about

"the fairness and objectivity with which standards are applied across the various sectors in the developing mixed economy of care...it will need to consider further measures. These might involve a greater degree of central influence over inspection standards and procedures - for example the national registration of inspectors or the creation of a statutory national body combining the present inspection functions of local and central government but independent of both".[111]

We propose that inter-departmental inquiries, with appropriate representation from the voluntary and private sectors, should now consider the possibility of building on the Social Services Inspectorate and similar bodies in Scotland and Northern Ireland to establish inspectorates, including lay members, for all residential services for children. It appears to be already recognised, in line with recommendations from several major inquiries, that detailed standards and indicators should be available to inspectors, not just of building design, record-keeping and staff quality, but of the quality of life for children and young people, implementation of basic rights, and protection. Indicators of the types of regime that have tended to lead to abuse (isolated from community, high turnover of staff, high rate of running away, high number of violent confrontations, involvement of police etc) could well be included, although with an emphasis that they are not exhaustive. A working group chaired by Barbara Kahan which arose from the Wagner Committee is currently (February 1993) drafting a handbook of good practice for all those working in residential care. It is likely to provide a valuable guide for inspections too.

In relation to existing arrangements, we recommend that the Secretary of State's powers to arrange inspections should be extended to cover penal establishments for young people (in addition to inspections by the prisons' inspectorate), and that specific duties to arrange inspections in certain circumstances should replace ministerial discretion. There should also be explicit duties to monitor the inspectorial role of local authorities, and all individual inspection reports (akin to the role of HM Inspectorate of Schools in relation to the new "registered inspectors"). In the special case of places where children's liberty is restricted, there should be a requirement to seek approval (which already exists in relation to secure accommodation in residential child care) and for appropriate inspection by the Secretary of State.

We share the concerns expressed in other reports about the degree of independence of local authority inspection units, charged with inspecting their own institutions as well as private ones. Mandatory involvement of lay people, including young people with appropriate experience, certainly mark a movement towards independence. There should clearly be consistency in the basic requirements regarding frequency of inspection, and the instances in which an immediate inspection should be arranged (similarly, there should be consistency in the parallel arrangements for "visits" to foster homes).

Direct access of children and young people to inspectors is an issue of particular importance in the context of their protection from ill-treatment and abuse: inspectors should always talk with and listen to some children and young people in private, and also ensure that any individual child, young person or staff member who wishes to talk to an inspector in private has an opportunity to do so.

The Scottish report *Another Kind of Home* emphatically recommended that

"Local authority inspection procedures should always include some interviews with young people and children and their parents".

The report also proposed that inspection units should review at least annually the adherence of each children's home to guidance on "care sanctions and constraints",

"and should involve young people and children in this review. They should also review staff training undertaken in respect of implementing the guidance".[112]

There has been a general move towards publication of inspection reports, both in education and child care, and while there is as yet no legislative requirement for publication, it appears that there is a growing assumption of openness. But it is important to remember that inspection reports on residential care homes are in a real sense reports on children's "homes", and while it is certainly right that the children themselves, relevant authorities and in most cases parents should see reports, there may be a case against general publication. But the important rights to privacy and confidentiality of individuals must not be used as excuses for preventing publication of non-identifying material that should be in the public domain.

The consultation document on inspections issued by the Department of Health in October 1992 emphasised that

"All inspection reports - whether by the SSI or local inspection units - should be directed as much at the local authority or other body with responsibility for the service provided, and at the public which uses and finances the service, as at the professional managers...Unless exceptionally there are legal reasons for keeping them confidential, or unavoidable risks to the confidentiality of client information, the reports should be distributed at least in summary to and considered by the full local authority social services committee if they are responsible for or contract with the service being inspected. They should actively be made available to users and their carers, and to the wider public at least in summary".[113]

Summary of current arrangements of inspection

The following section summarises the current arrangements for inspection and formal "visits".

"Inspection" is not an appropriate concept for children living at home with parent(s) or guardian(s). Arrangements for reviewing such children, including those who are subject to court orders, were therefore covered in section 2.4 (page 158). But this section does cover the arrangements for visits to children in foster care.

Secretary of State's powers to inspect residential settings for children

England and Wales

The Children Act (section 80) gives the Secretary of State for Health wide powers to cause residential homes and other places where children and young people are living to be inspected. They do not cover penal institutions. The settings specified in section 80 include:

local authority, voluntary and private children's homes; residential care homes; nursing homes and mental nursing homes; independent schools providing accommodation.

They also cover premises where any child is living who:

is being looked after by a local authority;

is being accommodated by or on behalf of a local education authority or voluntary organisation (this includes maintained boarding schools and hostels, and non-maintained special boarding schools);

is being accommodated by or on behalf of a health authority;

and any premises registered for daycare including childminding, or used for private fostering etc.

Any person authorised to inspect by the Secretary of State may inspect children and

"make such examinations into the state and management of the home or premises and the treatment of the children there as he thinks fit".

It is an offence to wilfully obstruct these inspections, which will normally be carried out by the Social Services Inspectorate.

Reports of the Social Services Inspectorate are normally made available, although there is no requirement to publish them in legislation. Since 1985 there have been three categories of "availability":

"Category A relates to reports that are documents of public access, and as such are available to anyone as long as there are copies available (SSI inspection reports of secure accommodation fall into this category).

"Category B involves reports which are not immediately available to anyone outside the Department of Health other than the responsible management body for the service inspected. This would include SSI's inspection of voluntary children's homes. No embargo is, however, placed on further distribution of such reports by managers, and indeed in relation to voluntary children's homes, they are actively encouraged to distribute them more widely, for example to placing authorities. In practice many SSI reports in Category B are "published" in the context of reports being presented to social services committees.

"Category C reports are not available to anyone outside and only on a limited basis within the Department of Health. This category includes reports to the Secretary of State on voluntary adoption agencies for approval purposes".[114]

As indicated above (page 175), a consultation document issued by the Department of Health in 1992 emphasised the importance of publication. The consultation document also emphasised the importance the Government now places in the involvement of lay people in all inspections, and in reviewing programmes and policies for inspection. It states that the Chief Social Services Inspector will be including lay people in all social services inspections during 1993, and that lay and consumer representatives are to be invited by the Department of Health to join the Joint Steering Group which scrutinises the annual programme of the Social Services Inspectorate.[115]

Foster care

There are arrangements for local authorities (ie social workers) to "visit" children in both local authority and private foster care, which are clearly intended to perform similar functions to the inspection arrangements for institutional settings.

Local authority foster care

England and Wales

Regulations issued under the Children Act (The Foster Placement (Children) Regulations) insist that local authorities must satisfy themselves that the welfare of each child placed by them "continues to be suitably provided for by the placement", and must arrange for a person authorised by them to visit the child in the home in which s/he is placed:

from time to time as circumstances require;

when reasonably requested by the child or foster parent;

in the first year of placement, within one week of placement and then at intervals of not more than six weeks;

subsequently, at intervals of not more than three months;

in the case of what is termed an emergency placement, the child must be visited at least once a week.[116]

The authorised person must on each visit arrange to see the child alone "if they consider it appropriate". A report must be written.

The report of an inquiry into the death of a child in foster care recommended that

"Statutory requirements for reviews, visits and medical examination of children should be strictly observed. Delays and omissions should be a matter of concern for supervisory staff".[117]

Foster care arranged by voluntary organisations

England and Wales

Where a child is placed with a foster parent by or on behalf of a voluntary organisation, the local authority must arrange for an officer to visit the child within 28 days of placement, or if requested by the voluntary organisation, within 14 days of the request. If informed that the welfare of the child may not be being adequately safeguarded or promoted, they must arrange a visit as soon as reasonably practicable and in any event within seven days. If satisfied following a visit that the child's welfare is being adequately safeguarded and promoted, they must arrange subsequent visits at intervals of not more than six months.[118]

Scotland

In Scotland arrangements for local authority and voluntary organisation fostering are covered by the Boarding Out and Fostering of Children (Scotland) Regulations 1985. These require at least one visit to the foster home within the first week of placement. Following that, visits should be made at least every three months.[119] Guidance emphasises that

"frequent visits are essential to maintain contact with the foster home and give the necessary support...social workers should ensure that they have an opportunity to speak with the child on his own..." [120]

Northern Ireland

In Northern Ireland there are similar arrangements for visits under the Children and Young Persons Boarding Out Regulations 1976.[121]

Private foster care

England and Wales

Those proposing to privately foster a child must inform the local social services department which must satisfy itself that the child's welfare is being suitably safeguarded. Visits must occur, as with local authority foster care, within one week of the beginning of the arrangement and then at intervals of not more than six weeks in the first year, and in subsequent years at intervals of not more than three months. There must also be visits if "reasonably requested" by the child or foster parent. The officer visiting must if considered appropriate arrange to see the child alone.

The regulations (Children (Private Arrangements for Fostering) Regulations 1991) set out a list of matters to be considered on visits, if relevant in the particular circumstances. These include the wishes and feelings of the child regarding the fostering arrangements, purpose, duration and suitability of the arrangement, health (including ensuring that the child is included on the list of a GP), education, standards of care, accommodation etc.[122] Guidance sets out in detail the purpose of visits, giving prominence to child protection.[123]

Scotland

Similar arrangements apply in Scotland under the Foster Children (Private Fostering) (Scotland) Regulations 1985.[124] Visits must take place within a week of placement, and then during the first year at least every three months and thereafter at least twice a year.

Northern Ireland

There are no arrangements for monitoring private fostering in Northern Ireland. The law is under review (February 1993).

Children's homes

England and Wales

Community Homes

There is no statutory requirement for inspection of community homes, although the local authority maintaining a maintained community home is required to arrange for it to be visited once a month, and for a report to be submitted to the authority (Children's Homes Regulations 1991).[125] This does not appear to apply to controlled or assisted community homes; there is no duty to inspect these homes. Although "assisted" homes are effectively run by voluntary organisations they have a management committee and are assisted by local authorities. They are not categorised as voluntary homes.

An inquiry report into a London children's home in which the officer in charge had taken indecent photographs of children over a 10 year period revealed that less than half the required monthly visits had taken place, and that guidelines on the purpose of visits had been lost.[126]

Guidance issued under the Children Act emphasises:

"In the interests of ensuring that good practice is consistently sustained in the home and of demonstrating that the well-being of children is protected, the work of all homes should be regularly inspected...Ideally, inspection is one part of a comprehensive system of quality assurance to make sure that the service delivered meets its intended objectives and standards. Inspections should normally be carried out by the social services department's independent (inspection) unit..." [127]

In his review of residential child care, *Children in the Public Care*, Sir William Utting, then Chief Inspector of the Social Services Inspectorate, underlined that community homes lacked any system of external regulatory inspection. He proposed that they should be inspected by the local authority inspection units, and that the Secretary of State should issue a "direction" requiring them to be subject to arm's length inspection.

"A condition of this new arrangement should be that the inspection units should include staff experienced in work with children, and in the management of residential homes. Some should have experience in independent agencies".[128]

A Department of Health circular summarising the Utting report and giving the Department's initial response said that the Department would be having discussions with local authority associations and other interests with a view to issuing brief guidance on the role of local authority inspection units in relation to children's homes. It also stated that

"authorities will wish to start preparations to address three specific recommendations, including the inspection of local authority children's homes by their independent inspection units".[129]

In 1991 the Social Services Inspectorate published guidance on practice for inspection units in social services departments and other agencies. This did not specifically cover inspection of children's services, except to state that further advice would be issued in due course. The guidance does emphasise that "users' experience of services should be a major focus of evaluation".[130]

A further brief circular on inspection of maintained, controlled and assisted community homes by local authority inspection units was issued by the Department of Health in November 1992. This emphasises that local authorities should arrange inspection of all categories of community home, as well as registered (private) children's homes. Inspections should be undertaken twice a year (at least one visit unannounced). Individual children's right to privacy and to confidentiality should be respected throughout the inspection process. Reports should be published, at least in summary, and local authorities should consider clearing any inspection report with their legal advisers before releasing it into the public domain. (As indicated above, a consultation paper issued by the Department of Health in 1992 emphasises the importance of publication, see page 175.)

The circular indicates that the Department of Health is

"currently devising explicit methodologies and a set of standards and criteria for the inspection of children's homes. This material is to be piloted and tested within the Social Services Inspectorate and will be published within the next 12 months" (ie by the end of 1993).

Local authorities are advised that inspection teams should include people with experience of providing residential care. They should also include at least one lay person:

"...local authorities will wish to consider the contribution to this process by young people who have experienced residential care, and may have much to offer in defining standards and criteria and advising on effective techniques for gathering reliable information".

Inspection unit advisory committees should have members representative of both professionals and consumers representing children's interests.

"The consumer viewpoint should be represented by someone who has lived in a residential child care setting within the last 10 years".[131]

The consultation document issued by the Department of Health in 1992 indicated that the Government intends that by Autumn 1993 the teams for all local inspections should include **at least** one lay member with the status of "independent assessor" and the right to participate fully in the inspection and express their own views in the inspection report.[132]

The Howe Report, *The Quality of Care*, recommended that local authorities should establish formal systems for reviewing inspection reports, including reports of statutory visits to children's homes and other information concerning the quality of services being provided

"so that they can satisfy themselves that services are being offered consistent with statutory regulations and their own policies".

It also proposed that there should be arrangements for elected members to visit homes on a regular but informal basis:

"The overall management policies are approved by elected councillors. It is important they understand the effects of their decisions. Councillors should also provide an additional ear for residents (and staff if necessary)".[133]

The consultation document issued by the Department of Health in 1992 proposes that

"the important objective of the units' independence would be more clearly established if the reporting line at officer level were to be to the Chief Executive"

rather than, as is normally the case at present, through the director of social services to the social services committee.[134]

The survey of children's homes commissioned by the Warner Inquiry included questions about visits to homes by inspectors. The survey was conducted about six months after the arrangements came into force. Homes were asked about pre-arranged, unannounced and night visits. While 88 per cent of local authority homes had had unannounced visits, only 67 per cent of voluntary homes and 64 per cent of private homes had. Night visits were reported by 81 per cent of local authority homes, 64 per cent of voluntary homes and 49 per cent of private homes. The report commented:

"Thus there is a significant proportion of private and voluntary homes not receiving visits from independent inspectors, while over 10 per cent of local authority homes had not been visited at the time of the survey. This caused us some concern, given that local authorities claim that independent inspection of homes will be made no less than six monthly. Moreover, less than a quarter of authorities reported that they have mechanisms or checks to ensure that their policy requirements regarding inspection are being carried out. We recognise that it is still early days for the new inspection arrangements, but given the publicity given to concerns about children's homes, we consider that the performance should have been better".[135]

Voluntary homes

Voluntary children's homes are registered by the Secretary of State under section 60 of the Children Act 1989. They are inspected by the Social Services Inspectorate on behalf of the Secretary of State. There is no statutory obligation to inspect, nor regulations setting out frequency of inspections, matters to be inspected etc. According to Sir William Utting's report *Children in the Public Care*, current SSI practice is to inspect homes run by the three largest voluntary agencies every three years, and other homes annually. The report suggests that if community homes are to be inspected by the new local authority inspection units, which are already obliged to inspect registered children's homes,

"it would be anomalous for individual voluntary homes to continue to be registered by the Secretary of State; accordingly I recommend that these homes should also come within the remit of the local authority's inspection units and be subject to the same frequency of inspection as for other homes".[136]

The voluntary sector has expressed strong opposition to transfer of responsibility for inspection from the Social Services Inspectorate (SSI) to local authorities. Organisations with children's homes in more than one authority have found very different standards being applied by different authorities. Some large voluntary organisations have many more children's homes than any local authority, and believe that the knowledge-base of some local authority inspection units is insufficient. If inspection of voluntary homes is not to stay with SSI, the voluntary sector has proposed an independent "hands off" voluntary sector inspection unit, working in the same way as local authority units.

But from the perspective of children in homes, if there are criticisms of the quality of local authority inspection units, they are as relevant to their task of inspecting local authority homes as to inspection of voluntary homes.

Local authorities must satisfy themselves (Children Act section 62) that voluntary organisations providing accommodation for children in their area are satisfactorily promoting and safeguarding the children's welfare; they must arrange for such children to be visited from time to time "in the interests of their welfare". The Children's Homes Regulations set out "circumstances necessitating visits by local authorities" to children in voluntary homes (and registered children's homes - see below).

Registered (private) homes

Local authority social services departments are responsible for the registration of private children's homes. The Children's Homes Regulations oblige registering authorities to arrange an inspection of homes before registering them.[137] They must then arrange inspections "within the period of one month ending on the anniversary of the registration", and may inform the person in charge of the home of their intention to inspect. They must also arrange an inspection "on at least one other occasion in any year", and not notify the person in charge in advance. Inspection reports must be considered when deciding whether registration of the home should be reviewed or cancelled. The regulations do not indicate what matters should be covered by the inspection.

Scotland

From April 1992, local social work department inspection units were required to extend their functions to include residential child care. The report *Another Kind of Home* states:

"This means that for the first time since 1968 the care provided in children's homes and schools will be regularly inspected. A regular inspection programme of residential child care is clearly essential to ensure the well being of young people and children in care".

The report proposes that the Social Work Services Inspectorate should develop standards and guidance, in consultation with local authorities and other agencies, for evaluating residential child care:

"The development of these standards should draw on analysis of the experiences of young people, children and their parents. The standards should be applied by managers and local inspection units to ensure a consistently good quality of residential child care provision".

It emphasises that

"For any inspection it is essential that the views of some young people and children living in homes are obtained and also the views of parents. Such interviews must be conducted sensitively and arranged appropriately to the age and circumstances of the individuals...Inspectors must also ask unexpected questions, they must probe discrepancies, look for information that may be being suppressed..."

The consultation that preceded the report found that views on whether local social work departments should retain responsibility for inspecting their own services were mixed:

"Written submissions to the review commenting on this fell fairly equally between those in favour of local social work departments holding this responsibility and those who considered that greater independence from local social work departments was required".

The report emphasises that the independence of inspectors must be assessed in some way.[138]

The earlier *Review of Child Care Law in Scotland* considered the option of establishing a separate, independent system of inspection and registration of child care establishments, but felt that it was "more practicable" to recommend that inspection units of local social work departments should undertake the task. It also suggested that if the review's proposals for a Child Welfare Commission (see page 105) are taken up,

"such a Commission could, with advantage, provide the degree of impartiality necessary in monitoring the effectiveness of inspection units and their operation across the whole range of residential provision for children".[139]

Northern Ireland

A circular from the Northern Ireland Department of Health and Social Services in 1983 required Health and Social Services Boards and voluntary bodies to submit to the Department annual monitoring statements on their residential child care services. A further circular issued in October 1988 reviewed these arrangements.[140] An annual monitoring report must be produced for consideration by the Board, and to be copied for consideration by the Department, which may raise matters of concern. Visits by social workers to children's homes are required at least once a month; quarterly visits to statutory children's homes must be carried out by a member of the Board or one of its committees or sub-committees. The Department suggests that there are no private children's homes in Northern Ireland.

Rules applying to the four training schools in Northern Ireland (see page 44) state that

"...the school shall be open at all times to inspection by or on behalf of the Department..."

In recent years the Department of Health and Social Services has arranged for inspections to be carried out on its behalf by the Social Services Inspectorate. Education provision at the schools is inspected by the Department of Education. The Board of Management of each school is required to ensure that

"the condition of the school and the training, welfare and education of the boys and girls under their care is satisfactory and for this purpose they shall pay frequent visits to the school" (under review together with all relevant legislation in Northern Ireland, 1992).[141]

Secure accommodation

In community homes

The Secretary of State must approve secure accommodation in a community home (see section 1.3, page 86) before it is used, and approval is subject to "such terms and conditions as he sees fit" (The Children (Secure Accommodation) Regulations 1991).[142] Secure accommodation in community homes is inspected by the Social Services Inspectorate, but there are no regulations on frequency of inspections, matters to be inspected etc.

In his report *Children in the Public Care* Sir William Utting recommends that responsibility for approving and inspecting secure accommodation should remain with the Secretary of State,

"since arrangements affecting the liberty of the citizen are properly for central government, and the associated inspection is properly undertaken by SSI".[143]

In other settings

This report proposes (see page 97) that wherever restriction of liberty of children is permitted under section 25 of the Children Act accommodation used to restrict liberty should be subject to approval by the Secretary of State. This would imply inspection too. The powers to inspect under section 80 of the Children Act (see page 175) do allow inspection by the Secretary of State of any secure settings in education and health settings, residential care homes and private health institutions. But we suggest that there should be clear requirements for inspection and approval of any accommodation used for the restriction of liberty, setting out frequency of inspections etc.

Youth treatment centres

There is no duty to inspect the two youth treatment centres in England, which provide mainly secure accommodation. In practice they are inspected on behalf of the Secretary of State by the Social Services Inspectorate.[144]

Scotland

In Scotland residential units with secure accommodation are inspected by the Secretary of State's Social Work Services Inspectorate (as well as by Her Majesty's Inspectorate of Schools), and if satisfactory are approved for three years. The *Review of Child Care Law in Scotland* found no need to change these arrangements,

"but as the inspection units become better established there may be a case for bringing secure units within their remit".[145]

Residential care homes

These are registered by local authorities and must be inspected at least once in every period of 12 months (Residential Care Homes Regulations 1984).[146] The legislation does not further specify matters to be inspected or other requirements. Similar legislation covers homes in Scotland.

Health service

National Health Service accommodation

There are no duties on central government or health authorities to inspect NHS provision, including any provision for children. As indicated above (page 175) the Secretary of State has powers under section 80 of the Children Act to cause premises in England and Wales where any child is being accommodated by or on behalf of a health authority to be inspected. The Social Services Inspectorate has taken part in inspection of various health units which accommodate young people, including the secure Gardener Unit in Manchester. Community Health Councils have a right to inspect NHS accommodation, but no duties.

Some inspections of provision for mental illness are carried out by the Health Advisory Service, which was founded in 1969 and operates independently of government and the Department of Health. Visits are conducted jointly with the Social Services Inspectorate, reviewing hospital and community services for mentally ill people in each health district. Occasionally, the HAS has undertaken a special project; for example, in 1986 it produced a report on services for disturbed adolescents.[147] In the field of mental handicap, the National Development Team has a similar function.

Nursing homes and mental nursing homes

Applications for registration of these private health institutions are made to the Secretary of State, who has delegated registration functions to district health authorities. Inspection of homes *"may be made on such occasions and at such intervals as the Secretary of State may decide, but he shall cause every home to be inspected not less than twice in every period of 12 months"* (Nursing Homes and Mental Nursing Homes Regulations 1984).[148]

Section 35 of the Registered Homes Act 1984 enables anyone authorised for the purpose by the Secretary of State to enter and inspect premises which are or may be being used as a mental nursing home, and interview in private any resident patient who is or appears to be suffering from a mental disorder. Section 80 of the Children Act also empowers the Secretary of State to arrange inspections of these institutions, and the Social Services Inspectorate has taken part in inspections of various provision for children, including Langton House in Dorset (now closed - see page 91) and St Andrew's Hospital in Northampton.

Scotland

In Scotland Health Boards are required to arrange inspections of private health institutions not less than twice a year (The Nursing Homes Registration (Scotland) Regulations 1990).[149] Boards can authorise any suitably qualified individual to undertake inspections.

Education

Maintained schools (including non-maintained special schools)

A new statutory framework for school inspections in England and Wales was introduced by the Education (Schools) Act 1992. It separated HM Inspectorate into HM Inspectorate for England and for Wales, and introduced for the first time teams of "registered" inspectors.

A new Office for Standards in Education (OFSTED) has been established. HM Inspectors can carry out inspections, and retain responsibility for inspecting independent schools - see below. Her Majesty's Chief Inspector of Schools has responsibility for registering inspectors and monitoring inspections. Private and voluntary bodies as well as local authorities can tender to provide inspectors (local authorities retain limited rights to inspect schools which they are maintaining - section 14). The categories of schools covered by the new registered inspectors are:

county, voluntary and special schools (including non-maintained special schools); grant-maintained schools; independent schools approved to take children with statements of special educational needs; city technology colleges and city colleges for the technology of the arts, and maintained nursery schools.

Draft regulations due to be issued shortly (February 1993) propose that all secondary schools should be inspected by 1 September 1997, and other schools before 1 September 1998, and thereafter at intervals of four years.[150]

Inspectors should report on quality and standards of education, whether financial resources are managed effectively and on

"the spiritual, moral, social and cultural development of pupils at the school" (section 9).

They should make arrangements to meet parents, but no meetings or interviews with pupils are proposed. Lay inspectors (who have not had personal experience of managing a school or providing education in a school - except as a governor or in a voluntary capacity - will be involved in each local inspection team.[151]

Under the Children Act, the Secretary of State for Health has powers to inspect premises provided by local education authorities to accommodate children (see above, page 175).

Scotland

In Scotland HM Inspectors retain full responsibility for inspecting all schools, both maintained, self-governing and independent. There is no legislation governing frequency or scope of inspections.

Independent Schools

HMI has powers to inspect all independent schools. Schools are initially inspected following provisional registration, prior to registration. Then the target has been to inspect between 15 and 20 per cent of all independent schools each year. Many of these inspections have not led to a published report. The intention is to publish more reports and to inspect a "structured sample" of independent schools annually.[152]

In England and Wales, the Secretary of State for Health also has powers to arrange inspection of any independent school providing accommodation (Children Act section 80). In addition the Children Act (section 87) requires social services departments to "take such steps as are reasonably practicable" to determine whether the welfare of children accommodated in an independent school in their area is being adequately safeguarded and promoted (see also page 55). Anyone authorised by the local authority has powers to enter schools, and to carry out inspection of premises, children and records. Regulations provide further detail of what inspections may and may not cover (Inspection of Premises, Children and Records (Independent Schools) Regulations 1991).[153]

Independent schools accommodating less than 51 children are required to register as children's homes and will be subject to inspection by the registering authority (see above, page 183). The Children's Homes Regulations applying to homes also oblige social services departments to visit every child privately placed in a registered children's home within 28 days, but amendments to the regulations proposed in a Department of Health consultation in March 1992 would remove this requirement for independent schools registered as homes.

It is likely that the Education Bill currently before Parliament (February 1993) will be used to limit the definition of independent school required to register as a children's home, so that only schools which keep children during the holidays are required to register.

Other independent schools are registered as residential care homes, and will be subject to inspection by the registering authority (see page 186).

The report following serious abuse at Castle Hill School (an independent school taking children with special needs) emphasised the importance of defining the duties and responsibilities of registration and inspection in relation to the child protection role of the local authority.[154]

Penal institutions

The Prison Inspectorate has powers to inspect all penal institutions, and can be directed to do so by the Home Secretary. There is no legislation setting out frequency of inspections or what must be inspected.

The Board of Visitors for a young offender institution is obliged to visit the institution "frequently". Members must have access to every part of the institution and to every inmate, and may interview any inmate out of the sight and hearing of officers, and have access to records. The board must satisfy itself as to "the state of the premises, the administration of the institution and the treatment of the inmates". While Boards are obliged to meet at the institution at least once a month, the regulations do not specify a frequency for inspection (The Young Offender Institution Rules 1988).[155]

Scotland

In Scotland the Young Offenders (Scotland) Rules 1965 provide similar arrangements for visits by a Visiting Committee appointed by the Secretary of State.[156]

Recommendations

2.5 Arrangements for inspection of institutions and quasi-institutional settings

General

The arrangements for inspection of institutional and quasi-institutional settings used by children and young people should be rationalised to ensure that there are clear and consistent powers and duties on central and local government to arrange appropriate inspections at regular prescribed intervals. In particular the arrangements must ensure that the primary purpose is to safeguard and promote the welfare of children. They must also ensure that they listen to children and young people, and provide an opportunity for individual children and those who work/live with them to speak in private to inspectors.

In addition, inspectors should be required to monitor particular aspects of care, among them the various matters covered in other sections of this report.

The following recommendations aim to move towards this overall objective.

Central government

1 An inter-departmental inquiry should consider the possibility of building on the Social Services Inspectorate (and similar bodies in Scotland and Northern Ireland) to establish at central government level an appropriately trained inspectorate, including lay members, for all residential services for children, whose primary purpose would be to ensure that the welfare of children is adequately safeguarded in all institutional and quasi-institutional settings.

Meanwhile...

2 Section 80 of the Children Act 1989 gives the Secretary of State welcome powers to arrange inspection of most residential institutional settings for children, including those provided by health and education authorities, independent schools and private health institutions. The powers should be extended to cover penal institutions which include children and young people, to supplement the functions of HM Inspectorate of Prisons. Similar powers should be available in Scotland and Northern Ireland.

3 In addition to these general powers, the Secretary of State should have a duty to arrange inspections of any such setting within a specified period or periods in cases where s/he has reason to believe a child's/children's welfare is not being adequately safeguarded, unless satisfied that the responsible local authority has inspected and that appropriate action is being taken to protect the children's welfare. There should also be an obligation to arrange an inspection when requested to do so on reasonable grounds by a local authority, voluntary organisation or private body responsible for providing accommodation for children.

4 There should also be an explicit duty to monitor the inspectorial role of local authorities, and all individual inspection reports from local inspection units.

5 The requirement that the Secretary of State should approve any secure accommodation provided in a community home should be expanded to require that inspections are arranged before approval, and at intervals of not more than six months, throughout the UK. The secure youth treatment centres in England should be inspected at similar intervals. In section 1.3 we propose that all accommodation provided for the restriction of liberty should be subject to approval by the Secretary of State: the requirements for inspection outlined here should apply.

6 Boards of Visitors of young offender institutions should be required to inspect them at similar specified intervals.

Local government

7 Legislation should set out duties for local authorities/health authorities to arrange inspection of all the settings referred to in section 80 as expanded. Thus the inspection units of local authorities would in particular be responsible, in addition to their current responsibilities, for inspecting maintained, assisted and controlled community homes, (including any secure accommodation provided in such homes - in addition to the Secretary of State's duty to arrange inspections proposed above) and voluntary children's homes (which local authorities rather than the Secretary of State should be responsible for registering). The serious concerns within the voluntary sector about the adequacy of local authority inspection units should be taken into account, and could alternatively lead to the establishment of a national voluntary sector inspection unit, perhaps based on the National Council of Voluntary Child Care Organisations.

In particular further consideration should be given to enhancing the independence of local authority inspection units, by the mandatory involvement of independent lay members, including young people with experience of residential care.

8 Regulations should specify the same frequency of inspections for all settings (similar to that already required for registered children's homes: before registration and at least twice a year, once without advance warning). They should also set out matters to be covered by all inspections, to include in every case that inspectors must:

satisfy themselves that the welfare of the children being accommodated is being satisfactorily safeguarded and promoted;

talk to children and young people and ensure that any individual child and any staff member who wishes to has an opportunity to speak to an inspector in private.

Similarly, requirements to visit foster children should be rationalised to provide the same frequency of visits for placements arranged by voluntary organisations and private foster care as are required for local authority placements.

Guidance from the Social Services Inspectorate (SSI) on inspection of children's services, and similar guidance in Scotland and Northern Ireland should pay particular attention to children's rights: the section on rights of elderly residents in the SSI report *Homes Are For Living In* (HMSO 1989) provides an impressive and relevant model.

9 All inspection reports, arranged by both central and local government should be published - ie made available to the institution/setting, and through local authority offices and public libraries to children, parents and the public. In certain cases it may be necessary to keep confidential certain parts of reports relating to individuals (any such material should be made available to the subjects of it). It should be borne in mind that children's homes in the child care system are in a real sense "homes", and the privacy of children in them must be respected.

10 In the case of every local authority inspection, a report should be sent immediately to SSI, or the central government agency responsible for inspections.

Summary of recommendations

Part One

1.1 Protecting children's and young people's physical and personal integrity

1 Laws concerning the upbringing of children in England and Wales, Scotland and Northern Ireland should be prefaced by a statement of positive principles for caring, addressed to parents, others with parental responsibility and all those having care and control of children.

These principles, which would, as appropriate, provide parents and others with parental responsibility with corresponding rights, should include the following:

Children are entitled to care, security and a good upbringing.

Safeguarding and promoting the welfare of the child shall be a primary consideration in all matters concerning the child.

Caring for the child shall be based on respect for his or her person and individuality, and for the child's evolving capacity to make decisions for him/herself.

The child's views regarding any major decision shall be ascertained and given due consideration having regard to the child's age and understanding.

The child shall not be subjected to corporal punishment or any other humiliating or degrading treatment or punishment (corporal punishment shall be defined as in the Education (No 2) Act 1986).

(An alternative approach would be to include in legislation a "Parenthood Code" including these and other similar principles which all those with parental responsibility and others caring for children would be required to pay due regard to.)

2 Section 1 of the Children and Young Persons Act 1933, barring cruelty (and similar acts affecting Scotland and Northern Ireland), must be amended to remove the current implied justification of "necessary" suffering or injury to health caused by assault, ill-treatment or neglect of children.

(Section 1 currently begins:

"If any person who has attained the age of 16 and has the custody, charge or care of any child or young person under that age, wilfully assaults, ill-treats, neglects, abandons or exposes him, or causes or procures him to be assaulted, ill-treated, neglected, abandoned or exposed, in a manner likely to cause him unnecessary suffering or injury to health...that person shall be guilty of a misdemeanour...")

Section 1(7) of the Act, which confirms the common law freedom of parents and other carers to use "reasonable" physical punishment, and similar provisions in the law affecting Scotland and Northern Ireland, must be repealed.

3 The current common law defence of "reasonable chastisement", in so far as it justifies corporal punishment or other humiliating treatment or punishment should **either** be explicitly removed for the purposes of both criminal and civil proceedings, **or** it should be removed for the purposes of civil proceedings, and in the criminal law the defence should be limited along similar lines to those proposed by the Scottish Law Commission.

We favour removing the concept of "reasonable chastisement" altogether, as inappropriate and anachronistic, in the context of developing concepts of parental responsibility and respect for children's rights. It should be replaced by parental duties to guide and safeguard their children according to their evolving capacity.

4 Definitions of physical and sexual child abuse used in child protection should be based clearly on the child's right to physical and personal integrity, and should not condone any level of physical or mental violence to children. This should be emphasised in inter-departmental guidance, and local procedural handbooks.

5 We emphasise that the purpose of these reforms is to change attitudes and practice, not to increase prosecution of parents or intervention in family life, which are unlikely to benefit children. We therefore recommend that the Government should use all appropriate channels to clearly discourage physical punishment and other humiliating treatment of children, and provide and/or support information campaigns aimed at encouraging positive non-violent child-rearing.

6 In addition to the general prohibition on physical punishment and other humiliating treatment and punishment proposed above which would apply to all carers, legislation applying to all institutional and other formal placements - day and residential, including foster care, childminding etc - should include a section prohibiting other specified sanctions. The Children's Homes Regulations 1991 issued under the Children Act for England and Wales (SI 1991 No 1506) contain an appropriate list for all residential institutions (see page 38): this could be amended for application to day institutions including schools, and to foster care, daycare etc.

It should be emphasised and made explicit in regulations and guidance that prohibited sanctions are no more acceptable if they form part of a behaviour modification programme, or are described as "treatment" rather than punishment.

7 Where temporary or permanent exclusion from a day or boarding institution (whether state-maintained, voluntary or private) is a permitted sanction, the right to exclude must be limited by appropriate criteria, and excluded children must have a right to appeal to an appropriate tribunal operating on principles of natural justice.

8 The legislation applying to all institutional and quasi-institutional settings must ensure that children and young people are not involved in the administration of sanctions against other children and young people (see also section 1.2 on bullying, page 70).

9 All institutions should be required to ensure as far as possible that all children and young people, their parents/guardians etc and all those working in the institution are aware of the positive principles of care outlined above, of the legislation protecting children from physical punishment and other humiliating treatment, and from other specific prohibited sanctions. They should be encouraged to involve children and young people directly in reviewing behaviour and discipline policies.

10 All "formal" carers (eg those working with children in institutions, and those whom the state is involved in registering or regulating, including eg foster carers, childminders etc) should be required in legislation to sign an agreement to indicate that they are aware of and will respect the legal provisions to protect children from ill-treatment and abuse, and also the positive principles of care outlined above.

11 Sufficient evidence of any breach of the legal provisions to protect children from ill-treatment and abuse should provide justification for dismissal for breach of contract, whether or not a prosecution and conviction follows. Serious breaches should be grounds for preventing the perpetrator from gaining further employment giving access to children (see also section 2.3, page 132). Hopefully, such issues can be built into codes of conduct for those professions which are able to regulate their members who are caring for children and young people (eg see the proposal for a General Social Services Council, supported in section 2.3, page 152).

Proof of such a breach should provide the employer with a defence against any claim for unfair dismissal. Information about any such breach should, after the worker has been given an opportunity to see and challenge it, be forwarded to an appropriately-constituted professional committee (similar to the "three wise men" procedure which adjudicates in relation to certain misconduct by doctors). This Committee would decide whether the information should be forwarded to the office or departments maintaining lists of people considered unsuitable for work involving substantial access to children (see section 2.3, page 132).

Gross or repetitive breaches of the provisions, whether or not they lead to any prosecution or conviction, must be regarded as providing evidence of unsuitability to work with children.

12 Codes of practice or guidance should be issued to all those working with children in institutional settings, day and boarding, on positive methods of encouraging acceptable behaviour. Guidance should also be issued to appropriate institutions on responding to challenging behaviour, and the minimum use of force in restraining children and young people who are a danger to themselves or others. This guidance should emphasise that "control" should be based on positive relationships between carers and children and young people, and that carers should aim to encourage acceptable behaviour through example, encouragement and reward rather than by punishment. Where rules of conduct are necessary, they should be clearly explained in ways that are readily understandable to the children and young people concerned. Enforcement of any sanctions should be subject to appeal and principles of natural justice. (The draft guidance on "permissible forms of control in children's residential care", issued by the Department of Health, and the draft guidance from the Social Work Services Inspectorate for Scotland, both issued in 1992, provide a valuable start).

13 The Department of Health should be designated the lead government department with overall responsibility for all aspects of child protection, charged with co-ordinating policy and action across government. The Scottish, Welsh and Northern Ireland Offices should designate lead departments for co-ordination of policy.

14 Children's law in Northern Ireland and Scotland should allow the development of "refuges" similar to those covered by section 51 of the Children Act 1989 in England and Wales.

1.2 Protection from bullying by children/ young people

1 All institutional settings for children and young people, both day and boarding, should be required in relevant legislation to have a written policy on protecting children and young people in them from bullying and preventing bullying, which should be defined broadly to include physical assault and intimidation, theft and extortion, verbal abuse including teasing, racial and sexual harassment, harassment on grounds of religion, gender, sexuality etc.

2 Policies must cover:

arrangements to ensure that everyone in the institution is aware of the importance of reporting bullying and the importance of ensuring that those bullied are not blamed in any way;

specific strategies for preventing bullying;

provision of appropriate protection and support for those who are bullied;

appropriate responses to those who bully (with a strong emphasis on non-stigmatising and non-punitive approaches);

arrangements for responding to those forms of bullying that appear to involve criminal offences.

(See also recommendations in section 2.1, page 125 on access to confidential advice and counselling.)

3 Children themselves should be actively consulted and involved in the drafting, implementation (but see 6 below) and monitoring of the policies.

For schools, we commend the Elton Report's general emphasis on ascertaining pupils' views, and on ensuring pupils' active participation and involvement in schools and in the formulation and review of behaviour policies. The curriculum should also appropriately reflect the need to value and respect others, human rights, anti-discrimination perspectives etc. A sensitivity to the issue should also be built into training for teaching and non-teaching staff.

4 The policy should be made available to all those in the institution including children, in a form they can understand.

5 Those responsible for inspecting the institution should be obliged to review the operation of the anti-bullying policy.

6 Children and young people should never be involved in the administration of sanctions for other children and young people: this should be forbidden in legislation on discipline and sanctions applying to all institutional settings.

1.3 Protection against arbitrary and/or unlawful restriction of liberty

1 Restriction of a child's liberty by a parent or other informal carer should be lawful only in so far as it is necessary for the safety and welfare of the child, and in line with the child's evolving capacities. Parents and other informal carers should be warned that, for example, locking a child in a room or space alone, even for short periods, is dangerous and could render them liable to prosecution for cruelty and/or false imprisonment. Punitive practices which involve formal restriction of liberty of children in their homes should be clearly unlawful. (This is an additional argument for removing the current defence of "reasonable chastisement": see section 1.1 page 62). It implies revision of the law on unlawful detention.

2 As in section 1.1 (page 62) we recommend that positive advice should be available to all those caring for children to limit unnecessary and unlawful restriction of liberty. In particular there should be further guidance on permissible forms of restraint in institutional settings.

Some children and young people with complex and multiple disabilities and challenging behaviour may occasionally pose major risks to themselves or others without some form of restraint. Parents and other informal carers may be very isolated when attempting to care for such children and may, without support, use inappropriate methods. Such situations must be acknowledged and appropriate support and advice must be provided.

3 Legislation providing appropriate safeguards for children and young people whose liberty is restricted outside the penal system in Northern Ireland should be introduced without delay.

4 The statutory definition of "restriction of liberty" in section 25 of the Children Act 1989 (and in similar statutes applying to Scotland) should be revised to remove the implication that the provisions and safeguards only apply when a child is placed or kept in "accommodation provided for the purpose of restricting liberty". It should be made clear that any forced detention of a child is covered by the provisions, whether by locking doors, perimeter fences, physical restraints, staff presence or other means. Guidance should be expanded to reinforce the wider definition.

5 The prohibition on restriction of liberty of children in voluntary and registered (private) children's homes under the Children Act should be extended to apply to all voluntary and private institutions throughout the UK, including eg independent schools, non-maintained special schools, residential care homes and nursing homes and mental nursing homes (in these last two categories of private institution, the detention of children and young people under the Mental Health Act should also cease).

6 The extension of section 25 of the Children Act to apply to children accommodated by a local education authority (under regulation 7 of the Children (Secure Accommodation) Regulations 1991) should be repealed. We can see no grounds for allowing formal restriction of liberty of children in boarding schools, and local education authorities should thus be prohibited from restricting the liberty of children they are "accommodating".

7 Wherever restriction of liberty under section 25 of the Children Act (and similar provisions for Scotland) is permitted, the safeguards in the Children (Secure Accommodation) Regulations 1991 should apply. Currently certain safeguards only apply when the restriction of liberty is in secure accommodation in a community home, including the requirement that the accommodation must be approved by the Secretary of State; the minimum age limit of 13 without prior approval of Secretary of State; and arrangements for review and record-keeping. The statutory basis for the provision of youth treatment centres should be changed to ensure that such institutions can be properly regulated and the regulations enforced. The maximum period for restriction of liberty of a child covered by these provisions before a court hearing should be 72 hours.

8 The criteria for restriction of liberty in section 25 of the Children Act (and similar provisions for Scotland) should be carefully reviewed and tightened to ensure compliance with the UN Convention on the Rights of the Child and the European Convention on Human Rights.

The current criteria (see page 85) include absconding which renders a child "likely to suffer significant harm". Evidence of absconding would be relevant to proving that the above criteria applied to a particular child - but only where the risk was extreme.

9 Legislation should make clear that any restriction of liberty of children in day settings which falls within the definition under recommendation 4 above must not be used as a measure of punishment or treatment, but only as a reasonable measure of safety, whose use should be for the shortest possible time and should be recorded.

10 The placing of children in solitary confinement (eg use of "separation" or "seclusion") should be explicitly forbidden in all open institutions. In any secure institutions in which it is permitted, its use must be limited by strict criteria and detailed safeguards, similar to those applied to the use of "single separation rooms" in secure units in the child care system in England and Wales.

11 There should be an obligation to record restriction of liberty of children in all institutional settings; statistics including all applications to court for permission to restrict liberty, full details of the children involved, length of detention etc should be collected centrally and published regularly.

12 The *Gillick* principle, that children judged to have "sufficient understanding" have a right to consent or withhold consent to medical treatment (and thus, for example, to control their admission to and discharge from hospital) should be included in primary legislation, as it is already in Scotland, with a presumption that a child who has reached the age of 12 has sufficient understanding.

13 Medication or withholding of medication must not be used as punishment. The prohibition on the use or withholding of medication as a measure of control in children's homes, except in extreme circumstances, in regulations issued under the Children Act, should be extended to cover all placements.

14 Rules applying to young offender institutions throughout the UK should ensure that no inmate is placed in isolation without the express approval of the medical officer and for the shortest possible time.

Summary of recommendations

Part Two

2.1 Access to advice and counselling, advocacy, and effective complaints procedures

1 Current law, policy and practice should be reviewed to ensure that children in all settings have ready and well-publicised access to:

(a) confidential advice and counselling (including confidential access to their GP);

(b) help from an independent advocate or representative (distinct from independent visitors - see section 2.2);

(c) complaints procedures with an independent element;

(d) ultimate access when necessary to the courts.

In all cases, special provision should be made for disabled children and young people (see also section 2.2), and to enable representations to be made on behalf of disabled children and very young children.

(a) Confidential advice and counselling
All institutions and services for or used by children and young people should be required to display readily understandable details of confidential helplines, and ensure that children/young people are able to use a telephone in private (with special arrangements for those with special needs).

(b) Independent advocates or representatives
Children and young people in all settings should be told how they can contact an independent advocate or representative, who can advise them on important matters in confidence, and help them to seek redress for any wrongs they are suffering by guiding them through complaints procedures, and where appropriate representing them. In particular, information on how to contact an independent advocate or representative should be available through helplines for children, and in information about any complaints procedures they may use.

(c) Complaints procedures
All guidance on complaints procedures should emphasise that complaints and representations from children are to be welcomed for the contribution they can make to improving the quality of a service or an institution.

Children and young people themselves should always be adequately and continuously consulted about the design, implementation, dissemination of information about, and operation of complaints procedures.

All complaints procedures which may be used by children and young people should allow complaints by groups of children as well as individuals, and by others on behalf of children (if a child is of "sufficient understanding", complaints made on their behalf should only be considered with their consent; this does not of course prevent relatives or friends making complaints on their own behalf about eg the level of contact allowed with a young person).

(i) "Local" complaints procedures:
There should be clear procedures to encourage informal resolution of complaints whenever possible.

Children and young people in all settings must have ready access to well-publicised complaints procedures which include elements independent of the setting in which they are living or in which they are being provided with a service. Local authorities providing complaints procedures should use independent people recruited, trained and supported by a separate body. It is essential that children should not at the first stage have to complain **to** or through someone they are complaining **about**.

Short time limits, compatible with effective resolution of complaints and extendable in exceptional circumstances, should be set.

If a complainant is not satisfied with the resolution of a complaint locally he or she should always be informed how else to pursue it.

Fulfilling this recommendation will require reviewing existing complaints procedures as outlined above, and providing legal duties to ensure appropriate procedures are available in, for example, the education service and all private and voluntary institutions (and, for example, extending the role of the Mental Health Act Commission to cover "informal" child patients in NHS and other health provision).

The content and resolution of complaints must be monitored in order to take account of implications for policy and service development. Any complaints procedure should also be monitored to see whether children and young people know about it, and have confidence in it.

(ii) When local resolution of complaints fails:
Where complaints are not resolved to the satisfaction of the complainant at service or institution level, there needs to be a further avenue of complaint for children. This could be provided by:

a new UK-wide children's ombudsperson service, with regional offices and powers of investigation etc similar to those of the Commissioner for Local Administration, and covering local authority, voluntary and private services and institutions used by children and young people;

widening the powers of the Commissioners for Local Administration appropriately to cover services and institutions for children.

(d) Access to the courts

All children and young people, including those in care, should have the same rights as adult parties to have applications about aspects of their upbringing considered by the courts: this will require amendments to the Children Act (which currently gives courts discretion whether or not to hear applications from children, and specifically excludes applications from children in care) and to relevant legislation for Scotland (following the proposals for clarification of the Scottish Law Commission) and Northern Ireland.

2 All those involved in providing confidential advice and counselling to children, any independent advocates available to children, and those involved in complaints procedures should be subject to special recruitment and vetting procedures if their work involves significant unsupervised access to children and young people (see section 2.3).

3 Social services departments, the NSPCC and the police should be advised to ensure that children and young people are provided with readily understandable information on child protection procedures: on how children can approach these agencies, and on likely action that may follow a complaint of ill-treatment by a child or young person.

4 Conditions of employment and contracts for all those working with or for children should not limit in any way their right to inform appropriate authorities, to seek appropriate help and to take any other necessary action to safeguard and promote the welfare of children they are working with or for. Necessary whistle-blowing in children's services should be clearly protected.

2.2 Access to independent people

1 In addition to the current obligation in legislation applying to England and Wales to consider the appointment of an independent visitor for certain children and young people, there should be (in legislation applying throughout the UK):

(a) an obligation to consider the appointment of an independent visitor for any child whose accommodation by an education or health authority, or in a residential care home or nursing home or mental nursing home for three months or more is notified to a local authority;

(b) a requirement to appoint an independent visitor or representative for any child placed in secure accommodation, or in other accommodation to restrict liberty falling within section 25 of the Children Act (and similar provisions for Scotland and Northern Ireland), together with an obligation to ensure that the child is visited within two weeks of the placement and thereafter at regular intervals;

(c) a requirement to appoint an independent visitor for those children and young people who are judged unable to use the complaints procedures available to other children and young people in an institution.

(d) a requirement to appoint an independent visitor for any child or young person in need, wherever placed, if the authority has reasonable cause to believe that the child's emotional or behavioural difficulties or disability may cause the child at times to be at serious risk of harming self or others without some use of restraint;

(e) All these requirements should be subject to the child's consent, where judged to have "sufficient understanding".

2 Consideration should also be given to requiring all residential institutions to ensure the availability to children of independent representatives.

3 Consideration should be given to similar requirements in relation to institutional placements in Scotland and Northern Ireland.

2.3 Arrangements to prevent people who threaten children's welfare gaining inappropriate access to them

1 We echo the recommendations of other bodies that a code of practice should be drafted as soon as possible (or a series of codes) on the recruitment, induction and supervision of people working or volunteering in situations which give them substantial unsupervised access to children. An inter-departmental group involving representatives from the voluntary and private sectors should be appointed to oversee drafting and should review and monitor implementation. The group could draw on recommendations in *Choosing with Care* and other reports.

Following a short period of consultation, the code(s) should be disseminated very widely to all bodies employing or likely to employ people or use volunteers in positions giving them substantial unsupervised access to children.

2 All employers - local authority, health authority, voluntary and private - of relevant workers/volunteers should be required in primary legislation to follow these codes, which would include appropriate arrangements for police checks.

3 All relevant voluntary and private employers should be enabled to check the possible criminal background of those who apply or move to work in paid or voluntary posts which will give them substantial unsupervised access to children. We are particularly concerned about the need for checks for volunteers who work in a one-to-one situation with children with learning difficulties, and eg guardians appointed for children in boarding schools whose parents are abroad.

4 In relation to private and voluntary organisations, procedures should ensure in certain cases (eg independent schools) that those responsible for employment and supervision have themselves been checked, either when they applied for eg registration of an institution, or when they first apply to use the checking procedures.

5 We support the proposal of the Home Office Efficiency Scrutiny on collection of criminal records, and other reports, that once criminal records are centralised (as they are already in Scotland), a single agency should take on the task of collecting, storing and providing access in defined circumstances to criminal records and other agreed information relating to potential unsuitability. This agency would take over the roles of government departments (eg the DH Consultancy Service, DFE List 99 etc). It would be responsible for ensuring that no information was provided until the subject of it had had an opportunity to check and if necessary formally challenge it. There is a strong case for central government meeting the cost: it is essential in any case that charges do not become a disincentive to employers to use vetting procedures: thus they should be available free at least to voluntary organisations.

This agency could also take on some responsibility for ensuring that codes of practice on recruitment and employment procedures are implemented.

6 We support the case for a General Social Services Council, which could make a major contribution towards protecting children from people who threaten their welfare.

7 Increasing mobility of workers within Europe and beyond makes it essential that there are reciprocal arrangements for police checks across country boundaries, with appropriate safeguards for the subjects of checks.

8 The obligation on the responsible authority for a children's home to report to the Secretary of State any conduct of a member of staff suggesting that s/he is not or may not be "a suitable person to be employed in work involving children", and the similar duty on proprietors of independent schools to report misconduct should apply to all employers of people who may have substantial unsupervised access to children (such information would eventually be directed to the central agency referred to above). A process of appeal should be built in to ensure that the subject of such reports is shown the information before it is made available to potential employers, and can challenge the information.

9 The necessary review of existing legislation implied by recommendation 8 should also include consideration of the arrangements in the Children Act for disqualification of certain carers. It appears to us either that such arrangements should apply consistently to all forms of employment involving substantial access to children, or the arrangements should be harmonised with those for reporting and recording information about other potentially unsuitable staff.

10 All those working in institutions and quasi-institutional settings with children should receive detailed guidance on protection of children. Particular guidance will be required for those working with very young children and children with learning difficulties.

11 In all advice relating to employment of people in settings with children there should be an emphasis on the importance of enabling children to protect themselves (though this should never be seen as an alternative to the responsibilities of adults to provide protection), on adequate supervision, and on clear procedures in the event of suspicion of inappropriate conduct with children.

12 Those responsible for inspection of institutions and other settings including children and young people should be required to monitor compliance with the codes of practice on employment, and awareness of the guidance on child protection.

2.4 Arrangements for monitoring/reviewing placement and treatment of children

1 Throughout the UK, health legislation should ensure that there is a clear obligation to make available specified appropriate developmental checks for all children in their area between notification of birth and age of starting school, and (subject to the child's right to consent) at appropriate intervals during the period of compulsory schooling.

2 We support the NSPCC's call for a co-ordinated reviews of child protection procedures throughout the UK, which should take as their starting point fundamental principles of children's rights.

3 The obligation to maintain local child protection registers should be set out in legislation. Having a child protection plan should not be a pre-condition of placing a child's name on a register. Regulations should set out an obligation to devise a child protection plan within a short period of placing a child's name on the register (seven days perhaps) and also obligations to review children on the register at appropriate intervals.

4 Arrangements for formal review of placement and treatment of children, involving the children themselves and similar in frequency and scope to those set out in the Review of Children's Cases Regulations 1991, issued under the Children Act 1989, should extend to all children being accommodated in institutions and quasi-institutional settings throughout the UK - eg to those not already covered who are being accommodated by a local education authority or health authority, all those in residential care homes, nursing homes and mental nursing homes, independent schools in the case of children accommodated for substantial parts of holidays in addition to school terms, private foster care etc, and also to young offenders in penal institutions.

In addition to these arrangements, in the case of all placements away from home for a significant period, we propose that there should be an "exit-review", or "leaving interview", at which the child or young person would be invited to comment, if s/he wished, on the placement and its successes, any problems etc.

Reports of all reviews should be made available to the subjects of them, in appropriate cases to parents, and submitted as appropriate to the relevant social services/social work departments (as well as to other appropriate authorities - eg health or education) which should be under a duty to consider them and take any necessary action to ensure that the child's welfare is being adequately safeguarded and promoted. Children should be consulted about such dissemination of information about them, and their views taken account of, in line with Article 12 of the UN Convention.

5 Wherever a child is placed in "secure accommodation" (accommodation provided to restrict the liberty of children - see section 1.2, page 85) there should be an obligation on the appropriate body (but involving an independent element) to review the placement; arrangements should be equivalent in frequency etc to those set out in the Children (Secure Accommodation) Regulations 1991, issued under the Children Act.

2.5 Arrangements for inspection of institutions and quasi-institutional settings

General

The arrangements for inspection of institutional and quasi-institutional settings used by children and young people should be rationalised to ensure that there are clear and consistent powers and duties on central and local government to arrange appropriate inspections at regular prescribed intervals. In particular the arrangements must ensure that the primary purpose is to safeguard and promote the welfare of children. They must also ensure that they listen to children and young people, and provide an opportunity for individual children and those who work/live with them to speak in private to inspectors.

In addition, inspectors should be required to monitor particular aspects of care, among them the various matters covered in other sections of this report.

The following recommendations aim to move towards this overall objective.

Central government

1 An inter-departmental inquiry should consider the possibility of building on the Social Services Inspectorate (and similar bodies in Scotland and Northern Ireland) to establish at central government level an appropriately trained inspectorate, including lay members, for all residential services for children, whose primary purpose would be to ensure that the welfare of children is adequately safeguarded in all institutional and quasi-institutional settings.

Meanwhile...

2 Section 80 of the Children Act 1989 gives the Secretary of State welcome powers to arrange inspection of most residential institutional settings for children, including those provided by health and education authorities, independent schools and private health institutions. The powers should be extended to cover penal institutions which include children and young people, to supplement the functions of HM Inspectorate of Prisons. Similar powers should be available in Scotland and Northern Ireland.

3 In addition to these general powers, the Secretary of State should have a duty to arrange inspections of any such setting within a specified period or periods in cases where s/he has reason to believe a child's/children's welfare is not being adequately safeguarded, unless satisfied that the responsible local authority has inspected and that appropriate action is being taken to protect the children's welfare. There should also be an obligation to arrange an inspection when requested to do so on reasonable grounds by a local authority, voluntary organisation or private body responsible for providing accommodation for children.

4 There should also be an explicit duty to monitor the inspectorial role of local authorities, and all individual inspection reports from local inspection units.

5 The requirement that the Secretary of State should approve any secure accommodation provided in a community home should be expanded to require that inspections are arranged before approval, and at intervals of not more than six months, throughout the UK. The secure youth treatment centres in England should be inspected at similar intervals. In section 1.3 we propose that all accommodation provided for the restriction of liberty should be subject to approval by the Secretary of State: the requirements for inspection outlined here should apply.

6 Boards of Visitors of young offender institutions should be required to inspect them at similar specified intervals.

Local government

7 Legislation should set out duties for local authorities/health authorities to arrange inspection of all the settings referred to in section 80 as expanded. Thus the inspection units of local authorities would in particular be responsible, in addition to their current responsibilities, for inspecting maintained, assisted and controlled community homes, (including any secure accommodation provided in such homes - in addition to the Secretary of State's duty to arrange inspections proposed above) and voluntary children's homes (which local authorities rather than the Secretary of State should be responsible for registering). The serious concerns within the voluntary sector about the adequacy of local authority inspection units should be taken into account, and could alternatively lead to the establishment of a national voluntary sector inspection unit, perhaps based on the National Council of Voluntary Child Care Organisations.

In particular further consideration should be given to enhancing the independence of local authority inspection units, by the mandatory involvement of independent lay members, including young people with experience of residential care.

8 Regulations should specify the same frequency of inspections for all settings (similar to that already required for registered children's homes: before registration and at least twice a year, once without advance warning). They should also set out matters to be covered by all inspections, to include in every case that inspectors must:

satisfy themselves that the welfare of the children being accommodated is being satisfactorily safeguarded and promoted;

talk to children and young people and ensure that any individual child and any staff member who wishes to has an opportunity to speak to an inspector in private.

Similarly, requirements to visit foster children should be rationalised to provide the same frequency of visits for placements arranged by voluntary organisations, and private foster care as are required for local authority placements.

Guidance from the Social Services Inspectorate (SSI) on inspection of children's services, and similar guidance in Scotland and Northern Ireland should pay particular attention to children's rights: the section on rights of elderly residents in the SSI report *Homes Are For Living In* (HMSO 1989) provides an impressive and relevant model.

9 All inspection reports, arranged by both central and local government should be published - ie made available to the institution/setting, and through local authority offices and public libraries to children, parents and the public. In certain cases it may be necessary to keep confidential certain parts of reports relating to individuals (any such material should be made available to the subjects of it). It should be borne in mind that children's homes in the child care system are in a real sense "homes", and the privacy of children in them must be respected.

10 In the case of every local authority inspection, a report should be sent immediately to SSI, or the central government agency responsible for inspections.

References

Part 1

Section 1.1

(1) Gillick v West Norfolk and Wisbech AHA [1986]AC 112.

(2) *Report on Family Law*, Scottish Law Commission, HMSO, 1992.

(3) *Report of the Inquiry into Child Abuse in Cleveland 1987*, HMSO, 1988; *Report of the Inquiry into the Removal of Children from Orkney in February 1991*, HMSO, 1992.

(4) *Private Fostering and Miscellaneous*, Children Act Guidance Volume 8, Department of Health, HMSO, 1991, para 1.7.16; also *Working Together under the Children Act 1989*, HMSO 1991, para 3.9. The major voluntary organisation campaigning against genital mutilation is the Foundation for Women's Health Research and Development (FORWARD), c/o Africa Centre, 38 King Street, London WC2E 8JT.

(5) R v Hopley (1860) 2 F & F 202.

(6) *Parliamentary Debates*, 3rd series (1889), vol 338, col 956.

(7) *Hansard*, House of Lords, 16 February 1989, cols 346, 350-1; 16 March 1989, cols 407-10.

(8) *Offences against the Person*, 14th Report of the Criminal Law Revision Committee, Cmnd 7844, HMSO, 1980.

(9) *Law Commission Consultation Paper No 122, Legislating the Criminal Code, Offences against the Person and General Principles*, HMSO, February 1992.

(10) *Institutional Abuse of Children - From Research to Policy: a review*, Helen L Westcott, NSPCC, 1992, page 37.

(11) ibid, pages 5 and 11.

(12) see (2).

(13) ibid, paras 2.90, 2.95, 2.97, etc.

(14) ibid, para 2.90.

(15) ibid, para 2.89.

(16) ibid, para 2.87.

(17) ibid, para 2.87.

(18) Children's Homes Regulations 1991, SI 1991 No 1506, regulation 8.

(19) see (2), para 2.96.

(20) *Assessment of Swedish Reforms: Reducing Violence towards US Children: Transferring Positive Innovations from Sweden*, Adrienne Haeuser, University of Wisconsin, Milwaukee School of Social Welfare: a detailed report of the effects of Sweden's prohibition of all physical punishment of children, following interview research in 1981 and 1988.

(21) quoted in *The Ombudsman and Child Maltreatment*, report of an international seminar organised by Radda Barnen, Swedish Save the Children Federation in Geneva, Stockholm, March 1980.

(22) European Commission of Human Rights, admissibility decision, Application 8811/79: Seven individuals v Sweden, 13 May 1982.

(23) *Can You Bring Up Children Successfully Without Smacking and Spanking?*, Ministry of Justice, Stockholm, 1979.

(24) Information from ministries of justice in countries which have prohibited physical punishment.

(25) *Violence in the Family*, Recommendation R85(4), adopted by the Committee of Ministers of the Council of Europe on 26 March 1985.

(26) *Social Measures Concerning Violence in the Family*, Recommendation R(90)2, adopted by the Committee of Ministers on 15 January 1990.

(27) *Gewaltkommission*: Commission appointed by the West German government, before reunification, to investigate the causes of all forms of societal violence and make recommendations for reducing it. The Commission's recommendation to prohibit all physical punishment, made in its report in 1989, was later repeated by the Kinderkommission.

(28) Information from Kinderkommission, Bonn.

(29) *Violence - Directions for Australia*, report of the National Committee on Violence, 1989.

(30) *Children in the Public Care*, a review of residential child care, Sir William Utting, HMSO, 1991, paras 3.53, 3.58.

(31) *Choosing with Care*, report of the committee of inquiry into the selection, development and management of staff in children's homes, chaired by Norman Warner, HMSO, 1992, pages 155/156.

(32) *Guidance on Permissible Forms of Control in Children's Residential Care*, Department of Health Circular LAC(93)13, April 1993; *Another Kind of Home: a review of residential care*, Social Work Services Inspectorate for Scotland, Scottish Office, HMSO, 1992.

(33) *Care and Control of Pupils/Students*, National Association of Head Teachers Council memorandum, NAHT, January 1993.

(34) *The Extent of Parental Physical Punishment in the UK*, John and Elizabeth Newson, APPROACH Ltd, 1989.

(35) *Attitudes Towards Punishing Children*, 22 - 27 November 1989, Gallup Omnibus Report.

(36) 'Smacking? You tell us how you discipline your children', *Woman's Own*, 12 November 1990.

(37) 'Caning mother cleared', *Daily Mail*, 4 October 1991; 'Father - why I beat my sons', *North Avon Evening Post*, 19 March 1993.

(38) 'Mother who smacked son loses "at risk" appeal', *The Times*, 27 February 1990.

(39) 'Boys thrashed after row with step-mum', *Lincolnshire Echo*, 9 December 1992.

(40) B v Harris 1990 SLT 208.

(41) Peebles v MacPhail 1990 SLT 245.

(42) *The Scotsman*, 27 November 1991.

(43) see (2).

(44) *Parental Responsibilities and Rights, Guardianship and the Administration of Children's Property*, Scottish Law Commission Discussion Paper 88, October 1990.

(45) see (2), paras 2.100-102.

(46) ibid, para 2.105.

(47) ibid, para 2.95.

(48) ibid, paras 2.103-104.

(49) ibid, 2.1 et seq; 2.60 et seq.

(50) Leaflets include 'The no smacking guide to good behaviour', 'Smacking a short-cut to nowhere' etc; details available from EPOCH, 77 Holloway Road, London N7 8JZ.

(51) see (2), para 2.102.

(52) SI 1991 No 893.

(53) SI 1991 No 910.

(54) Communication from National Foster Care Association, 1992.

(55) *Family Placements*, Children Act Guidance Volume 3, Department of Health, HMSO, 1991, para 3.30.

(56) SI 1985 No 1799.

(57) SI 1991 No 2050.

(58) see (4), para 1.5.13.

(59) see (54).

(60) SI 1985 No 1798.

(61) Communication from Department of Health and Social Services, Northern Ireland.

(62) see (18).

(63) *Residential Care*, Children Act Guidance Volume 4, Department of Health, HMSO, 1991, paras 1.82-1.90 (para 1.91 discusses in detail the prohibited measures listed in regulation 8).

(64) see (32).

(65) Children Act 1989 section 51 and Refuges (Children's Homes and Foster Placements) Regulations 1991 (SI 1991 No 1507).

(66) SI 1987 No 2233.

(67) *The Social Work (Residential Establishments - Child Care) (Scotland) Regulations 1987*, Circular No SW1/1988, Scottish Social Work Services Group, 1988.

(68) see (32), recommendation 41, page 66.

(69) ibid, para 3.8.22.

(70) ibid, page 96 et seq.

(71) Conduct of Children's Homes Direction (Northern Ireland) 1975 and the Children and Young Persons (Voluntary Homes) Regulations (Northern Ireland) 1975.

(72) The Training School Rules, 1952.

(73) SI 1991 No 1505.

(74) *Youth Treatment Service Policy and Management Specification*, Department of Health, March 1992.

(75) SI 1984 No 1345.

(76) SI 1988 No 1192.

(77) *Home Life: a code of practice for residential care*, Centre for Policy on Ageing, 1984.

(78) *Family Support, Day Care and Educational Provision for Young Children*, Children Act Guidance Volume 2, Department of Health, HMSO, 1991, paras 6.21, 6.22.

(79) *The Children Act and Day Care for Young Children Registration*, Circular LAC(93)1, Department of Health, January 1993.

(80) *Regulation and Review of Childminding, Daycare and Education Services for Children under Eight*, Scottish Office, June 1991, Annex A para 23.

(81) *The Welfare of Children and Young People in Hospital*, Department of Health, HMSO, 1991, para 4.16.

(82) HSG(91)1, Department of Health, July 1991.

(83) SI 1984 No 1578.

(84) SI 1983 No 1499 and SI 1991 No 450.

(85) *The Approval of Special Schools*, Circular 3/91, Department of Education and Science, 1991, paras 23 and 24.

(86) *Exclusions*, a discussion paper, Department for Education, 1992.

(87) SI 1990 No 295.

(88) SI 1975 No 1135, as amended by SI 1982 No 56 and SI 1982 No 1735.

(89) see (84).

(90) SI 1991 No 890, SI 1991 No 895, SI 1991 No 894.

(91) The Education (Abolition of Corporal Punishment) (Independent Schools) Regulations 1987 (SI 1987 No 1183), and the Education (Abolition of Corporal Punishment) (Independent Schools) (Prescribed Categories of Persons) Regulations 1989 (SI 1989 No 1233).

(92) Letter from Department for Education, Schools Branch 2a, 6 August 1992.

(93) Jeremy Costello-Roberts v UK, Application 13134/87; Report of the European Commission of Human Rights adopted 8 October 1991; Costello-Roberts v UK, Judgment of the European Court of Human Rights, 25 March 1993.

(94) Y v UK, Judgment of the European Court of Human Rights, 29 October 1992; Application 14229/88.

(95) Y v UK, Report of the European Commission of Human Rights adopted 8 October 1991, paras 43, 44.

(96) *Independent Schools*, Children Act Guidance Volume 5, Department of Health, HMSO, 1991, paras 3.9.1 - 3.9.5

(97) SI 1991 No 975.

(98) "Proposed changes to section 63 of the Children Act 1989 in relation to certain boarding schools", letter from Department of Health, Community Services Division, 14 January 1993.

(99) SI 1991 No 449, Schedule 1, para 6(b).

(100) *The Education (Special Educational Needs) (Approval of Independent Schools) Regulations 1991*, DES Circular 2/91, Department of Education and Science 1991.

(101) SI 1988 No 1422.

(102) SI 1965 No 195, rule 44 (f).

(103) Northern Ireland Training School Rules 1952.

(104) SI 1958 No 1990, SI 1978 No 1919.

Section 1.2

(105) *Bullying: an annotated bibliography of literature and resources*, Alison Skinner, Youth Work Press, 17 - 23 Albion Street, Leicester LE1 6GD, 1992.

(106) Anti-Bullying Campaign, details of publications, advice line etc from ABC, 10 Borough High Street, London SE1 9QQ (071-378 1446).

(107) Kidscape - the campaign for children's safety, 152 Buckingham Palace Road, London SW1W 9TR (071-730 3300).

(108) The pack contained three publications: *Bullying: a positive response*, by Delwyn Tattum and Graham Herbert (available from Delwyn Tattum, Faculty of Education, Cardiff Institute of Higher Education, Cyncoed Road, Cardiff CF2 6XD); *Bullying: the child's view* (see (109) below); *Bullying for Governors*, an Advisory Centre for Education Information Sheet, (available from ACE, 1b Aberdeen Studios, 22 Highbury Grove, London N5 2EA).

(109) *Bullying: the child's view*, by Jean La Fontaine, published by Calouste Gulbenkian Foundation, 1991 (available through Turnaround Distribution Ltd, 27 Horsell Road, London N5 1XL).

(110) *The Boarding Schools Line, January - July 1991, a report from ChildLine to the DES*, by Jean La Fontaine and Sally Morris, ChildLine, 1991.

(111) *Race Relations in Schools*, a paper by HM Inspectorate, Department of Education and Science, 1984.

(112) *Learning in Terror*, Commission for Racial Equality, 1988.

(113) *Discipline in Schools*, report of the committee of inquiry chaired by Lord Elton, Department of Education and Science/Welsh Office, HMSO 1989.

(114) Department of Education and Science Press Notice, 18 May 1992.

(115) *Action Against Bullying: a support pack for schools*, prepared by the Scottish Council for Research in Education under contract from the Scottish Office Education Department, 1992.

(116) Association of Educational Psychologists submission to Department of Education and Science consultation on school corporal punishment, 1977.

(117) *No Blame Approach to Bullying*, video and materials; details from Lame Duck Publishing (Barbara Maines and George Robinson) c/o 71 South Road, Portishead, Avon BS20 9DY

(118) *Bully-Victim Problems among Schoolchildren: basic facts and effects of a school-based intervention programme*, Dan Olweus, Department of Personality Psychology, University of Bergen, Norway, 1988.

(119) *Boosting Educational Achievement*, report of the independent inquiry into educational achievement in the London Borough of Newham, chaired by Seamus Hegarty, Newham Council, 1989.

(120) see (30), recommendation 26, page 10.

(121) see (32), pages 21, 96-99.

(122) see (63), para 1.184.

(123) *Regimes in Young Offender Institutions*, NACRO (National Association for the Care and Resettlement of Offenders) briefing, November 1991.

(124) *Independent Schools*, see (96) paras 3.9.5 and 3.9.2.

(125) *Castle Hill Report Practice Guide*, C Brannan, J R Jones, J D Murch, Shropshire County Council, 1993, pages 7 and 10.

(126) see (110).

(127) The Young Offenders (Scotland) Rules 1965, SI 1965 No 195, Rule 33.

Section 1.3

(128) *Imprisonment in Western Europe*, a NACRO briefing, 169 Clapham Road, London SW9 OPU, 1992.

(129) '12 year old offenders to be locked up', *Sunday Times*, 27 December 1992; 'New secure training centres to hold persistent juvenile offenders', Home Office news release, 2 March 1993.

(130) *Locked Up in Care*, Children's Legal Centre, 20 Compton Terrace, London N1 2UN, 1982.

(131) *Bridges Over Troubled Waters*, a report from the NHS Health Advisory Service on Services for Disturbed Adolescents, HAS, March 1986, section 5 and recommendations.

(132) *Children in Custody*, by Gillian Stewart and Norman Tutt, Avebury, Gower Publishing Company, 1987, pages 215-6.

(133) *Special Issues and Differing Needs*, review of health and social services for mentally disordered offenders and others requiring similar services, Volume 5, Department of Health and Home Office Report of the Official Working Group on services for people with special needs, HMSO, 1993.

(134) Children (Secure Accommodation) Regulations 1991, SI 1991 No 1505, regulation 18.

(135) *The Pindown Experience and the Protection of Children*, Report of the Staffordshire Child Care Inquiry 1990, Allan Levy QC and Barbara Kahan, Staffordshire County Council 1991, para 12.55.

(136) ibid, paras 12.57 and 12.85.

(137) see (132), page 10.

(138) see (18).

(139) see (32), pages 64 and 96.

(140) see (132), page 10.

(141) Information from Children's Legal Centre and Family Rights Group.

(142) In re "W" [1992]3 WLR 758, CA.

(143) see (18), regulation 8 and (63) para 1.91(v).

(144) see (131), para 5.19.

(145) see (30), paras 4.48-9 and 4.51.

(146) see (132) page 11.

(147) 'Head locks up haircut boy', *The Star*, 10 December 1992.

(148) *Guidelines to Good Practice in the use of Behavioural Treatments*, Royal College of Psychiatrists Council Report CR9, October 1989.

(149) *Seclusion, Control and Restraint*, Royal College of Nursing guidelines, RCN, April 1992.

(150) R v Rahman [1985] 81 Cr.App R 349, CA.

(151) *Offences against the Person*, 14th Report of the Criminal Law Revision Committee, Cmnd 7844, HMSO, 1980.

(152) *Legislating the Criminal Code, Offences against the Person and General Principles: a consultation paper*, Law Commission, HMSO, 1992, draft Bill clause 14.

(153) see (1) and (142).

(154) Code of Practice on the Mental Health Act 1983, Mental Health Act Commission, HMSO, 1990.

(155) see (73).

(156) see (63), para 8.10 and 1.91, vi.

(157) *Secure Accommodation for Children and Young Persons, Guidance for Local Authorities*, Department of Health and Social Security, Social Services Inspectorate, 1986, Appendix 6.

(158) see (18), regulation 8.

(159) see (63), paras 1.91v and 1.102.

(160) Department of Health Circular LAC(83)18, issued 9 December 1983, paras 7 et seq (now replaced by guidance issued under the Children Act).

(161) Secure Accommodation (Scotland) Regulations 1983 (SI 1983 No 1912; Children's Hearings (Scotland) (Amendment - Secure Accommodation) Rules 1984 and the Secure Accommodation (Scotland) Amendment) Regulations 1988.

(162) see (32), pages 64-65, 96 et seq.

(163) Correspondence with Northern Ireland Office, Probation and Juveniles Branch, 1992.

(164) see (73), regulation 7.

(165) see (63), para 8.13.

(166) see (73), regulation 5.

(167) see (63), para 8.58.

(168) *Mobility proposals for young people detained under section 53(2) of the Children and Young Persons Act 1933*, note of guidance, Home Office, 1992.

(169) see (132), pages 188 et seq.

(170) 'Disturbed child centre to close after drug ban', *The Guardian*, 26 June 1991.

(171) see (63), para 1.196.

(172) see (77), para 4.5.4.

(173) Report on St Charles Youth Treatment Centre and Glenthorne Youth Treatment Centre, Social Services Inspectorate, Department of Health, 1988.

(174) *Outcome of an Investigation concerning St Charles Youth Treatment Centre*, Department of Health, 1991, paras 5 et seq.

(175) ibid, para 21 et seq.

(176) see (73), regulation 18.

(177) see (96), paras 3.10.1-3.

(178) Circular 2/91, Department of Education and Science, 1991.

(179) see (101).

(180) see (102).

Part 2

Section 2.1

(1) *Inspecting for Quality*, guidance on practice for inspection units in social services departments and other agencies, Social Services Inspectorate, Department of Health, 1991, page 18.

(2) *The Leicestershire Inquiry 1992*, Andrew Kirkwood QC, Leicestershire County Council, February 1993, page 312.

(3) *Inquiry into Police Investigation of Complaints of Child and Sexual Abuse in Leicestershire Children's Homes*, Police Complaints Authority, February 1993, pages 166 et seq.

(4) *Children in the Public Care*, a review of residential child care, Sir William Utting, HMSO, 1991, paras 3.18, 3.48.

(5) *Choosing with Care*, report of the committee of inquiry into the selection, development and management of staff in children's homes, chaired by Norman Warner, HMSO, 1992, para 6.44.

(6) see (4), paras 3.37 et seq.

(7) see (5), para 6.44.

(8) see (4), para 3.50 and recommendation 7.2, page 63.

(9) *Taking Children Seriously: a proposal for a Children's Rights Commissioner*, M Rosenbaum and P Newell, Gulbenkian Foundation, 1991.

(10) *Review of Child Care Law in Scotland*, Scottish Office, 1990, paras 23.3 et seq.

(11) *Report on Family Law*, Scottish Law Commission, HMSO, 1992, para 5.11.

(12) SI 1991 No 1506, regulation 7(5).

(13) *Residential Care*, Children Act Guidance Volume 4, Department of Health, 1991, para 1.64.

(14) see (4), para 3.18.

(15) see (5), page 105.

(16) *Another Kind of Home: a review of residential child care*, Social Work Services Inspectorate for Scotland, Scottish Office, HMSO, 1992, para 3.1.13.

(17) *A Practice Guide on the Welfare of Children in Boarding Schools*, Social Services Inspectorate, Department of Health, HMSO, 1991.

(18) see (4), para 3.39.

(19) *Residential Care: a positive choice*, report of the Independent Review of Residential Care, chaired by Gillian Wagner, National Institute for Social Work, HMSO, 1988.

(20) see (16), paras 3.2.23 et seq.

(21) see (5), para 6.48 and recommendation 52, page 105.

(22) *Advice, Advocacy and Representation Service for Children and Young People*, ASC, Information Pack, July 1992, 1 Sickle Street, Manchester M60 2AA (061 839 8442).

(23) Independent Representation for Children in Need, IRCHIN, 23A Hawthorne Drive, Heswall, Wirral, Merseyside, L61 6UP (051 342 7852).

(24) A Voice for the Child in Care, Unit 4, Pride Court, 80-82 White Lion Street, London N1 9PF.

(25) see (17).

(26) see (5), Appendix 3, paras 158/9.

(27) see (5), para 6.52-6.54, and recommendation 53, page 105.

(28) *Quality Standards in the NHS: the consumer focus*, National Consumer Council, September 1992, para 4.4.

(29) *Freedom of Speech for NHS Staff*, draft guidance, Department of Health, October 1992.

(30) *Working Together under the Children Act 1989: guide to arrangements for inter-agency co-operation for the protection of children*, Department of Health etc, HMSO 1991, para 4.11.

(31) see (11), para 5.11.

(32) correspondence from IRCHIN, see (23).

(33) see (5), para 6.49.

(34) SI 1991 No 894.

(35) see (13), chapter 5.

(36) information from A Voice for the Child in Care, see (24).

(37) see (13), para 5.26.

(38) see (5), Appendix 3, paras 154, 156-7.

(39) see (5), page 105.

(40) *National Health Service and Community Care Act 1990; Local Authority Complaints Procedures*, Scottish Office Circular No SW5/1991.

(41) *Community Care in Scotland: the introduction of local authority complaints procedures*, Scottish Office, 1992.

(42) see (16), paras 3.2.12, 3.2.15, 3.2.31 and 3.2.9.

(43) *Provision of Information to and a Complaints Procedure for Children in Residential Care and their Parents*, Northern Ireland DHSS Circular HSS(CC)2/85, 1985.

(44) Information from Northern Ireland Office, 1991, and *Guidelines for Schemes which provide Independent Representation for Young People in Secure Accommodation in Northern Ireland*, NIACRO, 169 Ormeau Road, Belfast BT7 1SQ.

(45) *Policy and Management Specification for the Youth Treatment Service*, Department of Health, March 1992.

(46) SI 1984 No 1345.

(47) Mental Health Act Commission, Second Biennial Report, HMSO, 1987.

(48) *When Things go Wrong at School - Redress Procedures in the Education Service*, National Consumer Council, September 1992.

(49) *Independent Schools*, Children Act Guidance Volume 5, Department of Health, HMSO, 1991, para 3.11.1.

(50) see (17).

(51) see (13), para 1.10.

(52) SI 1988 No 1422.

(53) SI 1965 No 195 as amended.

Section 2.2

(54) see (13), para 6.11.

(55) SI 1991 No 892.

(56) SI 1991 No 895, schedule 2.

(57) see (10) and (16).

(58) see (4), para 3.39 and rec 7.1, page 63.

(59) see (13), paras 6.47 et seq.

(60) *Outcome of an Investigation concerning St Charles Youth Treatment Centre*, Department of Health, 1991, recommendations.

Section 2.3

(61) *The Pindown Experience and the Protection of Children*, Report of the Staffordshire Child Care Inquiry 1990, Allan Levy QC and Barbara Kahan, Staffordshire County Council, 1991, chapters 14 - 16 and recommendations, paras 23.15-25.

(62) see (5), para 1.4.

(63) ibid, recommendation 33.

(64) *The Children Act and Day Care for Young Children Registration*, Circular LAC(93)1, Department of Health, January 1993.

(65) *General Social Services Council Action Group Final Report*, National Institute for Social Work, January 1993.

(66) Circulars: HOC 102/88; DES 12/88; DH - LAC 88(19); WOC 45/88.

(67) Circulars: HC(88)9; HN(FP)(88)3; HOC 8/88; WHC(88)10).

(68) HO Circular 58/1989.

(69) *Disclosure of Criminal Background to Voluntary Sector Organisations*, Home Office Circular 117/92.

(70) Department for Education, Consultative letter, 25 September 1992.

(71) *Castle Hill Report: practice guide*, C Brannan, J R Jones, J D Murch, Shropshire County Council, 1993, page 27.

(72) Scottish Social Work Services Group Circular SW9/1989, and Scottish Education

Department Circular, SED 5/89.

(73) see (30), paras 6.52-6.54.

(74) see (5), paras 5.23 and 5.27.

(75) DES Administrative Memorandum 3/82.

(76) SW9/1989, 24 July 1989.

(77) List No 1(R): information from Scottish Office Education Department, 1992.

(78) Circular HSS(CC)2/89 and amendments.

(79) see (12), regulation 19.

(80) *Report of the Inquiry into the Death of a Child in Care*, L Goodman, P Hughes, R Nicol, Derbyshire County Council, 1990, paras 15.21 and 15.59.

(81) see (5), Appendix 3 page 241, recommendation 19 page 58, para 5.25.

(82) see (69).

(83) SI 1991 No 1034.

(84) SI 1991 No 2094.

(85) *Private Fostering and Miscellaneous*, Children Act Guidance Volume 8, Department of Health, HMSO, page 33.

(86) see (5), para 5.9.

(87) *The National Collection of Criminal Records, report of an Efficiency Scrutiny*, Home Office, 1991.

(88) see (5), recommendation 31, page 77.

(89) see (3), pages 163-5

(90) *Criminal Record Checks within the Voluntary Sector: an evaluation of the pilot schemes*, Judith Unell, Volunteer Centre, 1992.

(91) *Disclosure of Criminal Background: Pilot Schemes for the Voluntary Sector: Monitoring and Evaluation Committee: Report to the National Steering Committee*, Home Office, VS(91)3, 1991.

(92) see (64), para 30.

(93) see (65).

Section 2.4

(94) see (30), para 4.47.

(95) see (16), para 3.8.4-5.

(96) see (30), para 6.3.

(97) see (11), paras 2.1 et seq.

(98) *Fit for the Future, the report of the Committee on Child Health Services*, chaired by Donald Court, HMSO, 1976.

(99) *Court Orders*, Children Act Guidance Volume 1, Department of Health, HMSO, 1991, para 4.8-10.

(100) SI 1991 No 895.

(101) see (80), recommendation 15.36.

(102) see (56).

(103) SWS Group Circular SW9/1984.

(104) see (10), pages 12/13.

(105) see (16), recommendation 19, page 91.

(106) SI 1991 No 205.

(107) SI 1991 No 1505.

(108) see (10), para 3.1 et seq.

(109) Home Office circular instructions nos 40/1988 and 44/1988 on young offenders.

Section 2.5

(110) see (19), page 55 and recommendation 31.

(111) *Inspecting Social Services*, a consultation document, Department of Health, October 1992, paras 23-29, 39-43.

(112) see (16), para 5.37 and recommendation 14 page 66.

(113) see (111), paras 20 et seq.

(114) Information provided by Social Services Inspectorate, Department of Health, October 1992.

(115) see (111), para 13 et seq.

(116) SI 1991 No 910.

(117) see (80), para 12.2.

(118) see (116).

(119) SI 1985 No 1799.

(120) *The Boarding Out and Fostering of Children (Scotland) Regulations 1985*, Social Work Services Group, Circular SW15/1985.

(121) SI 1976 19.

(122) SI 1991 No 2050.

(123) see (85), para 1.8.8 et seq.

(124) SI 1985 No 1798.

(125) see (12), regulation 22.

(126) *Leeways Inquiry Report*, Social Services Department, London Borough of Lewisham, 1985.

(127) see (13), para 1.14.

(128) see (4), para 4.41.

(129) *Sir William Utting's Review of Residential Care Services for Children*, Department of Health circular, LAC(91)13, 1991.

(130) *Inspecting for Quality*, Department of Health, Social Services Inspectorate, HMSO, 1991, paras 3.5 and 4.39.

(131) *Inspection of Community Homes*, Department of Health circular, LAC(92)14, 1992.

(132) see (111).

(133) *The Quality of Care*, report of the residential staffs inquiry chaired by Lady Howe, Local Government Management Board, 1992, recommendations 18 and 19.

(134) see (111), paras 23 et seq.

(135) see (5), para 6.61 et seq.

(136) see (4), para 4.35.

(137) see (12), regulation 28.

(138) see (16), para 5.36 et seq.

(139) see (10), paras 12.7-12.12.

(140) Northern Ireland Department of Health and Social Services circular, HSS(CC)2/88.

(141) Training School Rules 1952.

(142) see (107).

(143) see (4), para 4.42.

(144) see (45).

(145) see (10), para 12.13.

(146) SI 1984 No 1345.

(147) *Bridges Over Troubled Waters*, a report from the NHS Health Advisory Service on services for disturbed adolescents, Health Advisory Service, 1986.

(148) SI 1984 No 1578.

(149) SI 1990 No 1310, regulations 11 and 12.

(150) *Implementation of the New Inspection Arrangements under the Education (Schools) Act 1992*, draft circular and regulations, Department for Education, November 1992.

(151) *Assuring Quality and Standards in Education, a short guide to the work of OFSTED*, Department for Education, 1992.

(152) information from OFSTED, January 1993.

(153) SI 1991 No 975.

(154) see (71), page 28.

(155) see (52).

(156) see (53), rules 133 et seq.

Appendix

Checklist of settings for children

In planning and carrying out this project, the Working Group found it useful to try and list all the places where children and young people in the UK can spend significant periods of their lives: at home, and in institutions and quasi-institutional settings. The list is extraordinarily long, and is no doubt still very incomplete. It may be useful when considering to which settings changes in law, policy or practice should be applied.

It must also be remembered that children's legal status - in care, under supervision, ward of court etc - may affect their legal rights and their treatment.

At "home"

living with one or two parents
living with relatives, friends
living independently

in care and living in above settings
ward of court

Voluntary associations in which children live or spend time - with or without their families, eg religious communities.

Foster care

local authority
voluntary organisations
private
(includes family-based respite care for disabled children).

Child care system

community homes including assisted and controlled homes
other local authority accommodation - hostels etc
secure accommodation
voluntary children's homes
registered (private) children's homes

intermediate treatment projects
family centres/day centres
refuges (also Women's Aid refuges)
youth treatment centres
training schools in Northern Ireland (part penal)

residential care homes

residential holidays, adventure schemes etc

Daycare

residential nurseries

Group daycare
local authority day nurseries
private nurseries
playgroups
creches
nurseries in independent schools
nursery classes in maintained schools

Other daycare
childminding
nannies, au pairs
babysitters
holiday schemes etc

Education

maintained day and boarding primary, secondary, special schools
maintained hostels for pupils with special educational needs
voluntary day primary, secondary and special schools
voluntary boarding primary, secondary and special schools
grant-maintained primary and secondary schools
grant-maintained boarding schools
non-maintained special schools
independent day and boarding schools
language schools

Youth Service

clubs - LEA-provided and supported; voluntary and private

Health

NHS hospitals and units (including NHS trusts)
private nursing homes and mental nursing homes, private hospitals, hospices etc
community care settings including hostels
regional secure units
special hospitals

Penal system

adult prisons (including babies in prison as well as young people placed in prison
on remand and after sentence)
young offender institutions
remand homes
probation hostels
probation day centres
bail hostels
police cells
attendance centres
immigration detention centres